DEADLY PEAKS

Deadly Peaks

Mountaineering's Greatest Tragedies and Triumphs

Frederic V. Hartemann
and
Robert Hauptman

GUILFORD, CONNECTICUT
HELENA, MONTANA

FALCONGUIDES®

An imprint of Rowman & Littlefield

Falcon and FalconGuides are registered trademarks and Make Adventure Your Story is a trademark of Rowman & Littlefield.

Distributed by NATIONAL BOOK NETWORK

British Library Cataloguing-in-Publication Information available

Library of Congress Cataloging-in-Publication Data available

ISBN 978-1-5897-9841-0 (paperback)
ISBN 978-1-5897-9842-7 (e-book)

∞™ The paper used in this publication meets the minimum requirements of American National Standard for Information Sciences—Permanence of Paper for Printed Library Materials, ANSI/ NISO Z39.48-1992.

We dedicate this book to the brave people who have lost their lives in the mountains.

The defining thing about climbing is that it kills you.
—JOE SIMPSON

Contents

Acknowledgments

We especially thank Greg Glade, whose invaluable contributions helped to make this a successful venture. Katie Sauter of the American Alpine Club library provided excellent service. Thank you.

NOTE

We refer to ourselves as senior author (SA), Frederic Hartemann, and junior author (JA), Robert Hauptman.

Foreword by Kenneth Kamler

I'm often asked, "What's it like to climb Mount Everest?" I give a polite response but the real answer is, you have to do it to know what the experience is like; it can't be put into words. That may still be true but no book comes closer to making the reader feel what big-mountain climbing is like than this one. I can personally attest to that.

In 1996, I was at 24,000 ft. when the worst storm in Everest's human history battered the mountain for two days, killing eight climbers. As the only functioning doctor high up on the mountain, I took care of the survivors that were brought to me. That epic tragedy is here told with such detail and intensity that I felt as though I was re-living the experience.

There were various accounts of what happened during that violent storm. Even as the disaster was unfolding, our impressions of what was going on were confused and often conflicting. The authors present a compelling narrative of that disaster, but are careful to include the divergent recollections and interpretations of those who were caught up in the ordeal.

There are honest differences in the way climbers recount events, and there are dishonest differences as well—self-serving versions that promote climbers' images or obscure their ignoble behavior. There are even downright lies about summiting. The authors go boldly into this underside of climbing, to give a more realistic picture of the mountaineering world.

What really happened on the first ascent of Annapurna? I winced when I read the evidence, here summarized fairly and honestly. Maurice Herzog's classic account was the first climbing book I ever read. He was a French national hero, an inspiration and a role model for me. I spent time with him and his wife both before and after the controversial revelations. It was disheartening for them (and for me) to see his image tarnished, but now there is a more balanced sense of what occurred on that climb and in the larger picture, what may happen and sometimes does happen on any climb.

The stories tell the hard truth about hard climbs. The reader goes up each mountain with climbers who sometimes don't come down. We feel the challenge, the fear and exuberance, the exhaustion and exultation, the joy and disappointment of their victories and defeats—the entire range of emotions that are the essence of mountaineering.

This is not a book that you can't put down. Each story is so gripping, I felt I needed a rest after each one. But in the same way that exhausted climbers descending a mountain are already planning their next climb, I felt compelled to quickly pick up the book to not be left behind on the next climb.

Many adventures await you in this book. Climb on!

Introduction

This collection of essays deals with controversies, hoaxes, triumphs, and disasters in climbing, mountaineering, and skiing.

Serious technical rock climbing and formal mountaineering are extremely dangerous pursuits. Amateurs and especially professionals put their lives on the line each time they tie a rope on and head out and up, but even normal people risk their lives the moment they step onto a mountain. It is very difficult to accept, but of the estimated 320,000 climbers who attempted Mount Fuji in 2012, 25 died. Since this is an easy though fairly long ascent, many of these folks succumbed to heart attack, hypothermia, and falling (Belson), rather than the typical threats such as avalanche or unarrested descent. Nevertheless, and despite the many tea houses along the way, they died. Even worse, on September 27, 2014, Japan's Mount Ontake exploded, raining ash down on the hundreds of hikers out to enjoy the autumn foliage. At least 31 people may have perished (Fackler). There exist many possible goals and objectives in these sports and a diversity of ways to reach them. A severe rock or vertical ice climb might last only a few minutes, whereas it may take three months to reach the summit of one of the fourteen 8,000-meter (26,247-foot) peaks. In both instances, a lifetime of commitment is invested, and there is ample emotional and physical opportunity to disagree, dissemble, or make sometimes fatal blunders.

In most activities and especially in athletic endeavors, there are almost always witnesses: competitors or spectators, coaches or referees. Success (or failure) is observed, recorded, and televised. In climbing and mountaineering, where success can have a dramatic effect on the life of the climber, where reputation, fame, and sponsorships are enhanced and financial security is assured, the achievement's validity may rest entirely in the word of the claimant. And until suspicions are raised or confirmed, we believe. If someone claims to have reached a summit via a new route and this is confirmed by his partner, we offer congratulations. If they are deceiving us, the truth will usually reveal itself. Nevertheless, despite the many controversial cases that litter the history of climbing, some people (like their scientific counterparts who refuse to admit that ethical breaches in research occur) deny that problems exist. Mark Allen insists that "There's a lot of integrity in the climbing community, and there are very few examples of people who didn't achieve what they claimed to achieve" (McMillan, quoting Allen, B11). Well, we will see.

The authors of this volume have surveyed the extremely broad and replete literature and chosen a group of extraordinary cases to present to the reader. We have supplemented these detailed overviews with some briefer instances of adventures that have resulted in disagreement, distortion, triumph, or catastrophe.

Even participants in these often-trying pursuits may sometimes wonder why they continue to risk their bodies, and their lives. Those who never leave the protective cocoon of their living rooms probably cannot comprehend the motivation or necessity to climb high or ski steeply and swiftly. On the most basic level, there is great joy in accommodating oneself to nature, its beauties, and its demands, pushing one's body, using one's skills, and accomplishing one's goals. In skiing and snowboarding, whether inbounds or in extreme environments, there is the thrill of speed, and the excitement of danger, something that inheres in climbing and mountaineering as well. But the intense tension or stress that accompanies the most extreme pursuits is not a concomitant for all participants. Nor is the need to be self-reliant, a frequently cited reason for climbing. Acting alone on the edge of the precipice seduces some, but not all of those who participate in difficult or dangerous adventures. Sometimes the coward is braver than the warrior; sometimes the former survives while the headstrong tumbles down the slope. Here, at least, W. H. Auden is wrong: Don't leap before you look! You won't last long if you do.

Controversial claims, outright hoaxes, and calamitous tragedies are all clear, easily discernible, and even comprehensible, although their etiologies and denouements may always remain unresolved. We read about, view, and discuss these issues frequently. What is often left unsaid is the misery that follows. *Where the Mountain Casts Its Shadow*, Maria Coffey's groundbreaking study, makes this much too palpable. A person leaves home, climbs, and dies, and therefore never returns to his wife or her husband or young children. The general tragedy of the loss of a great climber (such as Alex Lowe) is magnified a thousand times for those left behind (both Westerners as well as local porters' and climbers' relatives) to fend for themselves—emotionally, physically, and financially devastated. Some may never recover. Many years after John Harlin died on the Eiger, his son, also encumbered with dependent little children, decided that he must expiate the death by also climbing the dreaded north face. He was tracked by cameras, succeeded, and returned with a magnificent (IMAX) film, thus avoiding a second real tragedy. This was not the positive result obtained in countless other instances, many of which Coffey describes in painful, harrowing detail. There are other Annapurnas in the lives of men, and some of these are the (broken) bodies that litter the world's peaks, crags, walls, and slopes—mourned eternally by those left behind, including their many young children.

Astonishingly, there is even extreme trauma for successful mountaineers who return from expedition after expedition. This concerns guilt and sadness not only because fellow climbers have perished, but also because they have failed in some way to be there for their loved ones. And soon thereafter, the next trip calls and they must leave once again (Coffey, passim). But there is even more: Far too often the returnee is ill or maimed. Life continues, but without a lung or foot or toes or fingers. Those who are whole may know or read about these people, but they can forget. It is hard for the stricken to lose sight of their impediments. Maurice Herzog had a successful life after his return from Annapurna, but he did so without fingers; just so has Reinhold Messner continued without toes. As Coffey observes, these dedicated people are willing to suffer the loss of arms, fingers, toes, as well as other horrors, but many of them are not deterred: They return to the mountains (Coffey, 149), not the lower peaks of New England or the higher slopes of the western United States, but the dangerous heights of the Himalaya. Dedication easily slips into uncontrollable obsession. Very few serious mountaineers simply give up. The single important exception is Charles Houston; after K2 in 1953, he stopped climbing.

Coffey's prescient study preceded a major change that is still expanding, and this is the overwhelming desire of mountaineers, but especially skiers and snowboarders, to push the limits of their skills for the ever-increasing thrill that comes from doing things that were previously thought to be impossible: climbing very high mountains speedily, doing a series of peaks in quick succession, extreme out-of-bounds skiing or boarding on 80-degree cliffs, heli-skiing in avalanche country. Not surprisingly, the people often harmed or killed are skillful and knowledgeable guides who do these things on an ongoing basis. No matter how carefully one examines matters, an avalanche can surprise a single person or a large group, and this occurs much more often and in popular areas than most people realize. On March 6, 2013, the *New York Times* ran a detailed piece on how the parents and families of those harmed or killed are horribly affected; they are hurt and saddened, but also angry. Cases include the well-known snowboarder Kevin Pearce, who had a traumatic brain injury, and the guide Rob Liberman and his client Nickolay Dodov, who were both killed in an avalanche. Dodov's parents are actively pursuing (legal) changes in heli-skiing, which is basically unregulated. *The Alaskan Way*, a short documentary, includes footage of the avalanche that inundated these men, whose parents continue to suffer the painful loss of their sons (Amdur).

To compound matters, weather conditions are more severe than they were in the past (due to global warming), and hordes of novices now depend on GPS, locater beacons, or cell phones rather than their honed and tested skills. The well-known climber and mountaineering historian, David Roberts, laments this harmful development. People who are in no real danger foolishly call for help, which puts the rescuers at risk.[1] He cites the extreme case of some hikers who signaled on three successive occasions and called out helicopters because, for example, their water tasted salty! Their "leader was cited."

It is obvious to anyone even vaguely familiar with Nepal or the mountaineering literature that Sherpa names are very limited and therefore repetitive. Some people may understand why, but it is worth briefly explaining this. Jonathan Neale offers an excellent and detailed summary. A new baby is named for the day on which he or she is born: Nima is Sunday; Dawa, Monday; Mingma, Tuesday; Lhakpa, Wednesday; Phurbu, Thursday; Pasang, Friday; and Pemba, Saturday. There are many additional complications, necessitated by familial duplication, death, nicknames, and religion. Neale also notes the diversity of languages in the Himalaya and how they are interrelated: Sherpas speak Sherpa, which is Tibetan in origin; Nepali, the official language of the country, is a dialect of Hindi, the major national language of India (Neale, 8, 28). Even today some Nepalese Sherpas may not know Nepali. Many other languages and dialects turn up in the mountaineering literature, both because climbers come from many diverse countries (China, Kazakhstan, Japan, Korea, Austria, Spain, Mexico, ad infinitum), and because the indigenous peoples hired as porters, animal herders, cooks, and so on present a Babel of languages so that even local people who reside near each other (in the tribal areas of Pakistan, for example), may not understand each other. Today, most (though not all) people speak at least some English, which is not merely the lingua franca of virtually all international travelers, but also the official language of global air traffic control and the Norwegian navy![2]

We list our sources at the conclusion of each entry. Readers can thus more easily follow up on the individual cases than if a single comprehensive bibliography had been compiled. In some instances, many additional works exist, but since we did not consult them, we do not include them here. A web search engine or a library catalog will lead directly to other apposite sources. The American Alpine Club (americanalpineclub.org/library/) probably holds the single most comprehensive collection of relevant monographs, journals, magazines, and videos. Members may check out materials by mail.

NOTES

1 The most embarrassing moment the authors of this book ever experienced, in many hundreds of climbs during more than half a century, occurred after calling for automobile help, high on Colorado's Torrey's and Gray's on a stunningly beautiful winter day, only to discover upon reaching the bottom of the road that somehow a rescue vehicle had come to meet them. The men were preparing to climb or snowmobile up to perform a rescue, though it was the big lumbering SUV that needed help. The senior author (SA) once called for a helicopter rescue in the Alps, but this was warranted because the other members of the group were in severe trouble.

2 Both authors of this book are familiar with various languages and have traveled extensively in most parts of the world. The junior author (JA) has been in some forty countries, and has found that it is often (though not always) possible to communicate in English. Nevertheless, he has usually endeavored to learn some basic terminology and how to count whenever he planned to visit a new land. This is just a courtesy to those from whom he is soliciting help. It is well-known that Americans do not usually bother to learn additional languages, but this is not the case for people whose native tongues are fairly esoteric. JA recalls that fifty years ago, he met an eighteen-year-old traveler in Istanbul. This young man spoke Dutch, German, English, and two other languages.

Sources

Amdur, Neil. "Extreme Grief," *New York Times*. March 6, 2013: B11–B12.

Belson, Ken. "Mount Fuji, So Popular It Hurts," *New York Times*. August 18, 2013: 2 TR.

Clark, Ben. *The Alaskan Way*. Telluride, CO: GoDu Productions, 2013.

Coffey, Maria. *Where the Mountain Casts Its Shadow: The Dark Side of Extreme Adventure*. New York: St. Martin's Griffin, 2005.

Fackler, Martin. "Dozens of Hikers Feared Dead on Volcano," *New York Times*. September 29, 2014: A4.

McMillan, Kelley. "The Hard Way Up," *New York Times*. April 5, 2014: B9, B11.

Neale, Jonathan. *Tigers of the Snow: How One Fateful Climb Made the Sherpas Mountaineering Legends*. New York: Thomas Dunne Books, 2002.

Roberts, David. "When GPS Leads to SOS," *New York Times*. August 14, 2012: A17.

PART ONE:
MAJOR CALAMITIES AND
EXTRAORDINARY TRIUMPHS

Section One:
The Matterhorn (14,692 feet)

CHAPTER 1

The Matterhorn, 1865:
Whymper and the Fall

EVEN PHYSICAL SUPERMEN OR INTELLECTUAL GENIUSES WHO WANT TO reach the pinnacles of their endeavors must be possessed, fully committed to whatever it is they wish to achieve. They must have an uncontrollable compulsion to push on, often in the face of the impossible. Many, perhaps most, successful mountaineers lose rational control, return to the high mountains again and again, and refuse to turn back when they know that their lives depend upon it. When a superb mountaineer does call a halt in a consistent manner, as Ed Viesturs does, he stands out from his peers, sets an excellent example, and continues to prosper.

Edward Whymper was a mere amateur as opposed to the early professionals, all of whom were guides, or the current crop, who occasionally earn their living by guiding, but more frequently by doing ever more difficult and dangerous things, and are paid by sponsors, win competitions, make films or commercials, or present lectures (at $30,000 an hour). But Whymper liked to climb, and spent his vacations roaming the world doing first ascents. Like many of his predecessors and peers, he wanted desperately to reach the top of the Matterhorn, "the mountaineering world's most prized summit" (Henry, 100). Like Everest, it was a seemingly impossible goal, and like Everest, it is now climbed by elderly grandmothers in high heels. If this is an exaggeration, it is only slightly so.[1] Many hundreds of people now climb both of these peaks with little or no trouble, although, naturally, they both can still kill the unwary or careless, the overconfident or those who do not heed the signs of bad weather.[2]

Whymper's obsession with this mountain led him back again and again, nine times, before he finally reached the summit. The ensuing tumble on the descent must have seemed to both the climbers and the gawking world public to be a major catastrophe; as it turns out, it was a typical result, but a worthwhile sacrifice. It serves as an augury of what is to come: the maimings and deaths that occur in the world's mountains on an ongoing basis. Here, three climbers and one guide died; in 1990, in the Pamirs, forty-three people were killed in a single accident.

Whymper's first sally occurred in 1861, when famous guide Jean-Antoine Carrel was also on the mountain. Whymper was accompanied by only one man; guides were either rogues or hard to engage, since most people thought the Matterhorn to be unclimbable. He described the mountain and his attempt in great detail, but nothing came of all of his hard work, nor did anything radical occur, with a single exception, in the next many tries. He simply persevered. In 1862, he tried again, and as he turned a corner, he slipped and tumbled down a gully, bouncing along and hitting his head on ice and rocks over and over again. At one point he flew some 50 feet through the air. Had he not stopped he would have fallen 800 feet to the glacier. Bleeding from twenty lacerations, he fainted. Eventually, he carried himself almost 5,000 vertical feet, all the way down into the valley. He was embarrassed by his appearance when he reached the inn, inadvertently rousing everyone from sleep. This disastrous fall had a deleterious effect on his memory, but he was not deterred. He continued his quest.

To give the reader an idea of the extraordinary amount of climbing he managed, he noted that in the eighteen days preceding his July 1865 successful attempt (now celebrating its 150th anniversary), he ascended more than 100,000 vertical feet. Many human obstructions presented themselves, including trickery and a lack of help as he prepared for this climb, but eventually he hired Peter Taugwalder, his son, also Peter, and a second son; Lord Francis Douglas, his old and well-known guide Michel Croz, Charles Hudson, and Douglas Hadow decided to join him and attempt the Matterhorn. They departed from Zermatt early in the morning of July 13. They took their time and set camp at 11,000 feet. By 10:00 the next morning, they had reached 14,000. After resting, they continued, overcame some difficulties, and, on Whymper's ninth attempt, reached the summit at 1:40 p.m. They had beaten Carrel and his group, and now held the first ascent of the Matterhorn. They could see the others far below and hurtled shouts and rocks to attract their attention. Carrel retreated but later returned and reached the summit on July 17.

Except for older people with bad knees, the descent is always easier, at least physically, than the ascent. Naturally, some descents are overwhelmingly difficult and dangerous technically, but when moving downward, gravity is an excellent benefactor. Indeed, it is often possible to rappel, glissade, or run downward speedily, if rather haphazardly. One is also both elated and tired. This being the case, it is well known that most accidents occur when one is on the way down. Thus, one is adjured to be especially careful at the end of a hard climb; the ascent is only half the journey.

The Whymper party apparently forgot this admonition. But it was a very different time, with very different (primitive) equipment, untrustworthy ropes (they had taken along 600 feet of various types), no harnesses, staffs sometimes in lieu of axes, less-effective crampons (if used at all), and bad attitudes. For example, guides were *embarrassed* to use ropes on glaciers. They liked to believe that the undulations on the ice would alert them to hidden crevasses.[3] They descended. Croz led the first rope; he was followed by Hadow, Hudson, Douglas, and Taugwalder. The second rope consisted of a younger Taugwalder and Whymper.

Whymper then tied into the main line. Croz and those in front were proceeding with extreme caution when Hadow slipped and knocked Croz over. They tumbled down, pulling Hudson and Douglas along. Taugwalder and Whymper braced themselves; the rope became taut, and there is a good chance that they might have held the others, except that the rope broke. The Taugwalders and Whymper remained in place; the others plummeted to their deaths on the glacier, which lay almost 4,000 feet below them. Whymper indicated that they stayed in place for thirty minutes. The Taugwalders were extremely frightened and trembled, lamented, and cried. One is fairly certain that Whymper did the same. Upon examining the rope, he discovered that it was the weakest of those brought along, and should not have been used for protection. They set up some belays and proceeded downward slowly, reaching the ridge where the dangers were minimized. They picked up some material left there, when suddenly a vision appeared in the sky, an arch, called a fog bow. It had a powerful effect on the men.

Once down, Whymper reported the catastrophe and a group of men went up to investigate. Others followed, including, amazingly, some famous guides: Franz Andermatten, Frédéric Payot, and Jean Tairraz (Henry, 202). Finally, the victims were interred in the snow; later they were brought down and reburied. The aftermath included hearings and accusations that Taugwalder had cut the rope, but Whymper insisted that it was frayed in such a way as to make that impossible. It was just that they had used weak sashline rather than the stronger hemp, of which they had hundreds of feet. Henry claims that the many attempts on the Matterhorn "meld into a dramatic story whose climax and tragic aftermath would in retrospect seem inevitable" (Henry, 125).

This conclusion seems unwarranted. Had a single person not slipped, it is probable that all seven men would have reached the valley in triumph. That the man who slipped lacked experience may have been a factor, but perhaps a minor one; well-known, skillful climbers and mountaineers make mistakes and often are hurt or killed with some frequency. The great rock climber Lynn Hill, for example, once forgot to knot her rope and fell 70 feet. The other determining factor was that although they had discussed securing fixed lines where necessary, they never actually did so; this might have averted the tragedy (Henry, 217).

This was a bad business, one that has haunted us for 150 years. As Emil Henry observes, the Matterhorn triumph and tragedy entranced the public, and continues to do so even today (Henry, 199). Thus, someone decided to produce a very short "documentary" on the climb and fall. It is amazing to see these men ascending, triumphing, and then falling. It requires a moment's reflection to make sure that one realizes that this antiquated film is a modern re-creation with authentic-looking actors. Other films of various types have also been made. It should be noted that Whymper was responsible for the innumerable lovely illustrations that adorn his many books.

Notes

1 Readers may recall that some years ago, a woman in her seventies climbed Mount Rainier from Paradise to the summit and then returned without the normal long rest at Camp Muir. Many conditioned athletes, who do sleep in the refuge or in a bivouac, fail, and sadly, some die.

2 Between 1865 and late 2010, 431 people died on the Matterhorn (Henry, 218).

3 JA is descending the glacier on the Aiguille du Tour, near Chamonix, France. SA leads on a long rope. Next to JA is Lindsey, a large independent climber, a former guide in Nepal. We move along. Lindsey says, "Hold back!" SA is crossing a hidden crevasse. Suddenly, Lindsey, unroped, falls in. JA grabs him by the shoulder; luckily, Lindsey only sinks in a few feet. JA would never have been able to hold him with one hand; he would have plummeted downward and pulled JA along with him. One may suppose that SA would have taken up all of the weight, but since he was downhill, it would have turned out quite well.

Sources

The primary source for this chapter is Whymper's Scrambles. *Others are cited in the text.*

Henry, Emil. *Triumph and Tragedy: The Life of Edward Whymper.* Leicester, UK: Matador, 2011

Whymper, Edward. *Scrambles Amongst the Alps in the Years 1860–69.* Berkeley, CA: Ten Speed Press, 1981 (reprint).

Whymper's First Ascent Matterhorn. YouTube.com. 2013. www.youtube.com/watch?v=V7PLaJlq0uA.

Section Two:
Denali (20,320 feet)

Because Denali (The Great One, formerly Mount McKinley) is North America's highest peak, and because it is such a powerful and enticing mountain, climbers from all over the world attempt it every year. Even half a century ago, when far fewer people were found at base camp, horrible accidents occurred, including one in 1960 involving the Whittaker brothers (Jim was the first American to summit Everest) and Pete Schoening (who famously had held six climbers on "The Belay"). The rescue work was a debacle and two people were killed. Subsequent disasters number in the hundreds.

CHAPTER 2

Denali, 1967:
First Winter Expedition: Art Davidson

In late 1966, after an extended period of intense climbing, twenty-two-year-old Art Davidson[1] continued with his plan to climb Denali in winter. He invited mountaineers, most of whom declined to participate. Denali is difficult and deadly enough in spring and summer. It would take a very special person (even today) to try a winter climb in one of the harshest environments on Earth. Nevertheless, Davidson found five men who wished to participate in the expedition. Before leaving, two additional men joined them.

The climb in February and March of 1967 took place just before the deadly Wilcox expedition arrived on the mountain (see below). Davidson chose the West Buttress route; pioneered by Bradford Washburn, this is the easiest means of ascending Denali, though it, too, is difficult, and always dangerous because of storms, acute mountain sickness or edema, and accidents. People used to high climbing in the lower forty-eight states, Mexico, South America, or the Himalaya do not realize (or conveniently ignore) the fact that Denali is close to the North Pole (as opposed to the Himalaya), and oxygenation is far more proscribed than it is closer to the equator. Someone who can easily climb Mount Whitney (remeasured at 14,505 feet) or even Orizaba (18,800 feet) may think that a few thousand more feet might be attainable with little effort or discomfort. But Denali's 20,320 physical feet are analogous to 24,000 physiological feet in the Himalaya; it is also often extremely cold and windy. McKinley is very different than an analogous peak closer to the equator, and that is why many climbers fail, and some die.

At least 11 miles of difficult work lay ahead of these men when they landed on the Kahiltna Glacier, ferried in by Don Sheldon, the legendary pilot. They no sooner began to move than bad things occurred. It was dark for the last arrivals, although everything went well. One man fell harmlessly into a crevasse, but it was a potent augury of what was to come. They tried to do everything correctly, but they were unlucky, on this, the first winter ascent. Davidson, in his personal remarks to the authors, makes this clear: "This was the first time anyone had been on Denali in winter—the first time anyone had been at that altitude on a glacier at this latitude in winter. No one anywhere in the world knew how to read the winter conditions on these glaciers. Conditions during the normal climbing season are quite different; crevasses are evident. In winter there was no evidence of crevasses in the vicinity. They were apparently filled with snow that had been accumulating for six months. No one knew—and there was no way of telling—that instead of being filled with snow, some had wind-packed snow bridges built up over the top" (Davidson, pc).

Despite these conditions, along with the very early loss of another man who fell into a crevasse and succumbed, this was a unique expedition because the men appeared to suffer fear, hunger, thirst, cold, wind, pain, and crippling frostbite—although apparently this was not the case (Davidson, pc). In some of the other tragedies recounted in this volume, maiming and/or death occurred with great frequency. Here the suffering and endurance led to a successful summit, a triumph rather than a disaster.

The eight (now seven) men did not always agree with each other, and sometimes one was annoyed, but minimally. Generally speaking, they got along well. In such trying circumstances, they supported each other, and at the high camp, after summiting, Dave Johnston acted as Davidson's and Ray Pirate Genet's hands, doing everything that the others' frostbitten extremities were no longer capable of doing.

They moved upward, slowly ferrying "moderate loads" that weighed between 50 and 60 pounds.[2] Early on, some of the men had frequent crevasse encounters because they were untethered, but "[o]nce aware of winter crevasse conditions, we exercised all appropriate caution and did quite well" (Davidson, pc). Jacques "Farine" Batkin died; another was rescued. Davidson managed to extract himself, though he makes it clear that it was very difficult and frightening. Naturally, they were all extremely upset by Batkin's death, and even considered aborting the expedition before deciding to carry on. It is at this early point in the story that Davidson begins to intercalate passages from the other men's journals and diaries. These brief entries obviously differ stylistically from Davidson's polished prose because they were hastily composed high on the mountain in trying conditions (when even holding a pen may have been almost impossible). But they offer a true sense of how their authors felt as they had these dramatic experiences and reacted physically and emotionally.

The first storm arrived. Some men spent the time in an igloo, others in a tent. Then they continued their upward movement. Upon reaching some boxes that they had previously cached, they discovered that the infamous Denali ravens had scattered their Jell-O, potatoes, candy, cheese, and other foodstuffs across the terrain. Although aware of this possibility, they had thought this would only occur during the summer months rather than high on the mountain in winter. At this point in the climb, it was only minimally important, but if a cache were destroyed when famished climbers reached it upon descent, it could be disastrous.[3]

Subsequently, they took appropriate measures. During the early days, the temperatures were often bitter, 20 below, 42 below, and with a windchill of 50 below. It would get worse, although these optimistic men actually contemplated spending a night on the summit. And this, despite the fact that Davidson suffered from the altitude: He was weak, tired, and breathless just below 17,000 feet. Johnston also indicated that he felt very weak. The next morning, Davidson was so ill (nauseous, dizzy) that they decided to descend to 14,400 feet. Four men helped him since he was often dizzy and unsteady. As he descended he regained his strength. The next day, two went back up and three remained until the evening, when they too began to climb. They often left late in the day. Davidson, who had just been ill, decided to sleep along the route, and for no *apparent* reason—but as he notes, he was entranced by the beauty of the full moon illuminating the landscape (Davidson, pc).

The next day, he moved up strongly, carrying 50 pounds; now he wanted to catch the others and possibly summit: "I climbed at ease; the unrestrained passion that had started me up the wall had been replaced by a lighthearted sense of well-being. I'd just take a look at the pass, go up to meet the others as they came down from the summit. It would be fine if I reached the summit, but not necessary."

It is at this approximate point that they broke up into separate groups. Two men quickly returned to camp after trying for the top; Johnston, Genet, and Davidson continued upward, reaching the summit after a great deal of hard work, panting and resting, and then going on again. Finally, gazing out into the darkness, all they could see were Anchorage's distant lights. It was 7:00 p.m. and 58 degrees below zero when they started down, but they were tired, and for other reasons they decided, fatefully, to bivouac at Denali Pass.

Here, the structure of this unusual book alters: The next eight chapter titles are a sequence of dates.

March 1, 1967: The three men who reached the apex of North America were at the pass. The others were at their 17,300-foot camp. They were separated and incommunicado for many days. They had no way of knowing what was happening elsewhere. Since the weather was horrendous, they were all extremely worried about their friends' safety. Davidson relates what he and his two comrades experienced, while reproduced journal and diary entries, provided by the men who were lower on the mountain, inform the reader concerning the others' activities. An extended period of extreme misery, fear, and pain now followed.

An astonishing event occurred when one of the men camped at 17,300 feet managed to get up just below the pass (at 18,200 feet) to check on Davidson and the others. He was so close that he could see a sleeping bag "less than 100 feet away," but could not reach them because of the devastating 100-mile-per-hour wind. They were in the open in their bags, covered with a parachute blowing wildly. Johnston crawled in his bag to a more-protected spot; this untethered the parachute, which then flew away. Davidson and Genet huddled together, trying desperately to stop themselves from sliding downward on the ice. Then Davidson attempted to reach Johnston among the rocks, which offered some purchase, but it was no better at this new location. Davidson's left hand had become uncovered and froze so that all he could do was stop himself from sliding. Somehow Johnston dug a tiny ice cave, Genet came over, and they all took refuge inside. Some supplies were lost. Only Johnston had the full use of his hands. The wind was blowing at 130 miles per hour, which produced a temperature of 148 degrees below zero. The men who were camped below remained there, both because of the weather, but also in case those trapped above needed help.

March 2: The wind continued to howl and the two groups could not leave. Davidson's and Genet's frostbitten toes and fingers were in extremely bad shape, worsening as they remained on the mountain.

March 3: The interminable waiting continued. They discovered that some cans of food they had found were porous, and so the food was spoiled. They had very little left to eat. They, of course, craved water, but their gas supply was low; amazingly, Johnston had recently seen a gas container that he had left just 200 feet away, three years prior to this climb. But the wind was so intense that no one dared attempt to retrieve it. Somehow, two of the four men at 17,200 retreated to igloos at 14,400. The descent was extremely difficult in the wind, but at least the temperature increased to 10 below.

March 4: The interminable and painful days went by. The wind finally seemed to die down, and then they heard a helicopter, but it was a delusion, wishful thinking. The mental and physical pain of their frozen extremities was compounded by cracked lips, rawness of the mouth, tightened leg ligaments, penetrating cold, almost no food, and thirst leading to extreme dehydration. They needed the gas that might still have been in the container. Finally, during a series of lulls, Genet went to retrieve it, crawling along using two ice axes. He succeeded, and they reveled in their melted ice water.

March 5: The two men still at 17,200 went down; the two at 14,400 headed toward 7,500, but had trouble with heavy packs and deep snow and were forced to bivouac at 8,000. Davidson, Johnston, and Genet slept; they awoke in the dark to silence. The wind had finally stopped blowing.

March 6: They prepared to descend, but this took a lot of time because of swollen or frozen feet and hands. Johnston had to help the others with many tasks. Incredibly, they stopped to take some mental tests which showed they had major problems doing subtraction. One of the men stepped out of the cave and discovered that although the wind was calm, they were in a whiteout. Weak, uncoordinated, and physically beaten down, they looked much older; they also lacked the strength and balance to descend, but knew that failing to try would result in death. Indeed, the four men below basically had given up hope for the men high above. At one point, Davidson, despite his difficulty in standing, wanted to descend alone—in order to save himself, but "[o]nly momentarily, which is a natural impulse. . . . [W]e all stayed together and survived together" (Davidson, pc). Hours passed as they waited for the whiteout to dissipate.

Finally, they realized that they had to descend despite the very real possibility of getting lost. Returning to their cave would have resulted in starvation. Davidson managed to drag himself over to an old food cache and wildly slashed at the iced-over materials with his ax. His slashing and digging hurt his hands, but he was in a frenzy. He desperately wanted to locate some food, and miraculously he did: very old but edible dried potatoes, raisins, and ham. They returned to their icy home and feasted, looking forward to leaving in the morning.

March 7: They awoke to a perfect weather day for descent. With swollen feet, frostbitten extremities, weakness, and pain, everything was very difficult to accomplish. (Sometimes swollen feet force mountaineers to cut their boots.) They managed to get dressed and ready. Before descending, they once again had to practice walking on their damaged feet. At one point, when using their packs to block the cave's entrance, the wind had whipped them away. Now they were forced to drape their iced-over, heavy sleeping bags awkwardly across their shoulders; at times, they caught on their crampons. If this had occurred on the steep, icy section of the slope, the roped-up men would have been killed. But Davidson makes it clear that potential disaster is not part of his story: "[T]his might have happened. But it didn't! Yes, things could have ended in 'disaster.' But they didn't. . . . No, we climbed down. With Fortitude, Endurance, Caution, and by Helping each other, and never giving up, we Survived!" (Davidson, pc).

Belaying was difficult, since only Johnson had real use of his hands. They reached the lower cave and found a stove and some food, left not for them, as they thought, but for their spirits, since the others thought that they had perished (Leonard). As they ate, a plane spotted them; next came Sheldon's smaller plane, which dropped some supplies, including a malfunctioning radio. They continued down, suffering terribly as they descended the fixed ropes, but their happiness and relief predominated.

Then they were in a confusing total whiteout; they continued, fearing that they would miss their compound, but "With luck or an astonishing instinct he [Johnston] had led us straight to the igloos." They were extremely disappointed to find them deserted, but at least they had a new supply of food on which they gorged.

March 8: Their feet were badly discolored and swollen, and it was very difficult to get their boots back on, but eventually they succeeded. The sun was shining brightly and the temperature was a balmy 16 below zero. They moved down toward Windy Corner, made radio contact with rescuers, and eventually decided to be airlifted out by helicopter. The others also left. The three men had each lost about 35 pounds. Two days later, Davidson ate a normal breakfast, plus nineteen eggs! Johnston spent forty-five days in the hospital. They all basically survived fairly intact and went on to many other adventures.

Accounts of dreadful experiences or tragedies may sometimes be hyperbolically rendered, exaggerated for effect, and more or less so during varying cultural periods. The Denali men survived as the windchill plummeted to 148 degrees below zero, in an environment perhaps never before or since experienced by human beings.[4] Reality was so overwhelming that there was no need to embellish or exaggerate. The story is presented here as it truly occurred.

No one should have to endure the pain and suffering that these men experienced, which Davidson has rendered so powerfully in this extraordinary tale, in an often lyrical prose that both overpowers and stuns: "In my mind the full moon is still rising over the Kahiltna and that silent world of glaciers, ice and rock. The stars are still burning in the black sky we looked up to from the summit. I can see the northern lights swirling out beyond the mountain and the sun breaking cold and golden over an icy ridge. Shimmering ice crystals are falling out of a clear sky. And there is the wind, ripping and pounding on the slopes, and in our heads."

These men accepted a challenge, endured, and triumphed.

NOTES

1 When inviting climbers to participate in the interviews that led to the current authors' *Grasping for Heaven*, JA spoke at some length by phone with this extraordinary person (who still lives in the Alaskan mountains). It turned out that the two men have a number of unusual things in common.

2 We do not think that 60 pounds is a moderate load. As noted below, carrying extremely heavy packs (50, 75, or even 100 pounds) at altitude is difficult and draining, and probably indirectly causes many problems, and sometimes, tragedies.

3 Because ravens are the most intelligent birds, burying cardboard boxes and even wooden crates may be ineffective. The sites must be marked with flags so that they can be located later, after a big storm, and the ravens thereby know precisely where to dig, peck, tear, and feast. They reward climbers' generosity by scattering whatever they reject.

4 Naturally, other people have suffered in exigent situations. Nansen and a colleague once spent eighteen months in an igloo they constructed when marooned in the Arctic, but the weather (temperature and wind) was not as intense, and they were able to provide food for themselves.

SOURCES

This account is based primarily on Davidson's mountaineering classic, including his corrections. Ancillary sources and interviews are accessible via the Internet.

Davidson, Art. *Minus 148°: First Winter Ascent of Mount McKinley.* Seattle: The Mountaineers, 2007.

Davidson, Art. Personal communication. We are extremely grateful to Mr. Davidson for his kind and extensive comments on (and corrections to) this chapter. They are, for the most part, included silently in the account. When documented, they read "Davidson, pc."

Leonard, Brendan. "Climber Art Davidson on the 1st Winter Ascent of Denali . . . ," *Adventure Journal.* November 20, 2013. www.adventure-journal.com/2013/11/climber-art-davidson-on-the-1st-winter-ascent-of-denali-adventure-and-surviving-minus-148-degrees/.

CHAPTER 3

Denali, 1967:
The Wilcox Expedition

In June of 1967, two groups of competent climbers decided to attempt McKinley. The two leaders had discussed sharing some of the expenses and tasks, but Joe Wilcox's group's members were not really interested in climbing with strangers. Then disaster struck: Howard Snyder's small team lost a member because he had had an automobile accident. Now down to three, they could not proceed with their climb because park regulations demanded a minimum of four people for each expedition. In desperation, Snyder called Wilcox, and they decided that the teams would meet for some preliminary work on Mount Rainier. This decision turned out to have fatal consequences for seven of the Wilcox mountaineers and emotionally devastating repercussions for everyone else, in a controversy that can have no true resolution.

Although Wilcox had acquiesced, his eight teammates were against the merger with the three Coloradoans, all of whom were much bigger physically and more experienced than some of the comparative novices who had joined Wilcox. Although it is claimed that experience is not necessarily a good indicator of failure or disaster, it might have been a good idea if all of the climbers had known what an ice screw is and how to employ one (Snyder, 43). In any case, the Coloradoans had climbed, and even some of the Wilcox men had done quite a bit of mountaineering (Snyder, 4, 5, 14–16). The entire business got off to a horrible start because Wilcox had written to Bradford Washburn,[1] the dean of McKinley climbing, and one of the foremost photographers and cartographers of the mountain environment. Wilcox managed to antagonize Washburn (always somewhat curmudgeonly), and they had an unpleasant series of epistolary altercations, the result of which was that Washburn attempted to derail Wilcox's expedition. This was then compounded by the fact that Wilcox and Snyder disliked each other on sight. Nevertheless, after they all met on Rainier, they agreed to join forces, and then headed north for the long trip to Alaska, but in separate vehicles.

Major mountaineering calamities can be divided into two distinct types. At times, an unexpected occurrence, such as the arrival of a severe weather system, will catch diverse individuals or groups at different points on a mountain. Each will contend with the adversity in different ways. These people are separated from each other and cope with their problems with varying degrees of success. Some survive; others perish. This, for example, is what occurred during the 2008 K2 tragedy (see below). In the other instance, a sometimes large number of climbers are caught together in a deteriorating situation and act in unison. This was the case in 1953 on K2 (also discussed below), when all the climbers except Art Gilkey survived. Lamentably, here on Denali, the seven men trapped high on the mountain all perished.

As they proceeded with their hike to base camp, commencing at Wonder Lake on June 18, and heading up the mountain toward the Muldrow Glacier on July 4 in order to set up additional camps, they fought among themselves. Sometimes the two groups were at loggerheads, but it also came to pass that members of Wilcox's group hassled and berated each other. Two of Snyder's group walked in at a very fast pace, allowing a Wilcox man to fall way behind a number of times; this obviously can be a very dangerous thing to do, but as it happens, this man would stop to rest for very long periods (Snyder, 28–30). In another instance, one climber was ill but failed to inform others; when he carried less weight, he was publicly berated by his peers.[2] These two early incidents are indicative of the roiling discontent that was an ongoing feature of the expedition.

And they could be stubborn: A skier refused to change to snowshoes even though he found it extremely difficult to make uphill progress, thereby holding up his rope-mates. And because the men had different strengths and abilities, speed was a constant irritant. A few moved quickly; others begged them to slow down. It is easy to sympathize, because the going could be exhausting. It took five hours to go from 11,000 feet to 11,550 in deep snow with light loads; the return took twenty minutes. (Wilcox claims that at times they forced their way through hip-, waist-, chest-, and shoulder-deep snow [Wilcox, 97].) Some commentators think that this dissension might have been a contributing factor to the ensuing tragedy. Others disagree.

As low as 12,000 feet, a few of the men began to feel the effects of altitude, the result of which was irritability, but it seems improbable that altitude could have had a truly harmful effect on the men's personalities until they reached considerably higher elevations. The usual physiological reactions (acute mountain sickness, hypothermia, hypoxia, snow blindness) may also have played a role here. There additionally exists a minor controversy concerning whether they knew about an impending storm. After a debacle everything is magnified in the participants' attempt to assign or deny culpability. But even if a potential storm had been mentioned (Snyder quotes Wilcox to the effect that there was one approaching [Wilcox, 93]), we wonder whether they would have decided to sit in their tents while the sun was brightly shining, although four of the nine Wilcox group members ultimately but inexplicably decided to wait a day to summit. (Snyder had been in favor of a single group of twelve attempting the summit, and Wilcox seemed to agree [Wilcox, 91]). And, finally, Washburn insisted that the twelve men underestimated Denali's potency. Additional minor factors were nastiness, failure to read Washburn's guide, and a general malaise—all on the part of the Wilcox group (Snyder, passim). While these were all possible influences, the only thing that truly mattered was the overwhelming storm (one of the worst to ever hit Denali) that made descent impossible.

Just before they moved up from Camp Six to Seven, a stove ignited the cook tent and destroyed it; this set some of the climbers on edge. Then Snyder raced along, pushing a few of his rope-mates beyond their capacity. Finally, they set up Camp Seven out in the open, where it was highly susceptible to devastating winds, rather than a bit higher where Washburn had suggested it would have some protection. Around noon on July 15, the three Coloradoans and Wilcox departed from Camp Seven, but with an inadequate supply of wands, some of which they had forgotten below. They moved slowly in shirtsleeve weather but still made excellent progress, and at 6:29 p.m., the four men reached the summit. They were all extremely happy except for Wilcox, who was tired and fearful, and felt alone because his friends were still at Camp Seven.

After a long time on the summit, they headed down only to find themselves in stormy conditions. They reached camp just before ten. July 16 was clear but windy, so the other Wilcox men, who were now also at Seven, rested. They decided to leave for the summit on July 17, but lingered far too long: Six men started up at 3:00 p.m. (when traditionally one leaves for summits at 3:00 a.m., or even earlier; had they done so, they might have survived). By 8:00 p.m., they were lost in a whiteout. Wands that Snyder's group had set were too short to be seen or had been blown away, and others that had been placed by climbers coming up the West Buttress route were now also invisible. At 19,550, they were not far from the summit, but since they could not safely navigate, they decided to bivouac, perhaps dig snow caves, and proceed when conditions improved (Snyder, 121–22). Wilcox also conjectures that they dug snow caves (Wilcox, 248). They called in at 9:30 p.m. and indicated that everyone was okay. What they ostensibly did not yet know was that a very bad storm was on the way.

On July 18, the weather had cleared, so five men headed for the summit, where they arrived a little before noon, according to a final call. John Russell apparently was too ill to continue, so they must have left him at the snow caves. No one mentions him. They then headed down and very soon found themselves in a suddenly worsening conflagration. Nevertheless, they reached the snow caves by 3:00 p.m., and stayed there. Russell was gone, presumably now ensconced at Camp Seven with Steve Taylor, who had decided not to try for the summit. The first team (the three Colorado climbers, Wilcox, and Anshel Schiff) were at Camp Six, which they had struggled to reach because three of the men were quite ill (Snyder, 117). Surprisingly, there was now another expedition on this side of the mountain: Bill Babcock's team was down on the glacier, at 8,600 feet.

Much that follows up high is at least partially undocumented and therefore speculative. James Tabor, in his expansive study, hypothesizes—that is, creatively imagines—various scenarios, but there is no way to know with any certainty what occurred. Tabor's thoughts, no matter how logical, are merely conjectures. What we do know is that "every expert" consulted criticized the men for bivouacking (although what they thought the climbers might have done otherwise in this harrowing situation is unclear).

On July 19, the storm continued, but at 10:00 a.m. it cleared. By 8:00 p.m., when there was no call from the men above, Wilcox wanted to go up, but Snyder refused to climb at night. Very early the following morning, Wilcox, Snyder, and Paul Schlichter tried, but were forced to turn back when the storm reasserted itself. Wilcox contacted the rangers for a fly-by drop of fuel, batteries, a radio, and a count of the men at Camp Seven. According to Tabor (it is not clear whether this is conjecture, and Snyder also hypothesizes [Snyder, 147]), a little thereafter (at noon), the men at the caves headed down, but the wind was so devastating that, horribly, it forced them to go back up. Time passed. On July 21, they were all in an "arctic hurricane," "one of the worst [storms] in park history," even at Wonder Lake (which was extremely tranquil when the current authors visited).

The wind was so devastating ("more than 100 miles per hour" [Wilcox, 148]) and the snow so fierce that Wilcox and Schiff were incapable of shoveling fast enough to keep their tent clear. They were forced out and into Snyder's tent, which means that five people were squeezed into a two-man unit. At about the same time, the Babcock group somehow made a carry from 11,550 and then returned to their igloo, but they too were in lamentable shape. Things were so bad that a ranger attempted to mount an all-out rescue, but his superiors (at various hierarchical levels) were not entirely cooperative; things moved very slowly.

On July 22, there was partial clearing below, but the storm continued to rage on high; even the men at Camp Six were devastated (apathetic, hardly eating, drinking, sleeping, or communicating), and therefore incapable of mounting a rescue effort (which is what the higher-level authorities desired) for those at Camp Seven, as well as the men in the snow caves higher up (which Snyder and the others probably did not even know existed). Wilcox thought it might take as long as eighteen hours (in the new snow) to go from Six to Seven (Snyder, 148).

Once again, it was clear on July 23. Three of the five men at Camp Six were not well; Wilcox could neither feel nor move his hands, and despaired because he felt that he was about to abandon his friends (Wilcox, 159). Nevertheless, they prepared and then headed downward, all on a single rope, but with insuperable trouble, since some of them were very sick and weak. They fell constantly, and that was on the easy part. When they arrived at the steep slope, they found that the snow had blown away and the rock-hard ice was impassable. But they also found that the packed trail they had made when ascending was now a raised, softer, narrow "catwalk." They managed this difficult traverse. As they descended, the Babcock group spotted them and went to their aid. Eventually, they were ensconced in Babcock's tents. Snyder was incensed at Wilcox, and maintained his anger the next day, when, on the descent, they were joined by the ailing Babcock member, Grace Jansen-Hoeman. At the same time, there was much confusion concerning a rescue flight (for those higher up), and the authorities in charge refused to authorize a large plane until a smaller one had flown. Wilcox refused to formally request a rescue, although the men at high camp and the caves had been incommunicado for seven days.

The small group got down on July 25, while the Babcock expedition moved upward. Don Sheldon finally did a flyover, saw Babcock, and made a drop at 15,000 feet. (Even at the time, from a reasonable perspective, one must wonder how this could help anyone. If weakened climbers could get down to this material, they ostensibly could and would have simply continued to the lower areas on the mountain. And how would they know that a drop had occurred and where the supplies were located? It is, naturally, easy to comment and criticize in retrospect, but the entire business after the storm hit is most disconcerting.) Wayne Merry, the ranger with little authority and the only official to fully comprehend the import of the impending tragedy, continued to prod his superiors to mount a rescue, but he thus far had failed.

On July 26, Babcock continued to struggle toward Wilcox's Camp Seven, locating the airdrop. Wilcox himself, along with two others, made it to Clearwater Creek, but only he was capable of crossing the now fast-moving water. Next came the mile-wide McKinley River, a raging torrent and impassable, but Wilcox miraculously made it across, got to park headquarters, and ordered a helicopter to bring out the five remaining people stranded at the first water crossing.[3]

Finally, on July 27, Sheldon did two overflights but accomplished nothing. The park personnel and rescue group resumed efforts, but these were not coordinated and also accomplished nothing. It is astonishing that except for Merry, all of these people watched the days go by and never allowed that seven or more climbers were degenerating or dying high on the mountain. One reason may have been that some of them had never climbed, and so did not realize what it is like to be caught in a fierce storm, one of the worst in park history. They indicated that these competent men could rescue themselves!

Thus, it fell to the five exhausted remaining members of the Babcock group to set their own summit aspirations aside and concentrate on getting to the Wilcox men. On July 28, Sheldon flew again but insisted on a 14,300-foot drop, when the men were trapped above 17,000, and the Babcocks were thousands of feet above the drop point. The materials would do no one any good, but he refused to fly higher. Exactly like his good friend Washburn, Sheldon was extremely competent but curmudgeonly and stubborn. The Babcocks pressed on; suddenly they came upon an ice ax. They were stunned, and with good reason. Although mountaineers have given up (to anchor a line or help a climber), abandoned (due to mental aberration or fear), or dropped an ax (because it was untethered), this occurs so infrequently that instances in the history of mountaineering could be counted on a hand or two. The ax is the climber's lifeline. Without it, in steep, icy conditions, a fall will be fatal.[4]

This discovery was a very bad omen. They left it and continued. Soon they were shocked by another anomaly: an 8-foot pole, buried in the snow, and flying a sleeping bag and shell. Tabor expends much mental energy postulating the ways in which this bizarre occurrence had come to pass. Most reasonable is that a climber upon descending set it up because he could no longer carry it, or as a signal to rescuers. He then could have been blown off the mountain by the wind, which may have been howling at 150 miles per hour. They arrived at Wilcox's Camp Seven and were met by disorder and a bad stench. Beside the big tent was a decomposing body, but no one else.

The next day, July 29, they headed for the summit. Because of their fatigue, it was a real struggle. (The park personnel had inconsiderately asked these people to do more and thereby alienated them.) They reached the summit in windy and deteriorating conditions. As they descended, Sheldon informed them that there was a body below Archdeacon's Tower, and so two men dropped down on steep and dangerous terrain in very bad conditions to investigate. They then spotted another body, neither of which was accompanied by any equipment whatsoever. They re-climbed to their friends and rushed down to their snow caves in a windy whiteout. As they had moved upward early in the day, a larger plane than Sheldon's had made ten flyovers of Denali Pass, dropping a great deal of useful material, but, regrettably, on the wrong side of the pass.

After much struggle, the Babcocks got down, reached the river, which was now less turbulent but still bad enough, made it across, and retreated to civilization. Sometime thereafter, a group of climbers mounted a humanitarian expedition in order to bring some closure to the tragedy, but accomplished nothing because an enormous amount of new snow encapsulated everything. (The pole which had risen six feet above the surface now had only six inches of exposure.) Next came the sadness of parents and the horror of inquiring reporters. Even worse was an August 11 *Time* magazine story, quoting Washburn, that seemed to assign blame to the expedition members and Wilcox (rather than to the horrendous storm). A conference was convened, but, impossibly, the five survivors were not present. Washburn blamed Wilcox for the calamity, both here and later, in conjunction with Snyder. To add insult to injury, the report included in the 1967 edition of the American Alpine Club's influential *Accidents in North American Mountaineering* was riddled with innumerable errors, giving an extremely false picture of what had actually occurred.

Some of the men (the Coloradoans) were giants (6-foot-5, 225 pounds); others were quite diminutive (5-foot-5, 140 pounds). Many were skillful and experienced mountaineers; others were so lacking that at least one was initially rejected by the park service. They prided themselves not on how efficiently, easily, and skillfully they reached their various objectives, nor on their cooperation and camaraderie, nor, usually, on the joy that climbing and nature produce, but rather on their speed and how heavy their packs were. They brought an inordinate abundance of things (400 pounds for the smaller group, and some 1,500 pounds for the Wilcox contingent). Wilcox offers different numbers: 1,942 pounds via horse and 70 pounds on average on the twelve men's backs, which yields an additional 840 pounds (Wilcox, 69) that they naturally had to haul in obscenely heavy packs. Fording the raging McKinley River (which washed away a horse) with 80 pounds on one's back is simply stupid. (Göran Kropp may have carried 150 pounds to Everest base camp, but he was an anomaly, since he also rode a bicycle from Sweden to Nepal.) All of this extremely heavy hauling (up to 100 pounds in a single, steeply dangerous carry and 120 on easier ground [Snyder, 168; Wilcox, 80]) wore them down, exhausted them, and may have helped to lead to the disaster [5]

Another factor never discussed by anyone was the often-shoddy quality of their equipment. Almost thirty years after Charlie Houston's first attempt on K2, and almost fifteen years after Hillary and Norgay reached Everest's summit, both groups with adequate equipment, these men had at least three crampon breaks (which could have resulted in death), snow-tread (plastic snowshoe) hinge snaps (Wilcox, 97), different makes of badly malfunctioning stoves (which so frustrated the men that they would toss them out into the snow—sometimes after the stove had exploded and burnt or destroyed their tents), weak and broken supports (Wilcox, 102) on porous tents that would collapse under the snow burden or disintegrate in the wind, a leaking fuel container, various boots and gloves that failed to offer protection against the weather, pack straps that dug into their shoulders, sleeping bags that became waterlogged, and so on. [6]

Seven men died; they did not leave any diaries, so their final days are a blank. Wilcox and Schiff, as well as the three Coloradoans (Snyder, Lewis, and Schlichter) survived. Six years later, Snyder published *The Hall of the Mountain King*, which was not well received. Wilcox followed with *White Winds* in 1981 (supplemented with 230 pages of documentation and appendices—correspondence, radio and rescue logs, wind classification, McKinley fatalities, and so on), and simultaneously offered *A Reader's Guide to the Hall of the Mountain King*, a devastating critique of Snyder's book. Washburn, Fred Beckey, and Jonathan Waterman all devoted misleading chapters in their respective books to the tragedy, often blaming Wilcox for being a poor leader. But Snyder (ironically) described a number of instances in which Wilcox acted in a severely determinate fashion. When two of his men wanted to use skis, he demurred: "If any of you don't want to follow my orders, you can ... do Logan," and Wilcox ordered Snyder to locate a route and take specific men with him (Snyder, 38, 39).

There can be little doubt that these twelve men did not always see eye to eye, operated in different ways, and disliked each other, sometimes vehemently. But disagreements are part of human interaction in any venue (though heightened and exacerbated in the stressful environment one encounters in the high mountains). Had they had better luck with the weather, the Wilcox/Snyder Denali expedition would have faded from memory as so many other climbs naturally do. As it is, though, this was "one of the worst tragedies in mountaineering history."

Real culpability or guilt, if any does exist here, can never be truly assigned. If any people are guilty of something, it is the various park employees who insisted that the two disparate groups conjoin and later refused to mount an immediate rescue effort (after the men had been in extremis for ten days; Wilcox had called for an all-out rescue on July 23 [Wilcox, 162]), but even here it is necessary to qualify. Since the weather was so horrendous, the best-intentioned and strongest person could not have gone up on foot or by plane or helicopter. (The wind blew at 80 to 110 miles per hour, with gusts up to 150.) Nevertheless, the inept way in which the rescue efforts were carried out had a devastating effect on Merry, who eventually resigned from the park service.

When Wilcox finally reached Wonder Lake on July 26 and was apprised of the rescue's progress, he "literally exploded at how little had been done" (Wilcox, 175). Gerianne Hall, the daughter of park super-intendent George Hall, disagrees vehemently with Tabor's conclusions (based in part on Snyder and Wilcox), viz., that park personnel were responsible for the debacle, and adduces a torrent of evidence to prove her case (see georgehallsalaska.com). And in 2014, Andy Hall, Geri-anne's brother, published *Denali's Howl: The Deadliest Climbing Disaster on America's Wildest Peak*, in which he also comes to the defense of the park service. This was "the worst tragedy in North American mountaineering history," inexplicable and beyond human control and understanding.

NOTES

1 See the current authors' interview with Barbara Washburn, Brad's wife, in Frederic Hartemann and Robert Hauptman, *Grasping for Heaven: Interviews with North American Mountaineers* (Jefferson, NC: McFarland, 2011). Barbara was about ninety-five at the time of the interview. She would have been one hundred years old in November of 2014, but she died just before her birthday.

2 It is a simple truth, never learned, that if one treated others with real consideration, most interpersonal problems would be forestalled. Instead of jealously confronting or berating in a life-and-death situation, the stronger members should have offered compassion and help.

3 Bradford Washburn and his partner faced a similar impassable roging river upon their descent from Lucania. They had to walk upstream for many miles in order to cross.

4 Many years ago, as the current authors were descending Whitney, they met, at about 12,000 feet, a man carrying a calm baby; he was accompanied by his wife with their supplies. We had to traverse a short but steep chute of snow and ice, which SA had done on the way up with crampons. A fall would have caused the crampon-less man to tumble and his six-month-old child could have been killed. JA offered him his ax. (He could have put crampons on, had the man accepted.) He refused. JA averted his eyes as the man successfully crossed. These people were insane; they had no business carrying an altitude-sensitive infant to the 14,505-foot summit of the highest mountain in the contiguous forty-eight states, although this is not an unusual occurrence. On the summit of Utah's King's Peak, SA questioned a father carrying an infant who was crying hysterically. The man denied that the approximately 14,000-foot altitude was harming his child. SA became so incensed that he only avoided a physical confrontation by quickly going down.

5 Despite much of what is implied here, giantism is not a prerequisite for strength or success. The junior author of this book is seventy-three years old, 5-foot-6, and 135 pounds. He has conditioned himself by carrying 60 pounds of crushed rock on his walk to work and back, and hauled an enormous expedition pack to many sites, e.g., Rainier's Camp Muir and the refuge on the Aiguille du Tour. But JA finally realized that a heavy pack ruins one's pleasure, and so he now eliminates all of the superfluous stuff. While SA sleeps on a 6-inch air mattress inside a two-man tent on Mount Baker's moraine, JA lies outside on the hard ground under the stars. Go light; save a life!

6 Years before this 1967 debacle, JA traveled to Munich in order to purchase equipment, probably at SportScheck. The French mountaineering pack served him well for twenty-five years, as did the old-fashioned, comparatively heavy tent and the lightweight sleeping bag (which he soon replaced). The stove, at low altitude, was excellent. It is possible that at least some of the twelve men scrimped because of financial problems. At least one person sewed his own tent, and many made additions to their equipment by sewing on patches of various kinds.

SOURCES

Tabor's comprehensive, award-winning study forms the basis for the preceding account. Other sources are credited in the text.

Snyder, Howard H. *The Hall of the Mountain King*. New York: Charles Scribner's Sons, 1973.

Tabor, James M. *Forever on the Mountain: The Truth Behind One of Mountaineering's Most Controversial and Mysterious Disasters*. New York: W. W. Norton, 2007.

Wilcox, Joe. *White Winds*. Los Alamitos, CA: Hwong Publishing, 1981.

Section Three:
K2 (28,251 feet)

Every high and challenging mountain has presented sometimes insurmountable problems for those attempting a first or even second ascent. This is certainly true of K2, which began killing mountaineers soon after the first Westerners arrived. In *Mountain Men: The Ghosts of K2* (BBC, 2013), Ashish Chanda has produced a superb documentary overview of K2 attempts with original footage, re-creations, and some of the pioneers commenting on their expeditions of the distant past. Charles Houston and Bob Bates were there in 1938, followed by Fritz Wiessner in 1939, and Houston again in 1953. Then in 1954, Lino Lacedelli and Achille Compagnoni, accompanied to base camp by seven hundred porters, finally reached the summit. It is stunning to see and hear these legendary climbers remark on their travails and tragedies.

CHAPTER 4

K2, 1953:
The Savage Mountain: Charles Houston and Art Gilkey

CHARLES HOUSTON,[1] A MEDICAL DOCTOR, LED THE FIRST AMERICAN Karakoram Expedition in 1938; a second, without him, followed in 1939; and then in 1953, he was back for the Third. *K2, The Savage Mountain,* the account that he, Robert Bates, and other members of this tragic climb produced, is, like Maurice Herzog's *Annapurna,* one of the classic texts of mountaineering literature.[2] It is here that readers discover how, despite a devastating blizzard and the loss of a fellow climber's life, a group of dedicated and caring men managed to survive this horrific storm.[3]

The early stages of the expedition were taken up by planning, packing, traveling, and getting to base camp. There naturally followed weeks of route preparation. They climbed, hauled, and stocked their many camps. Although they had Balti porters to carry their 4,500 pounds of supplies to base camp and six Hunza mountain porters, the eight expedition members (plus one Pakistani colleague) did their own carrying once they moved up high on the mountain; therefore, much time was consumed, exacerbated by the intemperate weather that always hinders mountaineers in the Himalaya and Karakoram. These motivated, strong, well-conditioned, experienced, and cooperative men (including Houston, Bates, Pete Schoening, and Tony Streather) carried 30- to 40-pound packs as they stocked the camps, which seems reasonable, even at lower altitudes. (The insanely heavy—100-pound—packs that some of the climbers on Denali in 1967 hauled undoubtedly overwhelmed their physical abilities, and may have helped lead to the tragedy.)

June 20 found the men at base camp, ready to begin the assault. A beautiful day was followed by many more, with few exceptions. As late as July 10, the weather was still good. This means that they had almost three weeks of often superb weather. But that evening a storm hit, which continued to dump snow all of the following day. The men had to shovel the snow away from the tents (which sometimes were situated in the most precarious positions on precipices) every few hours. July 12 allowed for some movement, but then very early on July 13, snow and high winds returned, running through July 14. The men continued to rest on July 15 because of the 20 inches of new snow that had fallen. Many days passed, some stormy, others clear. They continued to move upward, slowly stocking their eight camps.

Finally, August 2 found all expedition members (except Pakistani liaison officer and colleague, Colonel M. Ata-Ullah, an ophthalmologist, who had stayed at base camp) ensconced at Camp Eight. The weather now turned extremely violent, and so they bided their time. On August 5, the wind tore the tent that Houston and George Bell occupied to pieces, so they had to crowd into other small units. Amazingly, despite their long hardship, thirst, and some frostbitten extremities, the eight men's morale was excellent. On August 7, the weather improved, and so they thought they might resume their attempt on the summit. Art Gilkey came out of his tent and immediately collapsed. He complained of a charley horse, but upon examining him, Houston discovered that he had thrombophlebitis: Here, blood clots cut off circulation in the legs and are extremely debilitating and dangerous, for they can break off and move from the legs into the lungs, a condition that even at sea level can be fatal . The men all realized that rather than continuing upward, they now had to descend in order to save Gilkey's life. They packed up, an activity that can take many hours under normal circumstances, but they did it quickly. Houston apparently had an obsession about leaving sites tidy, so he began to toss the extra food and material off the mountain. Someone told him to forget about aesthetics and get going. This simple admonition probably saved their lives.

They were high on K2, one of the most difficult mountains in the world, severely hard to descend in the best conditions, that is, when one is healthy and strong and the weather is excellent. These men were worn down, the weather had been terrible, and they had to haul a debilitated climber along with them over steep snow and ice and sometimes sheer rock and rubble, down and up and down. They all thought it was an impossible task, but they also knew they had to try. So they proceeded. After "a few hundred yards" they realized that the slope they were descending was ready to avalanche, so they turned back and worked very hard to get Gilkey back to the campsite that they had just abandoned. They were all now in desperate straits. They decided to investigate a different route along a ridge; two men went down in the wind and discovered that it was possible. Even though it was "difficult and dangerous," it would be free of avalanches.

The next morning was better, and some of the men once again thought about the summit; indeed, Schoening and Robert Craig spent a few hours climbing about 400 feet, to their highpoint of about 25,500 feet, but it was a futile gesture. They should have gone down, because August 9 was once again extremely bad, with wind and snow lashing the site. To make matters worse, the clots had moved into Gilkey's lungs; the pulmonary embolisms meant that he had to go down or die. So on August 10, despite the horrendous storm raging around them, they descended. Schoening and Dee Molenaar (whose superb drawings and maps can be found in many mountaineering accounts) left early in order to locate a viable route down (and eventually to base camp, 9,000 feet below); the others hauled Gilkey, whose ongoing good humor and uncomplaining nature were angelic, in a makeshift sled constructed out of a tent, backpack, and entwining ropes. The men either had to pull the sled through "knee-deep drifts" or hold it back lest it fly down and off the mountain. It was desperate work, especially since they could not see very far through the storm. They were bringing Gilkey down blindly when an avalanche poured over two of the men. The others then lowered Gilkey over a cliff; tied in to each other in different permutations, they were contemplating a difficult traverse when suddenly, Bell slipped and fell.

And now there occurred one of the most amazing feats in the history of mountaineering, even more extraordinary than either Joe Simpson's or Doug Scott's remarkable self-rescues despite their broken legs. The Belay is legendary: "Nothing like it, before or since, has ever been performed in the mountains," is how Ed Viesturs put it (Viesturs, 218). Five men fell, slipped, slid, tumbled, rolled, or plummeted downward on hard ice; they fell "150 to 300 feet down a 45-degree slope." Since they were tied in, in different configurations, even a single or double self-arrest might not have saved everyone. But this is moot because no one seemed able to find a purchase for his ax. They all continued tumbling. Bell, roped to Streather, pulled him down; they hit Houston and Bates on a second rope, and down they went as well; Molenaar and Streather were tied to Gilkey. As they slid, they became entangled in each other's ropes, which saved them, because when one was caught on something, they stopped.[4] Schoening had stuck his ax behind a rock and was belaying Gilkey; as the fall progressed, Schoening's rope took up all of the weight and he held it. Many years later, he recounted what had occurred:

I was in a belay position facing the ice slope . . . . Out of the corner of my eye I saw George slip, and thus knew I needed to brace against the impending impact. From this point on I concentrated solely on executing the belay; there was no looking around. I felt considerable force on the rope in stopping the fall. It was a long time before Art was anchored and the others secure so I could go off belay. (McDonald quoting Schoening, 134)

Schoening saved six men's lives, many of whom ended up hurt and in precarious positions on ledges. Houston was well below Bates, and unconscious. Bates climbed down to him and he revived but was unaware of his surroundings and incapable of movement. He was hurt and had a concussion. Bates tried to get him to move upward but Houston merely repeated, "Where are we?" Finally, Bates exclaimed, "Charlie . . . if you ever want to see Dorcas and Penny again [his wife and daughter], climb up there *right now!*" (Brackets and italics in original.) All of this occurred in extreme conditions: cold, wind, and biting snow were freezing the climbers, causing frostbite, and exhausting them.

They now had to get themselves up and over to their old Camp Seven, where they planned to bivouac for the night. (Thus far, all they had accomplished was to descend from Eight to Seven.) Craig, who had not been involved in the accident, went over to Gilkey and secured him firmly to an ice ax, which finally allowed Schoening to release the weight he had been holding and to try to warm up. Some of the men's packs had been swept away, but they still had a small tent; with great difficulty in the wind, they set it up, although part of it extended into the abyss. They then had to laboriously hack out a platform for a second small tent, which had been left at Seven. When set up, it too overhung into the void.[5] Three men now prepared to traverse back to Gilkey, who was tethered on the slope by two axes, 150 feet from the tents. They could not see him but he had yelled to them occasionally, although his words were indecipherable in the storm. When the men reached a point from which they could see the location where Gilkey was tethered, they were stunned: "The whole slope was bare of life. Art Gilkey was gone!"

This was a horrible shock to everyone, especially since they all liked Gilkey very much, but they were in dire straits and had to get down soon or die. They did not have much time to contemplate what had happened, but they thought an avalanche had ripped the axes out and thereby released Gilkey, who had slid down. Perhaps it was only later that they began to consider the possibility that Gilkey had somehow managed, in his weakened condition, to pull the axes out or otherwise extricate himself from his cocoon in order to save his friends the dangerous trouble of trying to get him down. In 2003, Houston changed his mind and insisted that Gilkey did release himself; Bates continued to hold that it was an accident (McDonald, 135).

Seven men, cold, exhausted, and some seriously injured, were now crammed into two tiny tents waiting for dawn. It seems almost impossible, but somehow they were able to make tea, which allayed their thirst and warmed them. When morning arrived, they knew that despite their injuries, frostbite, weakness, and exhaustion, they had no choice but to go down. They thought if they could safely reach Six on this most dangerous section, they would eventually be able to get to base camp. They struggled on the slippery, steep slabs, taking especial care of Houston, who was in a state of constant confusion. Had a single person on one of the two ropes (of four and three) slipped, the others would have been pulled off. After downclimbing some fixed ropes, they arrived at Six only to find the tents filled with snow, which they had to clear. In the morning, storm conditions held all but Schoening and Streather at Six. The next day was August 13, and stormy, but the remaining men gathered up their equipment, including one tent, and headed down. After a brief stop at Five, they continued.

Under normal circumstances, it only took five minutes to get from Five to the top of House's Chimney, a difficult sheer rock face. Now it took more than an hour, both because they were tired, but also because everything was coated with ice. They spent the night at Four. In the morning Bell was forced to slit his boots in order to get his badly frostbitten feet into them. Just above Two, on a precipitous slope, three Hunzas met them and they had a tearful reunion. They then spent some time resting at base camp. Before they left for home, they gathered at a point where two glaciers meet; it was here that the Hunzas had built a 10-foot cairn to commemorate Gilkey. It is still there for all visitors to K2 base camp to see.

They departed on August 17. The long walk was impossible for Bell, whose feet were in deplorable condition, and so he was carried on a litter. When the path became impossible for men abreast from each other, a single man carried the 170-pound Bell on his back. All of the rest were injured or depleted in some way, making the long, eleven-day walk out slow and painful.

Viesturs points out how rare thrombophlebitis is in the mountains (Viesturs, 212), and notes that in 1993, Gilkey's bones, carried down by the glacier, were discovered near base camp (225). Despite this tragedy, and the very real possibility that all members of this expedition might have perished in the storm and rescue attempt, the 1953 assault on K2 remains a glorious testament to caring cooperation: "In my opinion, the high point of American mountaineering remains the 1953 American Expedition to K2. The courage, devotion, and team spirit of that expedition have yet to be surpassed, and still represent the standards of conduct toward which all American mountaineers should aspire" (Viesturs, quoting Nick Clinch, 227). And of the nine men, the great Reinhold Messner observed: "They were decent. They were strong. And they failed in the most beautiful way you can imagine. This is the inspiration for a lifetime" (McDonald quoting Messner, 140). In 1978, seven men met for a twenty-five-year reunion.

Mountaineering historian Maurice Isserman has long maintained that the cooperative attitude and gallantry of earlier generations of climbers have been replaced by selfish individuals whose goal is to summit regardless of consequence: "[M]ountaineering has become more dangerous in recent decades as the traditional expeditionary culture of the early- and mid-20th century, which had emphasized mutual responsibility and common endeavor, gave way to an ethos stressing individualism and self-preservation." He contrasts Wilco van Rooijen's lament, following the 2008 K2 debacle (see below)—"Everybody was fighting for himself, and I still do not understand why everybody were [*sic*] leaving each other"— with the heroic actions of Houston and his fellow climbers (Isserman). His contention is valid in these cases, but I am still not certain that this is a generalizable conclusion. Some earlier mountaineers acted miserably (consider the treatment meted out to Walter Bonatti during the 1954 Italian conquest of K2—see below), whereas contemporary guides often make real sacrifices at their own peril to help or save their charges, or even complete strangers whom they encounter in passing. (In 1996, Rob Hall died on Everest because he did not want to abandon his clients.)

Nevertheless, the nine members of the 1953 K2 expedition outshined themselves in every way.

Notes

1 See Frederic Hartemann and Robert Hauptman, *Grasping for Heaven: Interviews with North American Mountaineers* (Jefferson, NC: McFarland, 2011) for an interview with Dr. Houston. This is probably one of his last formal conversations, for he died soon thereafter at the age of ninety-six.

2 Before he had begun climbing, Ed Viesturs read *K2: The Savage Mountain*, an experience that helped turn him into one of the world's elite mountaineers (Viesturs, 91).

3 Toward the end of his long life, and when he was almost completely blind, Dr. Houston somehow managed to edit the K2 films he had shot in 1938 and1953. These are viewable on a DVD that is included in Bernadette McDonald's *Brotherhood of the Rope*, a biography of Dr. Houston. As is often the case, these films (in color) complement the formal narrative and bring the people and events strikingly to life.

4 Roping up is standard practice in rock climbing: Belaying on vertical rock from a solid and protected stance is not merely reasonable; it is mandatory if one is to survive a bad fall. No one questions this. Belaying on steep snow or ice from one set ice screw or snow picket to another is also good practice, although extremely time-consuming. But moving belays in mountaineering (when all rope-mates climb simultaneously) has always struck me as potentially hazardous, especially when the surface is extremely steep and impenetrable. In case of a fall and when self-arrest is impossible, the tumbler will pull the other(s) down with him or her. In this unique case on K2, the practice initially did result in pandemonium, but then, miraculously, it averted a real tragedy. (About to descend a 70-degree, rock-hard, icy couloir on the South Teton [unroped, because we never considered roping up], SA slipped and tumbled down for perhaps 400 yards before he was able to self-arrest; had JA been tied in, he would have been pulled down as well. On his many hundreds of climbs over a thirty-five-year period in six countries, this was the only fall SA ever took.) It may be considered extremely iconoclastic advice, but there do exist occasions when a partner should wisely refuse to tie in. Consider that in 1986, near the summit of Orizaba, a climber slipped and pulled two friends along with him. They had to lie on the slope for three days before being rescued. The final result was death and horrible maiming (Coffey, 146). And the great Lionel Terray and his partner died because they were roped and one pulled the other along with him: "No doubt one man had slipped, pulling off the other" (Roberts, 203).

5 Their tents were primitive and inadequate in every way. It is truly astonishing that these flimsy and porous units were able to protect human beings in blizzards at 25,000 feet. When viewed in photographs, one can only shudder and thank tent designers for built-in floors, waterproof materials, flies, and aerodynamic mountain models.

SOURCES

The Houston/Bates text forms the basis for this recitation. When other authors provide material, they are noted in the text.

Coffey, Maria. *Where the Mountain Casts Its Shadow: The Dark Side of Extreme Adventure.* New York: St. Martin's Griffin, 2005.

Houston, Charles S., and Robert H. Bates. *K2: The Savage Mountain.* Seattle: The Mountaineers, 1979. Reprint (1954).

Isserman, Maurice. "The Descent of Men," *New York Times.* August 9, 2008. Accessed March 20, 2014. www.nytimes.com/2008/08/10/opinion/10isserman.html?_r=0.

McDonald, Bernadette. *Brotherhood of the Rope: The Biography of Charles Houston.* Seattle: The Mountaineers, 2007.

Roberts, David. *True Summit: What Really Happened on the Legendary Ascent of Annapurna.* New York: Simon & Schuster, 2000.

Viesturs, Ed, with David Roberts. *K2: Life and Death on the World's Most Dangerous Mountain.* New York: Broadway Books, 2009. (Contains a useful bibliography.)

CHAPTER 5

K2, 1954:

The First Ascent: Deception and Lies— Achille Compagnoni, Lino Lacedelli, and Walter Bonatti

ON JULY 31, 1954, ACHILLE COMPAGNONI AND LINO LACEDELLI reached the summit of K2; they were thus the first humans to stand on the top of the second-highest mountain on Earth. Like the English on Everest and the Germans on Nanga Parbat, these Italian climbers bought their conquest at a high price. English and German predecessors had offered their lives in order to fulfill what they thought was their rightful destinies. The Italians sacrificed their honor. They did reach the summit; this was no typical hoax à la Frederick Cook; rather, these two men conspired to keep Walter Bonatti from joining them in their triumph, caused a Hunza porter to lose parts of his hands and feet, and denied their culpability. It is an excellent example of how even the ostensibly idealistic and honorable mountaineers of the past sometimes acted as selfishly as Maurice Isserman contends we act today, allowing, for example, climbers to die rather than abort our own summit attempts to save them.

Bonatti was only in his early twenties and a mere amateur when his excellent reputation brought an invitation to join the 1954 Italian K2 expedition. The eleven men and thirteen Hunza HAPs (high-altitude porters) were led by Ardito Desio and supported by hundreds of Balti porters. Colonel Ata-Ullah, the very same Ata-Ullah who had been with Houston on K2 the preceding season, was once again the liaison officer. The men underwent the usual privations and took three months to reach the mountain, working their way up and setting camps as they went. On July 28, five climbers left from Camp Seven (at just over 23,000 feet). Bonatti was not among them, because he had eaten some tainted sardines and "felt shaken, listless, and useless." He was sorely disappointed. The men set up a single tent at Camp Eight (at 24,250 feet) and left Compagnoni and Lacedelli there to continue. The three others returned to Seven. Meanwhile, Bonatti decided to try to regain his strength by forcing himself to eat, though it nauseated him; he desperately wanted to rejoin his fellow climbers. About thirty minutes after the men left him, one of them returned; he was ill, unable to continue, and was forced to leave his pack on the slope above camp.

The next morning dawned splendidly, as Bonatti put it, and he was now feeling fine. The higher men were to continue, and set up a small tent at 25,800 feet. The others were to bring more provisions to Eight, but things went badly: Two of the climbers were worn out, dropped their loads, and descended. Bonatti exchanged his oxygen cylinders for some equipment they would need at Eight, and so they were forced to leave the heavy canisters sitting on the slope; these were crucial for the expedition's success, and were to play a seminal role in the controversy that followed.

After struggling through the mist, they finally located Compagnoni and Lacedelli, who were extremely tired from their own struggles. They decided that Bonatti and the other climber, Pino Gallotti, would descend in the morning and return all the way to the next camp (Nine), not yet set up, with the oxygen. Since the vertical descent and rise were enormous, the cylinders heavy, and the altitude extreme, they decided to place Nine a bit lower than originally planned. All in all, Bonatti calls this "almost an act of madness." Later, Bonatti noticed that Compagnoni was extremely tired and thought that maybe he could replace him on the summit team; Compagnoni even suggested that it was a possibility, though Bonatti psychoanalyzed all of this in negative terms.

In the morning, the potential summiters went up, and Bonatti and Gallotti went down slowly and carefully. At the point where the oxygen lay on the slope, they met three men, including the powerful HAP, Amir Mahdi. They retrieved the cylinders and all then went back up. Three of the five men—especially Gallotti, who fell constantly—were in bad shape. At Eight, only Bonatti and Mahdi could proceed. Bonatti realized that if he were to get the crucial oxygen up to the summiters, he would have to convince Mahdi to carry. This he did by offering money and suggesting that there was a chance that he too could join the summit team. It was ironic, given the developments that occurred during and long after the climb, and sad, because of what happened to Mahdi, that Bonatti admitted this was a deception, though he claimed that there was some truth to it. Mahdi agreed to continue, despite the fact that he did not have adequate boots.

Very slowly and laboriously they climbed toward their compatriots; a third man joined them for a while, and he alternated carrying the heavy canisters. They eventually surmounted a high wall of ice and then called out. Compagnoni and Lacedelli answered. They continued but could not locate the tent which they thought should have been lower than it apparently was. They nervously continued but were confused and fearful. They could not figure it out, despite the voices from above. The third man descended, leaving Bonatti and Mahdi alone on the slope from where they could see ascending tracks. But it was getting dark and Mahdi was extremely cold and in the early stages of hysteria. Bonatti called out again and again but there was no response. They struggled in great pain up a very steep, precipitous, and dangerous slope. Sadly, they had oxygen that could have alleviated their misery, but neither masks nor regulators; Bonatti mentioned the possibility of just allowing the gas to flow out around them, but that would have been very foolish and would have imperiled the expedition. Finally, he dropped his pack, crawled up higher, and saw that the tent was not there. He was very upset—indeed, in shock. Mahdi joined him. It was now dark and his light did not work. He retrieved the pack and they continued. Mahdi was in a state of uncontrolled madness, and Bonatti was fearful that Mahdi would slip and pull him off.

It was out of the question to attempt to return to Eight. The only alternative was to bivouac. Bonatti was now as deeply affected as Mahdi and felt "treacherously abandoned" and "betrayed." In this state he semi-consciously cleared a shelf, and it was here that they planned to wait until dawn. Before they settled in, they tried calling again and again, harming their throats. Suddenly, they saw a small light visible above. Bonatti asked why they had not answered their cries, and Lacedelli considerately replied, "Do you want us to stay out all night to freeze for you?" He asked about the oxygen, and when informed that they did have it, Lacedelli insisted they should leave it and return to Eight!

Bonatti said that Mahdi could not—that he was at that moment insanely climbing up the very dangerous slope toward the light, which suddenly disappeared. Mahdi returned to Bonatti and they realized that the others had purposely abandoned them—in the open, in the death zone![1] They waited in the intense and unbearable cold, which Bonatti allayed by beating himself with his ax. The night was clear and the surrounding peaks were visible. Nevertheless, a sudden blizzard inundated them and they had to fight for their lives. They lasted until sunrise and the storm's cessation, but were in very horrible shape, trembling and with little sensation.

Mahdi left for Eight before the sun was fully up, and managed to get down the dangerous slope without causing an avalanche. Even though Compagnoni and Lacedelli never appeared, Bonatti dug out the oxygen cylinders and then descended, first the very steep 700-foot slope, and then through the crevasse field. Soon he arrived at the tents shortly after Mahdi, whose limbs were badly frozen. Ironically, it was Mahdi who had carried the great but frozen Hermann Buhl off Nanga Parbat. In the evening, a Hunza announced that a climber was about to reach the summit. Astonishingly, those at Eight were close enough to the summit to see, without binoculars, the two tiny men summiting. Five hours later, all of the climbers were reunited at Eight, ecstatic in the victory. Bonatti set aside his feelings for the moment.

Later, in Karachi, a major controversy erupted when the press falsely claimed that Compagnoni had halted Mahdi just below the summit so that only the Italians would have the glory. An inquiry squelched this travesty. Upon his return to Italy, Bonatti inexplicably was ostracized. Neither the official report nor the film version mentioned the bivouac.

(A protest led to a generic cinematic insertion.) In both Desio's and Compagnoni's book-length accounts of the climb, Bonatti's contributions were diminished. Bonatti scrupulously questioned the accuracy of the reported "sites, altitudes, timetables, and oxygen usage," showing that "the official story is approximate and inexact." The summiters did not help Bonatti and Mahdi, and defended themselves by disingenuously insisting that "It was a misunderstanding, the north wind blew away their words."

Ten years later, two accusatory newspaper articles appeared. Based on Compagnoni's and Ata-Ullah's remarks, their author claimed that Bonatti had tried to beat the others to the summit, had used some of the oxygen, and had abandoned Mahdi. But the times offered by the summiters did not add up; nor was it explicable why the summiters would continue to carry the heavy cylinders if the oxygen had run out 600 feet from the top. The public overreacted and this forced Bonatti to file a suit, which he eventually won. For some reason, however, it was Bonatti who was thought to be "a liar, a malcontent, and a traitor." He bided his time, and after being incensed by a discrediting 1984 film, he wrote and published *Processo al K2*, in order to reveal the truth, correct the false official record, and expiate his pain.

Bonatti was especially angry at the Club Alpino Italiano (CAI), the Italian Alpine Club, which, even after thirty years and the court case, refused to alter the official narrative. He incisively observed that, "It is justly said that each of us has his or her own truth, but facts are facts and always stay the same. My accusations are neither interpretations nor hypotheses but precise facts, concrete data, well-authenticated evidence. But for thirty years I have been attacked, accused, provoked, and slandered—and all this because I had voluntarily offered my life in the service of my people and my country."

The world continued to deny him justice. Then, one day in 1993, Robert Marshall, the editor and translator of the book that provides the material upon which this brief account is based, looked at some published summit photos from 1955, images that he had viewed many times during the past forty years. He was stunned to now notice that Compagnoni still had his oxygen mask on, "two hours after he is supposed to have ripped it off to avoid suffocation." The line between the tanks on the ground and the mask is connected, which meant "the oxygen [was] still running." Lacedelli's face is covered with frost. Had it been previously unmasked, the frost would have melted.

The photos later included in Desio's book are different. It would have been impossible for these men to climb 600 feet with useless masks impeding their breathing. They did not run out of oxygen as claimed, and it appears that they fabricated a misleading and harmful narrative. When Marshall shared the images with Bonatti, he was astonished. The eventual publication of the "incriminating photographs" caused a furor, and Compagnoni did not fare well. (However, see below.) This seemed to be the end of the affair, which had dragged on for so long and caused so much travail for Bonatti, who, despite this, became one of the twentieth century's great mountaineers. Then a miracle occurred.

Lacedelli published *K2: Il Prezzo della Conquista* in 2004. Here, he revealed some critical points. For example, Desio was an egotistical, autocratic authoritarian, who refused to allow the great Ricardo Cassin to join the expedition, and turned out to be an inadequate leader. All of the expedition members, except for Compagnoni and Sergio Viotto, sent a letter to the CAI in which they indicated that they were dissatisfied with the expedition. Desio also did some very unsavory things (Lacedelli, 12, 13, 14). In a series of interviews that follow, Lacedelli insists that he was forced to sign the official report even though he knew that some things were false. And consider the minor point that Lacedelli always came up one short when counting tents. The missing unit was discovered in Compagnoni's tent; he explained that he had saved it for his children (Lacedelli, 56)!

When it came time to set up camp at Nine, at the agreed-upon location,[2] Compagnoni insisted that they make a long, unnecessary traverse to the left, one that had to be reversed the next day (Lacedelli, 62, 103). Lacedelli did not like this idea, but did not argue: "I only understood later . . . I believe he didn't want Bonatti to reach us." When asked why, Compagnoni "said that it was just the two of us that had to make the final climb to the summit" (Lacedelli, 62). Lacedelli disagreed, and even offered to sacrifice his oxygen if Bonatti could climb with them, but Compagnoni was adamant (Lacedelli, 63).

This is when Lacedelli spoke briefly with Bonatti (Lacedelli, 64). Giovanni Cenacchi, Lacedelli's coauthor, asked him to reaffirm his belief: "So you maintain that Compagnoni wanted to move Camp IX from the agreed position so that Bonatti wouldn't reach it." "Yes, but I understood this only much later" (Lacedelli, 65). He did not care if others also summited, and claimed that he only realized the following morning that Bonatti had bivouacked; he felt so guilty that he said, "Let's go back down" to Compagnoni (Lacedelli, 66). Cenacchi then asked if Bonatti had used oxygen, if he desired to precede them to the top, if he wanted to trick them. Lacedelli answered, "Absolutely not!" Bonatti did not have masks and he was an honest man and would never have gone back on his word. Lacedelli also confirmed Bonatti's times—that is, that they left to pick up the cylinders at around 6:00 a.m. rather than at about 4:00 a.m. (Lacedelli, 71).

The authors include a photo of Lacedelli putting his crampons on in the bright light of morning; the sun was not up at 4:30 a.m. (Lacedelli, 107)! He did, however, continue to insist that the oxygen had run out below the summit, and it was simply too hard to remove the heavy pack frames; additionally, it is claimed that climbers wore masks to protect against the cold even when no oxygen was available (Lacedelli, 71, 113). They had frostbitten fingers and some trouble descending, including a 90-foot fall, but eventually they successfully reached Camp Eight and their friends (Lacedelli, 75, 76). Lacedelli was "very angry" at Compagnoni, and appreciated the many things that Bonatti had done, and he reaffirms that "the accusations made against Bonatti were absolutely false" (Lacedelli, 77, 78).

In 1984, Bonatti had written that "if it takes a hundred years, the truth will have to be recognized." He was correct, and has now been fully vindicated. Although it is gratifying that he lived to experience this, it's sad that he was forced to suffer through the course of his long and successful climbing career because of the greed, treachery, and cowardice of his climbing partners.

NOTES

1 It seems obvious that what these men did was ethically horrific and legally actionable. It is miraculous that their purposeful failure to help at this point did not result in the deaths of two men. They naturally denied their guilt, but fifty years later, the truth was revealed. Compagnoni was more culpable than Lacedelli.

2 The site decided upon was next to the Bottleneck (Lacedelli, 62). This was the location of the horrible 2008 tragedy (see chapter 6).

SOURCES

The primary source for this chapter is Bonatti's The Mountains of My Life. *Other materials are cited in the text.*

Bonatti, Walter. *The Mountains of My Life*, tr. and ed. Robert Marshall. New York: The Modern Library, 2001 (chapters 6, 20–25).

Lacedelli, Lino, and Giovanni Cenacchi. *K2: The Price of Conquest*, tr. Mark Worthington. Seattle: The Mountaineers, 2006.

CHAPTER 6

K2, 2008:
Avalanche and Deaths: Wilco van Rooijen and Gerard McDonnell

In 2008, a concatenation of horrific events on K2 led to the deaths of eleven people, eight of whom died on a single day, in what Freddie Wilkinson describes as "one of the deadliest chapters in modern mountaineering history" (Wilkinson, 119). As with the well-known 1996 Everest debacle, many of the survivors, as well as unaffiliated authors, have written accounts. These vary not only because survivors were at different points on the mountain when disaster struck, but also because participants (and commentators) have very different needs, desires, emotional reactions, and perspectives. Sometimes, there exists a strong feeling of guilt or anger, and what appears to be mere articulation is in reality a defense of someone's actions.

In 2012, two uninvolved authors, Peter Zuckerman and Amanda Padoan, published *Buried in the Sky*, a most unusual account of what occurred here. Instead of concentrating on the many national teams attempting the summit, these authors offer extremely detailed remarks on the early and later lives of the accompanying Sherpa, Botia, and Hunza general and high-altitude porters or climbers, some of whom eventually died in this overwhelming tragedy. Because indigenous porters and climbers do not usually write memoirs, the perspective presented is almost always that of a Westerner who emphasizes his or her climb, and not the history and lives of those who make mountaineering in the Himalaya or Karakoram possible. Exceptions include Tenzing Norgay's *Tiger of the Snows* and Jamling Tenzing Norgay's *Touching My Father's Soul.* Sherry Ortner's sociological studies of the Sherpa are distant cousins. Other authors approach the calamity from either personal or purely scholarly perspectives.

K2 kills. Other mountains do too, but K2 is especially malevolent. Alison Hargreaves, the extraordinary British climber, died on K2, as did thirteen climbers in 1986, at least seven in 1995, and six in 2006. Over the years, more than sixty people have lost their lives here. Every time four people reach the summit, one dies in an attempt. K2 was first climbed in 1954 by two Italians, Achille Compagnoni and Lino Lacedelli. Subsequently, a major controversy erupted and lasted until 2013, when Lacedelli admitted that the two mountaineers had indeed deceived Walter Bonatti and his HAP, who was gravely harmed by their actions (see chapter 5). Four Americans were responsible for the third ascent.[1] K2 is more difficult and more dangerous than Everest and the other 8,000-meter peaks, which total fourteen in number.

During the summer of 2008, a series of unforeseen events led to a tragic loss of lives. The climbers were competent, caring, and cooperative, well positioned to succeed. There was little animosity among the many groups; indeed, they had worked out a most unusual agreement. And the individual members of each national expedition seemed to get along well with their teammates. Naturally, some people were stronger, more pressed, or ambitious, but even the Koreans did not wander around screaming (as they sometimes do) "Summit or die!" What happened was due primarily to an ill-timed occurrence.

As is often the case, a variety of unremarkable contingencies conspired here to build to a devastating climax. The different groups of porters spoke many mutually incomprehensible languages and could only communicate through a single individual; one man got sick, and he happened to be the translator; less-capable climbers remained on the mountain when they should have descended; some of the climbers were extremely aggressive; the perfect weather naturally degenerated and the tiny window slammed shut; an avalanche carried some climbers away, and also wiped out the fixed lines, which made descent extremely difficult; and whiteout conditions made navigation impossible, and people got lost.

This climbing season, thirteen expeditions set up their tents at base camp. There were eleven Koreans, seven Dutchmen, five Serbs, seven Americans, four Norwegians, two Italians, and Alberto Zerain, an individual Basque climber, among others. In addition, most groups had hired either Nepalese Sherpas or local Pakistani HAPs. As is often the case, the final ascent was dependent on a weather window, and when it arrived (a perfect, warm day, one in a million, as a climber in *The Summit* observed), each group began the push to the top. Between Friday, August 1, and Sunday, August 3, disaster struck again and again. Zerain forged on in front of the others, reached the summit, and descended. But later clustering at a narrow point, called the Bottleneck, high on the mountain, where the slopes are especially steep and dangerous, resulted in very slow going, because everyone was forced to move up and down a single set of fixed ropes.

At times, a string of climbers would just stand still for long periods while those above halted either to rest or for the emplacement of additional fixed lines. During one such frustrating halt, Dren Mandic, a Serb, tried to help the Norwegian climber, Cecilie Skog, put a rope into her pack. He unclipped from the fixed line, slipped, slid, and fell to his death. After much travail, four men tried to lower the body; one of them, a HAP named Jahan Baig, probably suffering from acute mountain sickness, slipped and he too plummeted to his death. This was but the beginning of a series of disasters caused later by an enormous falling chunk of ice that broke off from a serac; it tore out and buried the fixed ropes that had been placed along the Bottleneck and the Traverse, both extremely steep and difficult portions of the route very high up on the mountain. Without the aid of these lines, the descent was very difficult, dangerous, and for some, impossible. Four climbers died in the initial onslaught of ice. Five others perished later.

The many climbers struggled upward impeded by the altitude, their fatigue, and the interminable waiting. And as Graham Bowley observes, despite the external harmony and the unusual agreement among the expeditions, the individual climbers were annoyed and frustrated by the gridlock and disrespected their peers. It is also obvious that because many of the climbers spoke English badly, or not at all, it was at times difficult to communicate effectively.

Ascending, Dutchman Wilco van Rooijen had a hard time, especially since he refused to use oxygen. (He had previously tried K2 in 1995, when he was seriously injured, and again in 2006.) His was the first expedition on the mountain this year, and his group marked the way and set more than 10,000 feet of fixed line, working very hard. Eventually, they had to haul two tents, two 200-meter ropes, two 60-meter ropes, plus other heavy material to Camp Four on the way to the summit. They were cooperative and in good spirits, and actually contemplated a summit bid in late June or mid-July. Their first attempt was stymied by severe winds that threatened to tear their tent apart. When next they tried, they discovered an unfixed portion of the Bottleneck, and were forced to go down to remove some rope and bring it back up. Van Rooijen finally got frustrated waiting in line and unclipped and went around part of the Bottleneck unprotected. He was standing there when Mandic fell and he tried to save him, but failed. He continued, and the going was so difficult that he crawled in places (van Rooijen, 22, 29, 102, 103, 108, 109). When he finally reached the summit, three of his expedition teammates were there to greet him. Like most summiters everywhere, they rejoiced, celebrated, employed cameras and telephones, and then prepared to descend.

If climbs are excruciatingly hard, especially those on the higher, more-difficult peaks in the Himalaya, Karakoram, or Andes, the descents are far more dangerous. There are many obvious reasons for this: First, the climbers are exhausted; second, they have gone for long periods (ten, twenty, thirty hours) with little real nourishment; third, they are cold, thirsty, hypoxic, and sometimes have frostbitten extremities; and finally, they are partially or completely confused because of the altitude, and therefore often make very bad decisions (for example, sometimes removing gloves or other protective clothing when it is 20 below zero). Nevertheless, van Rooijen remarked that "descending in the dark should not be a problem" (van Rooijen, 115). He was very wrong there. As he went down, the other climbers passed him, and he soon found himself alone and lost (van Rooijen, 116, 117).

He had started down late at night on August 1. Eventually, he stumbled upon two climbers (Marco Confortola and Gerard McDonnell) who had decided to bivouac. They all waited. At first light, they searched for the missing ropes, but failed to find them (because they had been wiped out by the falling serac). Suddenly, van Rooijen began to descend. He was having trouble with his sight and knew that if it failed completely he would die; he had no choice but to try to get down unbelayed, despite the extreme danger. As he moved along, he suddenly noticed just a few feet away three people hanging in various positions from their entangling ropes. They were very badly hurt and unable to extricate themselves. Van Rooijen wanted to help, gave one a pair of gloves, but was otherwise incapable of disentangling them. His snow blindness was worsening, and so he continued down, trying to remain calm, and searching desperately for foot- and handholds on the steep slope, which eventually became vertical (van Rooijen, 124).

But he had made an error, and so despite his extreme tiredness and thirst, he was forced to re-climb to the entangled people, who turned out to be two Koreans and the Sherpa, Jumic Bothe (van Rooijen, 122). There he met up with the bivouackers again. He continued to downclimb but had more trouble: A series of phone calls to the Netherlands, back to base camp, and then to van Rooijen accomplished very little. He was exhausted and in a whiteout, facing horrific obstacles and thinking about death. He suffered greatly, and finally was forced to put some ice in his mouth (van Rooijen, 133). (Sucking on ice or eating snow is a very dangerous gamble because it reduces one's body heat as it concomitantly offers lifesaving moisture.)

He descended considerably and his eyesight improved (van Rooijen, 136). Someone in base camp spotted him high on the mountain, but this did little good, and incredibly, as night approached, he was forced to bivouac again. He sat down next to a dead climber! After a long night, the sun came up and he began to move. Suddenly, his phone (with dead battery) miraculously rang. He spoke with his wife and they were both overcome with emotion. He then spotted two tents and two climbers, Pemba Gyalje and Cas van de Gevel, his good friend. He had spent thirty hours above 8,000 meters and now he was safe. Lamentably, he paid a price for his amazing feat: After he and van de Gevel were flown out on helicopters, van Rooijen discovered that he had lost 22 pounds (Bowley, 197), and later, almost all of his toes (van Rooijen 137, 140, 141, 142, 147).

Cecilie Skog and Lars Flato Nessa reached the summit, celebrated, then descended, meeting Skog's husband, Rolf Bae, who had decided not to continue upward, near the Traverse. They went down the fixed lines together. Suddenly, there was a terrific icefall, and although Skog and Nessa were unaffected, Bae disappeared. When Mandic died, his teammates (and everyone else) were devastated. Naturally, the same emotional reaction occurred when Bae was killed. His wife, one of the outstanding climbers on the mountain, who had already successfully reached both poles and the seven summits, was inconsolable. Although it was a horrible shock to lose a husband and friend, they were high on K2, and unless they went down quickly, they too would suffer and perhaps die. It took a long time for Skog to move on, and she sometimes thought about simply staying in place or retreating. Somehow, she managed to take control of her emotions, her overwhelming sadness (perhaps bordering on despair), and she descended safely. This was not the case for many of the others who succeeded on K2. Some died; others did get back down, but it took a monumental struggle and a great deal of good luck. Despite this, some of these superb climbers suffered horrible emotional and physical damage.

Since the collapsing serac had wiped out the fixed lines, it was very difficult to proceed. Nessa suddenly recalled that, amazingly, he had a double coil of rope with him. He set it in place, anchored by an ice screw; they were now able to cross the Traverse. When they reached the Bottleneck, they discovered that the fixed lines were gone here, too. Somehow they were able to proceed, whereas a few of the climbers who followed were unable to do so safely.

For those readers who may have skipped K2 in their quest to reach heaven, and who do much of their climbing on their sofas, it is important to understand the crucial difference between fall-line movement on even a very steep slope and lateral movement on a traverse. Climbing straight up unbelayed on a 70- or 80-degree slope may be difficult and frightening, but climbers can protect themselves by grasping rock or with deep thrusts of their ice axes. By leaning forward into the slope, one can safely rest. Moving across the same extremely steep slope, perpendicular to the fall line, is much more dangerous because one is off balance, the lower leg extended far below the upper, with very little protection. A loss of concentration, a tiny error, may cause one to slip and tumble over and speed down the rocky, snowy, or, much worse, icy slope. Traversing is sometimes impossible without an ongoing belay or a fixed line that has previously been set in place. (In 1936, an impossible retreat, after a rope had been removed, caused the horrible tragedy on the Eiger's Hinterstoisser Traverse.)

Skog and Nessa, despite their unimaginable emotional strain, somehow managed to laboriously work their way down through the Bottleneck, although at one point, Skog fell and slid for more than 50 feet before self-arresting. After additional downclimbing, they stumbled onto the remaining fixed line and continued, guided by a bright, flashing beacon that had been set up at Camp Four. They were very lucky. Many catastrophes occur because climbers lose their way in darkness, storms, or whiteouts, and although they are close to camp, they fail to locate it. This was the major cause of the 1996 tragedy on Everest, and to some extent, here as well.

Marco Confortola, Gerard McDonnell, and the Koreans reached the area above the Traverse but could not locate the ropes. The Koreans proceeded but the others hesitated. Ironically, although camp was quite close and visible, it was almost impossible to reach in the dark and without the fixed lines. They decided to wait until morning light, even though bivouacking high on K2 is, of course, extremely detrimental to one's health. After van Rooijen left, and before he reencountered them, Confortola and McDonnell began an early-morning descent; they soon discovered the Koreans hanging in their ropes. They tried to help; then Confortola left and made it down (though he eventually lost all of his toes), with the help of Pemba Gyalje, who saved his life (Wilkinson, 141–42, 313). Apparently, McDonnell heroically freed the Koreans but was not lucky enough to survive. Later, the Koreans, Bhote, and another Sherpa were swept away in an avalanche (van Rooijen, 149).

As these events transpired, telephone calls were made to and from Holland, Italy, and France. Blogs were updated and had tens of thousands of hits. Many of the calls and postings occurred as the action unfolded on the mountain, so that it is possible that someone in Alaska or Holland knew more at a particular moment than a person just a short distance away from the suffering caller whose satellite phone coordinates were used to attempt to locate him. Occasionally, someone in base camp caught sight of one of the climbers through a high-powered telescope (Wilkinson 59, 65, 68, 81).

With very few exceptions, the thousands of accounts, memoirs, and autobiographical works written by climbers and mountaineers concentrate on Western adventurers who have had a singular extraordinary experience (think of Beck Weathers or Joe Simpson), or serious amateurs or professional climbers who have a lifetime of adventures to recount. But many of these expeditions would have been impossible, in the distant past, without the help of thousands of porters and guides, or, more recently, without Sherpa or HAP support. These men now sometimes climb on an equal footing with those who hire (or invite) them. As noted above, Tenzing Norgay and his son, Jamling, both wrote books from the Sherpa point of view. Peter Zuckerman and Amanda Padoan offer a detailed recital of this K2 tragedy, but they have chosen to emphasize the lives, histories, and contributions of the Sherpa, some of whom did not survive. When a Western climber perishes, it is sad and devastating for his or her friends and relatives, but often no financial exigency develops. When a Sherpa or HAP—often the sole support of an extended family—dies, financial catastrophe ensues. Even if a substantial insurance payment alleviates matters, eventually the money must run out, and by then the man's children will have matured and foolishly decided to follow in their father's footsteps, since guiding is one of the very few ways in which one can earn a decent living in the rural areas of Nepal or Pakistan.

Chhiring Dorje—who had summited Everest ten times (Zuckerman, 26)—reached the Traverse and discovered that the ropes were gone. He slipped, fell, slid some 70 feet, self-arrested, and then managed to locate a displaced partial rope. He continued down and eventually encountered Pemba Gyalje and Little Pasang, who were stuck on a small rock-and-ice ledge, because Pasang no longer had an ax. Although the descent here was extremely steep and dangerous, Dorje allowed the young, inexperienced, and frightened Pasang to attach himself to Dorje's harness. Pasang led and Dorje followed, facing inward, using his ax to protect himself and Pasang, whose additional weight pulled him downward. At one point, they fell and slid 90 feet; they thought that they would be unable to stop, which would have been fatal, but the ax finally caught and held. They eventually completed the Bottleneck safely and arrived at Camp Four. They were very lucky.

At about the same time, two other Sherpas, Chhiring Bhote and Big Pasang, left Camp Four with supplies in order to locate and help the missing Koreans. Two hours later they found the lost and weakened Go Mi-Sun. They carried her and then lowered her down. After they all returned to camp, the Sherpas went back up. In addition to saving Confortola's life, Pemba also helped to rescue van de Gevel and van Rooijen. For his heroic actions in the face of extreme danger and the deaths of his fellow guides, *National Geographic Adventure* chose him for its "Adventurer of the Year" award (Wilkinson, 212).

All in all, eighteen people reached K2's summit, but eleven died during this extended weekend, including those mentioned here, as well as Frenchman Hugues d'Aubarède and three Koreans. This tragedy generated a great deal of controversy and personal and media criticism. Naturally, defenders also spoke up (Wilkinson 111–13, 139), but the many stories told were often contradictory.

The Summit—the highly acclaimed, Sundance Film Festival–winning 2012 documentary, starring actors but also Wilco van Rooijen, Lars Flato Nessa, Marco Confortola, and Pasang Lama, among many others, as themselves—offers a dramatic visual overview of what occurred. Watching this film is almost like personally experiencing the overpowering wind and cold, the darkness, the avalanches, the fear, the suffering, and the horror of slipping, falling, tumbling, and finally, dying. The viewer also takes comfort in heartwarming human interactions, the sacrifices that others made, and the emotionally satisfying rescues. The historical footage of and commentary by Walter Bonatti is invaluable.

Notes

1 The authors of this book interviewed three of these men: Rick Ridgeway, Jim Wickwire, and John Roskelley. Their remarks may be found in Frederic Hartemann and Robert Hauptman, *Grasping for Heaven: Interviews with North American Mountaineers* (Jefferson, NC: McFarland, 2011). All four survived, though Wickwire suffered pulmonary problems after bivouacking near the summit. He subsequently had part of a lung removed.

Sources

As is sometimes the case, there exists a large number of personal and scholarly works on this tragedy. Marco Confortola contributed an account in Italian, and Cecilie Skog has two works, in Norwegian and German, respectively, that touch on the issues. Zuckerman and Padoan's volume includes a fairly comprehensive bibliography. Additionally, a plethora of relevant websites offer further information. The preceding narrative is indebted to and based (to some extent, but not exclusively) on Graham Bowley's No Way Down. *Other sources are cited in the text.*

Bowley, Graham. *No Way Down: Life and Death on K2*. New York: Harper, 2010.

Eleven Die in K2 Climb Tragedy. CBS. Accessed October 30, 2013. www.youtube.com/watch?v=8Mzpk2ygjf8.

The Summit. Dir., Nick Ryan. Image Now Films, etc. 2012.

van Rooijen, Wilco. *K2 Expedition 2008: Triumph & Tragedy*. YouTube. Accessed October 30, 2013. www.youtube.com/watch?v=KaHr1_5ujoM.

van Rooijen, Wilco. *Surviving K2*, tr. Roger Thurman, et al. Diemen, The Netherlands: G + J Publishing, 2010.

Wilkinson, Freddie. *One Mountain Thousand Summits: The Untold Story of Tragedy and True Heroism on K2*. New York: New American Library, 2010.

Zuckerman, Peter, and Amanda Padoan. *Buried in the Sky: The Extraordinary Story of the Sherpa Climbers on K2's Deadliest Day*. New York: W. W. Norton, 2012.

Section Four:
Cerro Torre (10,262 feet)

CHAPTER 7

Cerro Torre, 1959, 1970, 2012:
The Towering Shadow of Deception:
Maestri's Claimed Ascent

AT THE SOUTHERN TIP OF THE LONGEST MOUNTAIN RANGE ON EARTH lies Patagonia, where storms rage with unparalleled ferocity. The Andes are part of a still longer series of systems that span the entire Western Hemisphere, from Tierra del Fuego to the Aleutian Islands, along the geological feature known as the Great Rim of Fire, a series of volcanoes and fault lines encircling the Pacific Ocean. Cape Horn has long been known as one of the worst maritime areas in the world, due to powerful, uninterrupted atmospheric circulation along the Southern Ocean.

The Patagonian Andes are home to the Chaltén Range and the Hielo Continental, a large ice field connected to a beautiful system of fjords and the Pacific Ocean. The best-known mountain areas and summits in Patagonia include the Torres del Paine, a national park to the south of the Chaltén Range; Cerro Fitz Roy, the highest peak in the range proper, culminating at 3,405 meters (11,171 feet); and Cerro Sarmiento, 2,246 meters (7,369 feet), in Tierra del Fuego. The Torres, or towers, comprise Cerro Torre, 3,128 meters (10,262 feet), Torre Egger, Punta Herron, and Cerro Standhardt. Reinhold Messner, arguably the greatest mountaineer of all time, has beautifully described Cerro Torre: "A shriek turned to stone." Altitude is not the defining factor of these mountains; rather, it is sheer verticality, combined with truly brutal weather. Indeed, the Pacific-borne winds can reach well over 120 miles per hour, and plaster the western flank of the range with astonishing amounts of rime, hoar-frost, sleet, ice, and snow.

Vertical walls with extremely challenging routes can be found in a number of areas worldwide, including Yosemite in California, where El Capitan and Half Dome preside over a bounty of granite cliffs carved by glaciers a few tens of thousands of years ago. The Bugaboos in the Canadian Rockies; the Drus, the Aiguilles de Chamonix, and La Dibona in the French Alps; or the Dolomites in Italy present extremely difficult rock climbs. New areas such as Baffin Land in the Arctic, and the Trango region of the Karakorum, are also being explored in search of longer, more-sustained climbs requiring outstanding technical skills, endurance, and commitment. In Baffin Land, Mount Odin is the highest peak, with an elevation of 2,143 meters (7,031 feet); another prominent and impor-tant mountain is Asgard Tower, located in Auyuittuq National Park, with an elevation of 2,011 meters (6,598 feet). Mount Thor, with an elevation of 1,675 meters (5,495 feet), has perhaps the greatest purely vertical drop of any mountain, estimated at 1,250 meters (4,100 feet). Yet, the Torres still represent an astonishing combination of vertical continuity, nearly featureless granite, and extreme mixed climbing in very harsh conditions and a remote location. Thus, for over half a century they have attracted climbers seeking new lines and more-complex technical pitches, in what remains a true wilderness embodying "The Freedom of the Hills."

More ambiguously, they have also been the theater of an ongoing con-troversy that has embarrassed the climbing community for almost sixty years, at the time of this writing. At its very heart lies the simple question: Who performed the first climb of Cerro Torre, and when? In some cases, it is hard to ascertain the particulars of a first climb because the summit in question can easily be reached by basic, nontechnical means, and the local people have frequented it for religious or other reasons since time immemorial. This is not the case with Cerro Torre.

The chronicles of alpinism arguably begin with Petrarch's account of his climb to the summit of Mont Ventoux, in the Provencal Alps; Mount Fuji and Mount Aiguille have also inspired somewhat detailed descrip-tions of their ascents. Most folks were simply afraid of the mountains and carefully avoided these strange places where rock and ice seemed devoid of life, where storms could take entire armies in the blink of an eye, where snow dragons and other creatures were known to hide and prey on humans. The few people who dared venture toward the peaks then were chamois hunters, monks seeking isolation or rescuing lost travelers with the valiant help of their Saint Bernard dogs, especially bred for the task, or sheepherders seeking the lovely pastures and flowers of the pristine *alpages*.

The first ascent of the highest peak in the Alps, Mount Blanc, in 1786, by Jacques Balmat and Michel Paccard, marks the true beginning of mountaineering as a challenge, an adventure, and a personal as well as literal exploration. Indeed, the nineteenth century witnessed an incredible series of first ascents, mostly in the Alps, led by British gentlemen and their local French, Swiss, Italian, and Austrian guides. In North America, names like Agassiz, Muir, Wickersham, Humboldt, and Lyell are associated with peaks ranging from the California Sierras to the Rockies, Cascades, and Alaskan ranges. Many were first climbed there during the same period; by the twentieth century, the attention of climbers started to turn to the higher ranges of the world, while a few grand challenges remained in the Alps, including the North Faces of the Grandes Jorasses, Matterhorn, and Eiger.

Before the invention of photography, partly out of necessity, first ascents were ascertained and recorded based primarily on a code of honor among alpinists, but also in detailed descriptions of the climb, outlining the route, its main difficulties, and prominent landmarks. Later on, summit photographs became *de rigueur*; nowadays, videos and helmet cameras provide ever more detailed chronicles of new routes, or repeat climbs of important routes. A series of periodicals specializes in reporting new ascents and novel routes or variations, particularly in alpine countries, but also in the United States, Canada, Japan, and New Zealand. For example, in the United States, the *American Alpine Journal* is the prominent publication of record. There are also a few people, such as Elizabeth Hawley, who resides in Kathmandu, who records most Himalayan climbs for the benefit of the community at large. She is a historian of mountaineering in the world's highest range, and has served as an arbitrator when controversial claims have been posited. New technologies, including drones fitted with light video cameras and specialized software, are capable of recording athletes running, trekking, and climbing, among other possibilities, and will provide more documentation and evidence of mountaineering achievements.

During the establishment of alpinism, climbing techniques and equipment began to develop from the rudimentary tools used by chamois hunters and those searching for precious stones, called *cristalliers*. The first embodiment of the ice ax, simple hemp ropes, and hobnail shoes were part and parcel of Victorian climbing equipment. Warm clothing, alpenstock, and knickers were directly borrowed from the local designs, while inventive climbers and guides continually introduced variations and improvements. The same is true for climbing techniques proper: The Dülfer, a chimney-climbing method, bears the name of the climber who first used it; the Tyrolean traverse, the rappel or abseil, the use of protection, including pitons, carving steps in the ice—all of these and many others occurred in the nineteenth century.

The move toward higher altitudes came with the realization that, although challenging, the effects of decreasing barometric pressure and concomitant oxygen content could be overcome by physical preparation, endurance, and acclimatization, where the body naturally adapts over a period of up to three weeks, by changing blood oxygenation and other metabolic functions to alleviate the detrimental effects of elevation. In fact, high climbs were reported in 1802, on Chimborazo, 6,268 meters (20,564 feet), by Prussian geographer, naturalist, and explorer Alexander von Humboldt, while the Swiss guide Matthias Zürbriggen made the first ascent of Cerro Aconcagua, the highest peak in the Andes, at 6,961 meters (22,837 feet), in 1897. The question became whether a limit would appear at some yet-to-be-determined altitude. Early Himalayan climbs indicated the possible existence of a lethal zone, somewhere above 25,000 feet, where no amount of acclimatization proved sufficient to combat hypoxia and other debilitating effects.

Between the late 1800s and 1945, alpinism evolved from the fairly pure and somewhat naive spirit of the golden and silver ages of climbing to a more-politicized activity, as noted by Lee Wallace Holt: "During the Weimar Republic, mountaineering organizations sought to establish hegemony over the cultural narrative of mountaineering. Contemporary texts published by various alpine organizations positioned mountaineering as an activity reserved for a select elite, casting alpinists as masculine nationalists committed to the preservation of the Alps as their exclusive 'playground of Europe.' Until World War I, the German-Austrian Alpenverein, the largest alpine club in the world, maintained firm control over mountaineering's master narrative."

Nevertheless, this period also saw a great number of first ascents, spreading across the planet as means of transportation were undergoing a revolutionary transformation. A few of the more significant summits climbed during this era include Mount Saint Elias, in 1897; the Grand Teton, in 1898; Illimani (6,438 meters) in the Bolivian Andes, in 1898; North Palisade, in the California Sierras, in 1903; Mount Stanley (5,109 meters), in the Virunga Mountains, in 1906; in 1907, Trisul (7,120 meters), in India became the highest-altitude peak climbed at the time; Mount Erebus (3,794 meters), in Antarctica, was ascended in 1908; in 1913, Mount McKinley (6,168 meters) in Alaska, and Mount Robson (3,954 meters), in the Canadian Rockies; Gannett Peak (4,209 meters), the highest point in Wyoming, was first climbed in 1922; in 1928, Lenin Peak (7,134 meters) in the Pamirs; Kamet at (7,756 meters) in 1931 represented another altitude record, followed by Nanda Devi (7,816 meters), the highest point in India, in 1936; Peak Podieba (7,439 meters), in the Tien Shan Mountains, was ascended in 1938.

It is worth noting that, shortly after the end of the terrible conflagration of World War II, a number of European countries were in the process of reconstruction and the recovery of some form of dignity, and for the vanquished, even a modicum of national honor. One approach was to sublimate the anguish of war into the noble, friendly competition of being the first to summit a Himalayan 8,000-meter peak: France, with Annapurna in 1950 and Makalu in 1955; England, with Everest in 1953 and Kangchenjunga in 1955; Austria, beginning with Nanga Parbat in 1953, followed by Cho Oyu in 1954, Gasherbrum II in 1956, Broad Peak in 1957, and Dhaulagiri in 1960; Italy, with K2 in 1954; Japan, with Manaslu in 1956; Switzerland, with Lhotse in 1956; the USA, with Gasherbrum I in 1958; finally, China, with Shisha Pangma in 1964.

Nepal is also associated with a number of first ascents, including Everest, Cho Oyu, Dhaulagiri, and Manaslu. German climber Peter Diener was part of the team that summited Dhaulagiri in 1960. It is also well worth noting that Polish climbers, including Jerzy Kukuczka, Krzysztof Wielicki, and Maciej Berbeka, have established an amazing record of first climbs in winter: all 8,000-meter peaks, except Gasherbrum II and Makalu, climbed by Italian Simone Moro and Russian-Polish Denis Urubko. Finally, the first ascent of all fourteen 8,000-meter peaks without oxygen was performed by Reinhold Messner during 1970–1986, while Austrian climber Gerlinde Kaltenbrunner is the first woman to accomplish this amazing mountaineering feat, finishing in 2011.

Other peaks in foreign and remote locations were also tackled. In 1952, a French team attacked Cerro Fitz Roy, the highest peak in the Chaltén Range, a mountain reminiscent of the Drus in its topology, with wide and steep granite faces. The ascent was performed along a route on the south buttress, over a short time period, in what is now called *alpine style*, where logistics are minimal and the climb is performed by fair means. From his vantage point on the top of Cerro Fitz Roy, Lionel Terray estimated Cerro Torre impossible to climb, at least in the foreseeable future. Coming from such a noted mountaineer as Terray, this was a rather powerful statement. At the same time, it upped the ante considerably, as it created a sort of ultimate challenge: the next barrier to be broken in alpinism. At the time, Terray was already a well-recognized figure in the mountaineering world, having participated in the successful Annapurna ascent of 1950, and about to lead an expedition, with Jean Franco, to the first climb of Makalu, 8,485 meters (27,838 feet), in 1955.

At the time of the purported first ascent of Cerro Torre, in 1959, climbers using supplemental oxygen and very large expeditions with complex logistics were in the process of climbing the highest Himalayan peaks, including the fourteen summits above 8,000 meters. Annapurna, 8,091 meters (26,545 feet), was the first, climbed on June 3, 1950, by Frenchmen Maurice Herzog and Louis Lachenal; Everest, 8,848 meters (29,035 feet) was ascended on May 29, 1953, by Sir Edmund Hillary, and Tenzing Norgay; K2, or Chogori, 8,611 meters (28,251 feet), was climbed on July 31, 1956, by Lino Lacedelli and Achille Compagnoni, two Italians closely related to some of the main protagonists of the Cerro Torre saga.

These formidable mountaineering challenges were tackled by steering away, as much as possible, from technical climbing difficulties, by choosing a path of least resistance while avoiding unnecessary exposure to objective dangers: seracs, icefalls, avalanche-prone areas, couloirs and gullies, high altitude, and storms. The latter was particularly tricky, since no reliable forecasts existed then.

Cerro Torre presented a completely contrasting set of difficulties: extremely sustained technical climbing, but low altitude. It did share the potential for vicious storms, howling winds with terrifying force, extraordinary snow and ice conditions, and remoteness.

For Cesare Maestri, a renowned Italian rock climber from the region of Trentino-Alto Adige, Cerro Torre presented a perfect opportunity to make up for his being snubbed by the Italian Alpine Club (CAI), which did not include him on the team that was to conquer K2. While the K2 expedition was a very expensive, logistically involved affair, Cerro Torre offered an equally exotic location, with an ambitious climbing goal, at a fraction of the cost. Additionally, for a pure rock climber, Cerro Torre may well represent a more interesting objective. Finally, a strong Italian component of the Argentine population provided a local network that proved quite helpful in this endeavor; in particular, the Buenos Aires branch of the CAI provided local manpower and resources.

This is where a key protagonist appears: Cesarino Fava, an Italian émigré from Trentino, and a solid climber. He contacted Maestri and described the haunting beauty of Patagonia, with its ice fields, fjords, and many unclimbed peaks. Fava would be a big asset, because he had many contacts and could help organize a trip to what was a very remote area at the time. Meanwhile, Folco Doro Altán, who was familiar with the Hielo Continental and the Fitz Roy mountains, invited Walter Bonatti and Carlo Mauri to join his own expedition to Patagonia, with the goal of attempting the impossible: the ascent of Cerro Torre. The year 1958 thus saw two small expeditions to Cerro Torre: One led by Bruno Detassis, and including Maestri and Fava, and a second team under Doro Altán and Bonatti. Instead of joining forces, the two expeditions decided to attack the peak by different routes.

To the west of Cerro Torre lies a breach, which Bonatti and Mauri called the Col of Hope. Maestri famously declared: "In the mountains, there is no such thing as hope; only the will to conquer. Hope is the weapon of the weak." Maestri called the breach marking his chosen route to the east the Col of Conquest. Bonatti and Mauri made it up the Col of Hope, where they bivouacked, and further up the West Face, but the level of technical difficulty became so extreme that they had to turn back. They were also well aware of the destructive storms that they had already encountered on their way to the West Face, fully exposed to the fury of the howling winds charged with ice and sleet, forming hoarfrost and rime on contact. They realized that they had been lucky to climb during a lull, which would necessarily be followed by extreme weather. The name "Col of Hope" reflects their aspiration to come back for a successful first ascent.

On the Col of Conquest route, Maestri did not fare any better. Initially, upon sighting the eastern aspect of Cerro Torre, expedition leader Detassis actually forbade his climbers to even attempt the ascent. Maestri did a bit of reconnaissance and identified a possible route, up to the Col of Conquest, then veering toward the north face, where rock, mixed, and ice climbing on exceptionally steep terrain would lead to the summit of the impossible mountain. Maestri knew he would return as soon as possible, and bring a new weapon: one of the foremost ice climbers of the time, Austrian Toni Egger.

Egger had already made a name for himself by climbing most of the difficult, classic routes in the Alps, including the Petit Dru and the Piz Badile, at breakneck speed. In 1953, Egger performed the first climb of the south face of Laserz; in 1955, the first ascent of the south face of Cima Piccola, 2,857 meters (9,373 feet), in the Tre Cime di Lavaredo Dolomites. In the same year, Egger climbed the north wall of the Cima Ovest, 2,973 meters (9,754 feet), and the Cima Grande, 2,999 meters (9,839 feet), in a single day. In 1956, Egger climbed the Bonatti pillar on Mount Blanc with only one bivouac; he also performed the first ascent of the south Spigolo of the Punta d'Ombretta in the Marmolada. In 1957, he ascended Yerupaja Chico, 6,089 meters (19,977 feet). Among Egger's most noteworthy climbing achievements was his recent first ascent of Jirishanca, 6,094 meters (19,993 feet), in Peru.

Indeed, in 1959, the impossible climb was under way with the help of Fava, who had enrolled four college students from Buenos Aires to assist with carrying and ferrying equipment to base camp. The trip to Patagonia was still an arduous enterprise, which first led them to El Chaltén, and was followed by a long hike to Laguna Torre, at the glacier terminus where they established a supply camp. The final camp was set in an ice cave, up the Torre Glacier, 200 meters (600 feet) below the start of the climb to the Col of Conquest. The general approach followed a fairly direct line: 2,000 feet to the Col of Conquest, the small breach between Cerro Torre and an unnamed tower to the north; another 2,000 vertical feet on the north face proper led to the summit, mostly extremely steep granite slabs, with a slope averaging over 80 degrees. After a mixed climb to the col, 1,000 feet of headwall presented the crux of the climb, followed by unusual ice formations below the summit.

This particular route was chosen because it offered some protection from the terrible oceanic storms rolling over the Hielo Continental; by contrast, the Col of Hope route was directly exposed to the raging winds, and required a far longer approach. During the initial phase of the climb, Maestri and Fava installed fixed lines leading to a characteristic feature called the Triangular Snowfield, some 300 meters (1,000 feet) above the *bergschrund*, approximately 40 percent of the way to the col proper, while Egger was recuperating from an infected foot injury. Even this initial foray was very hard going, and presented difficult, exposed climbing. Maestri and Fava created a cache for the food and equipment that would be needed for the continuation of the climb, to the col, and the virgin north face. It required four climbing days for 300 meters of elevation gain, and seven days of poor weather or rest at base camp. This timeline outlines the technical difficulties and atmospheric conditions in the Chaltén Range. Indeed, this relative lull was followed by weeks of extreme weather, storm after storm, piling snow, ice, sleet, and rime over the granite spires hovering thousands of feet above the dejected climbers, waiting for the weather to change.

Better weather eventually arrived, but the storms had left the upper part of the climb covered with rime and ice. With renewed hope, they made their way back to the snow cave, carefully studying the north face, and the infamous mushroom cap of hoarfrost and rime, sometimes reaching well over 10 feet in thickness, but notoriously unstable and unreliable for climbing. These new climbing conditions implied that Egger, the finest ice climber, would be best positioned to decide on the technical approach to the ascent beyond the col.

Ice and rock climbing are very different: On rock, the lines of the climb are mostly dictated by the cracks, dihedrals, ledges, overhangs, slabs, and other topological aspects of the mountain; ice is largely a white canvas, where the climber can choose the best line depending on variable conditions. Ice climbing also requires specialized technical equipment, without which sustained slopes above 60 degrees become essentially impossible. This equipment includes synthetic ropes, twelve-point crampons, two short ice axes, and ice screws for protection. Nowadays, the most common protection for ice climbing are ice screws; these specialized devices are hollow tubes comprising sharp teeth on the front end, a hanger eye at the back to clip a carabiner into, and threading around the tube. There are two main types: hollow, as described above, and solid. The first is used when the ice is relatively soft, or with compacted snow; for hard, or black, ice, the solid screws are better adapted, but far more time-consuming to properly anchor and remove. They are screwed in and can provide very strong protection in solid ice; this is especially true if the ice locally melts around the screw due to mechanical work and friction, and quickly refreezes. In practice, because of the highly variable nature of ice, the strength of ice-screw placements can vary greatly.

Ice climbers also use the ice itself as protection. The two most common of such techniques are the *V-Thread*, also known as the "Abalakov anchor," named after a Russian climber who popularized the technique, and the *ice bollard*. In a V-Thread, two intersecting cuts are bored into the ice to form a V-shaped tunnel. A sling is then threaded through the V and tied in a loop, and the rope is passed through the sling, which remains in place after use. In the case of an ice bollard, ice is chipped away to create a teardrop-shaped protrusion, typically 1 to 2 feet in diameter. A sling is placed around the bollard and the main rope goes through the sling, which can be left behind. When ice conditions permit, the sling may be dispensed with. Natural formations, ice hooks, and ice pitons may also be used as protection anchors. For rock, pitons can already be in place if the route is a repeat, generally spaced 10 to 20 feet apart, depending on the vertical exposure and other factors. Ice is always changing, and no permanent protection can be implemented. If the conditions are ideal, climbing on ice can also be very fast, especially if both climbers ascend simultaneously, without setting belays. This is true today; in 1959, however, there was almost no differentiation between rock and ice equipment, and speed was not possible for extreme slopes because the purchase on a single ice ax was too tenuous, thereby forcing the lead climber to cut steps a time-consuming prospect.

In any event, Egger decided that they could forgo fixed ropes and take enough food and equipment for a few days, sufficient for the climb from the Col of Conquest to the summit, and back. This was a technique he had successfully used on Jirishanca, in Peru, and which provided a distinct speed advantage, time between storms being a precious commodity near the Hielo Continental.

In a single day, January 28, 1959, the three men ascended all the way to the col, with adequate equipment and supplies for five to seven days, retracing their path to the cache on the Triangular Snowfield, and forging ahead. Fava decided to go back to the snow cave, because he felt he would only hamper the rest of the climb. Their speed was on par with the faster climbs to the col nowadays. Early on January 29, they were in virgin territory, attacking the base of the ice-covered north face. For protection at belays, they had to get to the rock under the ice and use expansion bolts, because the granite slabs were devoid of cracks or chinks. They discovered that the face was "not as steep as you might expect," to quote Maestri, who also estimated an average slope of 45 to 50 degrees.

Photographs, or even direct views of a mountain face, can be deceiving; in general, a face seen head-on appears to be vertical, while a side view will often provide a better estimate of the actual slope. This is perhaps the first striking disjunction between Maestri's account and reality: First and foremost, the north face of Cerro Torre is factually far steeper, over 80 degrees in the crux pitches up the headwall. Next, a 45- to 50-degree slope would be akin to a much lesser climb, such as the Courtes, in the Mont Blanc Range, which were first climbed in the mid-1800s—impressive at the time, but easy a century later, and not worthy of the publicity and applause Maestri received after chronicling his sensational exploit. Perhaps these statements about exceptionally favorable ice conditions and a dangerous but technically less-challenging line than expected, projected humility and almost atonement for what remains a legendary climb; in any event, they seem to imply that, after all, the climb was not as impossible as first thought.

As Egger led the climb with *maestría* and boldness, they reached the bottom of the mushroom ice cap by the third day, and continued the ascent through phantasmagorical, terrifying rime formations on terrain Maestri estimated to be at 50 to 60 degrees. Finally, after a bivouac a few hundred feet below the summit, the fourth day arrived, with deteriorating weather conditions. This prompted a veritable sprint to the summit, with Egger opening vertical ice with a single, long ice ax, and very few pitons for protection: a truly extraordinary feat, driven by will and desperation. As Cerro Torre fell on January 31, Maestri felt no emotion, no happiness, rather more of a slightly depressed feeling, sometimes associated with the anticlimactic end of a very long quest. Fatigue and tension may also have darkened his mood, as winds strengthened with the impending storm. After a few summit photos, they rappelled down to their bivouac for a restless night in the building cyclone. Avalanches, snow, and hoarfrost became their constant companions in the bleak darkness, where the roaring winds danced with unforgiving intent. Descending and surviving was now their throbbing mantra.

With the storm came higher temperatures, foretold by the *foehn* blowing on the fourth day; the ice sheet that had made the climb possible in the first place had all but disappeared, leaving smooth, featureless granite slabs in its stead. This new state of affairs made the rappelling down beyond their bivouac a tedious, terrifying process, and it was even worse because of the extreme wind gusts and avalanching rime. Each abseil had to be protected by expansion bolts; each 120-foot pitch, rappelled down in minutes, required a lengthy setup in ever-deteriorating conditions. The alarmingly warm storm was dumping tons of heavy snow, melting the mushroom ice cap, and creating horrific avalanches and constant slides. The lack of sleep and exhaustion compounded their grim mood as they set out to rappel down toward the upper reach of their fixed rope; after much suffering, they stood 200 feet above the Triangular Snowfield, but the falling night forced them to find yet another location for a wretched bivouac.

After leaving the Col of Conquest, Fava related that during the following three days the mountains were engulfed in a storm of immense proportions, with furious winds howling at hurricane force, lashing at the peaks and spraying ice and rime on the granite towers rising from the ice field—dire, lonely times for Fava, waiting for Maestri and Egger in a snow cave, high up the Torre Glacier. After three long days, Fava had abandoned all hope and was ready to hike back to the world of the living, with dreadful news of utter disaster; then, at the base of the tower, a dark shadow appeared. It was Maestri, at the edge of death, muttering again and again: Egger was dead, taken by a horrific avalanche that had swept the tower as they were desperately looking for a place that offered a modicum of safety for a last bivouac. Maestri barely escaped; he had found that the rope connecting him to his climbing partner had snapped, sparing him. Cerro Torre had been conquered, but at such a cost! To compound the tragedy, the only summit photographs had been taken by Egger and disappeared with his body, deep within the shroud of snow and ice covering the upper Torre Glacier. Maestri, and, to a lesser extent, Fava, had to be taken at their word.

Maestri made a triumphal return to Italy, and his native Trentino-Alto Adige, where he received a hero's welcome. Egger's death, a sad shock to the mountaineering community, was accepted as another exacting sacrifice to the sometimes-cruel mountains. Initial doubts concerning the success surfaced only because of the truly revolutionary impact of the climb: Mastering such extreme degrees of technical difficulty, on sheer vertical slabs covered with unstable layers of ice and rime, at such an amazing pace, and surviving a Patagonian cyclone, seemed rather improbable, especially in view of the equipment and climbing techniques available at the time. Even in 2016, any climb of Cerro Torre is extremely difficult, although meteorology, climbing apparatus, and the concomitant techniques and methods have progressed tremendously.

Maestri and Fava insisted that the very special ice conditions on the north face, rarely repeated, and never at the level reported by the victorious team, combined with Egger's extraordinary ice-climbing abilities, had allowed for the impossible: A continuous layer of stable ice covered the entire face, allowing for fast climbing, with reasonable anchors and safe belays. Absent this ice, the final headwall would have consisted of pristine, smooth granite slabs, requiring extreme care in finding minuscule cracks or chinks in the rock, and much artificial climbing, which implies very slow, painful progress, and would have led to an aborted climb in the impending storm, or worse.

In the Chaltén Range, most of the ice on the towers is found in the form of rime or hoarfrost, both very delicate formations, unstable and transitory, and a nightmare medium to climb on. It should also be noted that unusual weather circumstances can lead to extraordinary climbing conditions. In the 1990s, continuous very hot weather in the Chamonix and Mont Blanc region led to ice melting on an enormous scale, and gigantic avalanches of rock and seracs. Blocks the size of houses were cascading down the north face of the Droites, plainly visible from across the Argentière Glacier, at an alarming rate; at the same time, some of the world's best climbers were tackling a series of new, ephemeral rock routes on the polished slabs that had been covered by ice for hundreds of years. What had recently been some of the most difficult mixed and ice terrain in the Alps suddenly became perfectly smooth, nearly vertical granite, with over 3,000 feet of vertical amplitude. With climate change, such occurrences are likely to happen more frequently, and the retreat of glaciers means that some routes are becoming increasingly longer, or changing character altogether.

A series of subsequent climbs on Cerro Torre and the discovery of Egger's body transformed initial doubts based on technical arguments into more-probing questions. This happened over many years, but Maestri became so fully frustrated that, in 1970, he returned to the impossible mountain and committed what many climbers consider a completely unethical corruption of Cerro Torre and the spirit of alpinism: He created a route on the southeast ridge comprising over four hundred bolts, which he affixed using an air compressor powered by a gasoline engine. The line was so continuous and closely spaced that the entire upper part of the route became a matter of artificial climbing, where short ladders could be secured on the bolts and used to progress upward systematically. Such methods are sometime necessary, for overhangs or slabs entirely devoid of holds, but generally over minimal distances. What made Maestri's move anathema to climbers is the fact that subsequent climbs revealed the completely unnecessary character of what became known as the Compressor Route. Numerous handholds were found that were quite adequate for the extreme climbing challenge offered by Cerro Torre. It seemed that Maestri's actions were borne out of frustration, anger, and a desire for revenge. He might as well have blown up the entire mountain.

Reinhold Messner has expressed his views on the ethics of climbing numerous times, and eloquently; perhaps the following passage, from *Free Spirit*, best encapsulates his views:

At that time [1967] there were two directions in extreme mountaineering: technical and free climbing. Some people used all imaginable aids to achieve their goal. Others—among whom I counted myself—imposed limits on themselves, so as not to make the relationship between man and mountain too incongruous. A mountaineer can, through training, skill, and experience, raise the limit of his performance and climb extremely difficult rock faces free, or he can overcome everything with technical aids without much risk and climbing skill. On repeat ascents I always endeavored to bang in fewer pitons than the original climbers had done. A new route was for me only justifiable if I managed to find a line on the face that was possible with slight use of pitons. Ideally, in my view, a route would have been one that was climbed in a direct line, under the greatest difficulties without any technical aid, and leading to an 8,000-meter summit. I knew this ideal was beyond human grasp; we could however approach it. In attempting that I see a possibility for the future development of mountaineering.

The bizarre technique used for this strange climb only increased and deepened the questions and doubts regarding the first ascent, and alienated Maestri from the mainstream mountaineering community. Between 1959 and 1970, the Chaltén Range saw climbing activity and new routes were opened, but the summit of Cerro Torre was not reached again, in spite of a number of attempts, including a 1968 British-Argentina expedition (this was long before the Falklands War) up what was to become the Compressor Route. In 1970, Carlo Mauri attempted the route above the Col of Hope, up the rime-covered West Face, that he had first contemplated with Walter Bonatti over a decade earlier. They reached a point some 200 meters (600 feet) below the summit, beyond which the climbing appeared completely impossible. The storm that concluded their aborted attempts was colossal, with winds so strong as to physically pluck climbers from the mountain, save for their being tied to ropes.

In 1974, the Ragni di Lecco—literally, the Spiders of Lecco—led by Casimiro Ferrari, who had been part of Mauri's team in 1970, set out to attempt Cerro Torre's West Face, the logical route above the Col of Hope. As noted earlier, this route involved a complex trek over the ice cap, and was directly exposed to storms; as a result, most of the climb was over ice and mixed terrain. The first half leading to the col was over sustained ice and snow, with moderately steep slopes, and a much higher inclination below the col proper. Beyond the col, which served as a cache, the second part began with a series of rock towers and gendarmes, covered with thick hoarfrost; a labyrinthine terrain of gargoyles, and other ice dragons, ethereal and dangerous, pregnant with danger. Fixed ropes were installed, since the frequent storms allow only a lucky, lightning-fast alpine climb, or a protracted, siege-like approach.

The next prominent feature on the line is called El Elmo, The Helmet, beyond which the climb steepened considerably, to become altogether vertical in the last pitches under the summit. At The Helmet, the summit team, comprising four climbers, waited out storms for over a week, before a final push. The violent winds danced, roared, ululated, shrieked, and howled, while the snow and ice plastered the face, building layer upon layer of delicate crystals, rime tubules, and hoarfrost mushrooms. On January 13 the storm abated, and they quickly reached their high point on the fixed lines, for a final attack of the tower. The rime was worse than anything they had imagined, ice layered to build enormous overhangs of brittle hoarfrost, a hundredfold bigger than formations seen after an ice storm. Stalactites projected into the void, creating yet another barrier protecting the summit. Compounded by sheer verticality, the ice formed a formidable, impregnable protection, forbidding access to the top. The four climbers inched their way up vertical pillars of rime, struggled through unimaginable inverted labyrinths of ice, overhanging mushrooms of hoarfrost; somehow, perhaps by sheer will, they summited Cerro Torre. For most in the mountaineering community, this was the true first ascent of the impossible Patagonian tower.

For Cerro Torre, 1974 was a momentous year: After the Ragni di Lecco route was successfully opened in January, Brian Wyvill discovered parts of Egger's body on the upper Torre Glacier, in December. Wyvill and Ben Campbell-Kelly were in the area when they met two American climbers they knew from Yosemite: John Bragg and Jim Donini. They decided to join forces and try the first ascent of Cerro Standhardt, which was aborted due to bad weather; however, they stayed in the Chaltén Range, and on December 26, a mountaineering boot made in Kitzbühel, Austria, with a tibia/peroneus sticking out, appeared on the glacial ice. A few scattered pieces of equipment surrounded the grim discovery, including a frayed hemp rope and a 1950s-style ice ax. They had no doubt about the corpse's identity; it had to be Egger. Significantly, the remnants of his backpack did not contain the camera that might have given irrefutable proof of the Maestri-Egger first ascent. Additionally, the rope told a different story than Maestri's description of Egger's demise; in particular, the specific knots and lengths of different segments were quite inconsistent with the rope configuration that one might use to lower a person in search of a bivouac location.

The next year, more questions arose. Torre Egger, the sheer tower on the south side of the Col of Conquest, was the climbing objective of Bragg and Donini, joined by Jay Wilson, during the 1975–1976 austral mountaineering season. This would require a repeat of the Egger-Maestri route to the breach, followed by virgin territory on the Torre Egger south face. The climb to the Triangular Snowfield was described as "a trip through

79

history" by Donini, because of the sheer number of old pieces of climbing equipment and protection gear they found. The route had clearly been equipped before, and notwithstanding the 1968 Anglo-Argentine expedition, they attributed most of the artifacts to Maestri and Egger. Rather mysteriously, no equipment was found above the Triangular Snowfield, in contradiction to Maestri's account, which indicated that the route had been equipped with fixed ropes all the way to the Col of Conquest. Another layer of mystery was added to the Cerro Torre enigma.

Far more puzzling and perplexing was the disjunction between Maestri's account of the route above the Triangular Snowfield and what the Donini party observed and photographed while climbing to the col, on their way to the first ascent of the south face of Torre Egger, which they reached on February 22, 1976. The first 300 meters (1,000 feet) of the climb, ending with a dihedral and the Triangular Snowfield, were faithfully similar to Maestri's description; the second half of the line to the col was described as relatively easy, until a traverse to the breach, whereupon the climb became very difficult. In reality, the pitches leading to the traverse were far trickier than described, with interspersed vertical segments and then a beautiful ledge, making the traverse to the col far simpler than it appeared: a simple scramble up easy terrain. This was a hidden traverse. Perhaps crucially, Maestri's account nicely matches the route, but as seen from below. Donini, Bragg, and Wilson came to the conclusion that the 1959 team had not reached the Col of Conquest, only climbing the first 1,000 feet of the 6,000-foot route to the summit.

In 1977, an American team comprising Bragg, Wilson, and Dave Carman performed a rapid repeat of the Ragni di Lecco route with modern ice-climbing equipment, and using the marteau-piolet technique. In contrast to the 1974 Italian team, the Americans had trained extensively on frozen waterfall and vertical ice, made possible by revolutionary progress, both in terms of equipment and technique, and they were able to perform the climb alpine-style, ascending fast during weather windows, and forgoing fixed ropes. This new approach made steep ice far easier, faster, and safer to climb, and opened the way to many repeats of classic routes in the Alps and elsewhere. The 60- to 80-degree ice on the north faces of the Droites, Courtes, Grandes Jorasses, Matterhorn, and other major peaks could now be ascended with precision and efficiency, and many "unclimbable" couloirs and gully routes were opened, including very long and sustained ice on vertical terrain.

In the 1978–1979 season, Jim Bridwell, a legendary Yosemite climber, set out to do the Compressor Route solo. Upon meeting Steve Brewer, a fellow American alpinist, they decided to climb the route together. In two hours, they ascended the steep terrain to the Col of Patience, and began tackling the more-difficult pitches above, leading to Maestri's 1970 bolt ladder. They moved quickly over a series of chimneys, mixed terrain, and bolt lines, to gain the final 150-meter (500-foot) headwall. They followed the bolts, all the way to Compressor, in its icy vertical grave, some 150 feet below the summit. After another 70 feet, the bolt line stopped; above, the remaining 80 feet presented highly polished, smooth, featureless, vertical granite. Bridwell opened the virgin pitch, using artificial climbing; after surmounting this crux, the two summited in elation. Later on, upon reflection, it became quite clear to Bridwell that Maestri's Compressor Route did not actually reach the summit of Cerro Torre. To this day, the extremely difficult Bridwell pitch is rarely free-climbed.

The year 2005 turned out to be another pivotal time in the Cerro Torre saga. Alessandro Beltrami, Rolando Garibotti, and Ermanno Salvaterra decided to climb Cerro Torre via the Col of Conquest and north face—the Egger-Maestri route. In less than seven hours, they had bypassed the col to a point about 100 feet higher, where the ascending traverse abuts the north face proper. As others had, they noted the distinct lack of old equipment beyond the first 1,000 feet of the ascent to the breach, and the difference in topology between the actual terrain and the description of the purported first ascent. The climb to a bivouac spot, high on the north face, followed natural lines of least resistance, presumably lines that Maestri and Egger would have followed. No artifacts were found on the virgin face. The next day, they climbed rapidly on extremely difficult terrain, until they reached the mushroom ice cap, where they fought for four hours before reaching the summit. The feat got them a nomination for best climb of the year, the French Piolet d'Or. The route, called El Arca de los Vientos, represented the first documented climb of the Egger-Maestri line. Maestri contested the award on the basis that it was merely a repetition of his first ascent; at the same time, his description of the route clashed with the photographs and account of Beltrami, Garibotti, and Salvaterra.

The 2007 Kelly Cordes / Colin Haley ascent, combining a sustained 2,600-foot ice line to the Col of Hope—first climbed in 1994 by Frenchman Francois Marsigny and Andy Parkin, from the United Kingdom, and called Los Tiempos Perdidos, to the Ragni di Lecco route proper—further pushed climbing boundaries on the legendary tower. Since then, new feats of fast and light alpinism have been performed on Cerro Torre, including winter climbing. As such, the impossible mountain of Terray remains an exacting benchmark for the world's very best mountaineers.

In January 2012, Hayden Kennedy and Jason Kruk, an American-Canadian team, performed the very first fair-means climb of the southwest ridge from the Col of Patience, ignoring Maestri's bolt line. On the way down, they removed most of the bolts, returning the route previously climbed by hundreds of lesser climbers to the beautiful line of a much higher degree of difficulty that they had just first ascended. While lauded by most, this move was decried by some, especially some local outfitters and businesses that feared it would lead to less adventure tourism and concomitant revenues. They, too, made observations that contradicted the author of the Compressor Route.

Although there is concrete, compelling evidence against a 1959 first ascent of Cerro Torre, could one look for a possible middle way to reconcile Maestri's claims with reality? Here, we can only speculate, and outline a few noteworthy points of fact that may offer a coherent solution to the Cerro Torre mystery. We know that the mountain was enshrouded like a tomb by horrendous weather in those fateful days of 1959; we know that Toni Egger died a terrible death; we know that all involved, Maestri, Egger, and Fava, were alone, wretchedly tired, in what remains a remote wilderness exposed to devastating storms. Would Egger's death have been in vain, only a few pitches above the ice cave? Could the hellish winds, nauseating fatigue, burrowing suffering, unfathomable weather, and the constant roar of avalanches have driven Egger and Maestri to truly believe they were much higher on the mountain than they actually were—perhaps even on the desolated summit? After all of this pain and suicidal commitment, Maestri felt no emotion, no happiness, at the top—only the melancholy of a catatonic anticlimax, tinged with utter fear.

SOURCES

Cordes, Kelly. *The Tower: A Chronicle of Climbing and Controversy on Cerro Torre.* Ventura, CA: Patagonia, 2014; and references therein.

Holt, Lee Wallace. "Mountains, Mountaineering and Modernity: A Cultural History of German and Austrian Mountaineering, 1900–1945." PhD Dissertation, University of Texas at Austin, 2008.

www.nationalgeographic.com/adventure/0604/whats_new/cerro-torre-garibotti.html.

www.nationalgeographic.com/adventure/0604/whats_new/cesare-maestri.html.

www.nytimes.com/2015/02/22/opinion/sunday/mountaineerings-greatest-climb-unravels.html?_r=0.

www.outsideonline.com/1983336/cerro-torre-snowballs-chance-hell.

www.outsideonline.com/1807171/new-doubts-swirl-around-1959-cerro-torre-ascent.

www.outsideonline.com/1898681/torre-torre-torre.

Section Five:
Everest (29,035 feet)

Mount Everest is the highest (though not the tallest) mountain on Earth. It pierces the atmosphere at a point where many large commercial jets fly. It is a difficult and dangerous climb, but by no means the most arduous. Nevertheless, it is often the objective of sometimes-obsessed amateur and professional adventurers. Summiters seem to revel in the fact that they are the highest entities on Earth, if only for a few moments. People who have never tested themselves in the higher ranges take on Everest, because they have the money and ambition, and are able to secure a place on a commercial expedition, one that may foolishly allow the inexperienced (and unconditioned) to attempt the climb. These folks may not know how to tie-in; belay; use crampons, ice ax, or ascenders; self-arrest; assess avalanche danger; perform rescues; or cross a tilting aluminum ladder above a deep crevasse without suffering from vertigo. All of this leads to catastrophes. What is truly stunning, as one may see in the 1996 debacle, is that superb professionals, such as Rob Hall and Scott Fischer, may die, while amateurs, like the experienced Jon Krakauer and Matt Dickinson, not only summit but survive unharmed.

Many trying years passed by before Tenzing Norgay and Sir Edmund Hillary finally summited in 1953. Since then, more than four thousand climbers have reached the top of the world, some more than once. This seems to imply that it is easy, and if they could do it, so can you. You probably cannot. Even trekking to Everest base camp can be fatal. It may be disheartening, but it is probably preferable to enjoy the climb vicariously, through an account or movie, such as the extraordinary IMAX *Everest*, which was filmed before, during, and after the 1996 tragedy. Narrated by Liam Neeson, it stars Jamling Tenzing

Norgay and Ed Viesturs, among many other outstanding mountaineers. Watching it in an IMAX theater is the next best thing to being on the mountain. At its conclusion, JA cried uncontrollably.

SOURCE

Everest. (IMAX film). Dir., David Breashears, et al. Laguna Beach, CA: MacGillivray
Freeman Films, et al., 1998.

CHAPTER 8

Everest, 1996:
Death and Rebirth: Rob Hall,
Beck Weathers, and Many Others

THE 1996 EVEREST DEBACLE IS UNDOUBTEDLY THE MOST FAMOUS mountaineering tragedy, at least as far as the general public is concerned. More than twenty of the involved and affected climbers wrote books on what occurred. The reasons that Jon Krakauer's *Into Thin Air* stands out and was so popular and influential are because it was the first overview to appear, and because it is beautifully articulated in a moving and enticing way. Although Krakauer has a perspective limited by his experience, he is honest and self-deprecating; if he was partially wrong or misleading about something, for example, Anatoli Boukreev, who corrected the record in his own excellent memoir, it was not entirely his fault; he simply was unaware of all of the details. As it turns out, however, an enormous controversy exists here, and we will return to it below.

Krakauer, subsidized by *Outside*, for which he was acting as a reporter, was a member of Rob Hall's commercial expedition. Hall's group of eight paying members was but one of fourteen expeditions comprising more than three hundred climbers present at Everest base camp that season. Some of these people were experienced, skillful, and caring; others, lamentably, were extremely incompetent or deceptive, discourteous, and nasty. Indeed, despite the sacrifices and commitment one must make to oneself, sponsors, and nation, three or four members of the South African expedition left before the climbing even began.[1] Hall was a highly respected mountaineer, owner of Adventure Consultants, and a guide, who preferred to control and protect his clients. His competitor, Scott Fisher, who owned Mountain Madness, was also respected, but allowed those in his group to roam with greater freedom. All of their clients, as well as everyone else on the mountain (including the Sherpas), were engaged in climbing, returning, and climbing again in order to acclimatize. Despite the constant immediate and historical reminders that nothing is more crucial than full and complete acclimatization, far too many of those who climb, whether to 15,000 feet or twice that high, fail to take this grueling necessity seriously. Even a Sherpa born halfway to Everest's 29,035-foot summit can succumb, as did Ang Dorje, early in the 1996 season. He eventually died from high-altitude pulmonary edema (HAPE).

Individuals and groups of independent mountaineers who manage to get a sometimes extremely expensive permit for any mountain in any country must deal with all of the logistics and arrangements necessary for the climb, including supplies, local help, medical support, and so on. But they do not have to pay as much as $65,000 to a guiding company, which, in exchange for the payment, takes care of everything and helps or leads the members to the summit. Before that can occur, in many locations (Aconcagua in the Andes, Vinson Massif in Antarctica, Annapurna in the Himalaya), the adventurers must wend their way to the base of the mountain (by helicopter, yak, goat, other creatures, on foot), and this takes patience, time, and energy. In third-world countries, the trekkers often get ill from the food, water, and altitude, as well as the extraordinarily unhygienic conditions in which human excrement litters the environment[2] and smoke fills the filthy guesthouses in which the mountaineers sleep along the way. They suffer a lot—with headaches, stomach cramps, diarrhea, and acute mountain sickness (AMS), or worse. This was the case here, as Krakauer and his fellow members trudged toward Everest base camp; it probably was also the case for many of the other people who eventually reached the bottom of the mountain. An additional obligation in certain countries, Nepal, for example, is to visit a Buddhist holy man, a lama, and receive a blessing. To refuse to participate in this ritual and a later *puja* ceremony, which takes place at the mountain, could alienate the Sherpa help, who might refuse to carry on.

So, during the first arduous weeks at base camp, the newly arrived must climb, return, and climb once more—over and over again. On many mountains, few impediments, other than storms and avalanches, provide distraction from the acclimatization process. But the south route on Everest is different: In order to move up above base camp, it is necessary to pass through the Khumbu Icefall, a notoriously dangerous, if beautiful, minefield of expanding and contracting crevasses, bridged by many aluminum ladders, reset in place each season, and overwhelmed below and above by enormous seracs, blocks of ice the size of houses, that can break off and crush and bury anyone caught in their path. Indeed, it was here that thirteen or more Sherpas were killed at the beginning of the 2014 season (see below). Everest climbers and readers familiar with the literature know all too well how enervating, even for professionals, this multi-hour passage can be, but Krakauer's description of his own terror, balancing on ladder rungs "bridging a sphincter-clenching chasm" in crampons, made it vividly clear: "There were many such crossings, and I never got used to them." Additionally, he suffered, as others do, from various ailments, including a very bad cough and an excruciatingly painful headache. Another fear, one that would have been unnecessary, if people were less foolish or arrogant, was that at least two groups would cause some real harm: The Taiwanese were incompetent, and the South Africans, through their leader, were dishonestly and offensively uncooperative.

Hall's clients, as well as everyone else, continued to acclimate. The distances and vertical rises (4 miles and 1,700 feet—on average, a mere 425 feet per mile—from Camp One to Two) are not great, but at 20,000 feet, they take a toll. As one moves higher, everything gets harder. And one of the most astonishing concomitants of an Everest climb is that the Western Cwm, a broad valley above the ice field, produces extremely variable temperatures. During the day, when the sun beats down, it may reach 100 degrees Fahrenheit (Krakauer kept a supply of snow under his cap to remain cool); at night and in the early-morning hours, when climbers begin to travel, it is frigidly cold. Three weeks after arriving, although he had lost some 20 pounds and was physically beaten down, Krakauer was fully acclimated.

On May 6, Hall's group began its multiday push to the summit, more than 10,000 vertical feet above. At Camp Three (24,000 feet), the climbers started using oxygen. On May 9, they left Three for Camp Four. As they moved up, they entered the death zone, the altitude at which it is difficult to get enough air into the lungs, where every step or action is exhausting, and where the body cannot recuperate but rather begins to die. Often, the wind and cold are more extreme. Here, on the 26,000-foot South Col, there were fifty-plus people, all planning, in just a few hours, to head for the top of the world. The astutely experienced must have realized that this would cause massive logjams at various constricted points. A mere 3,000 vertical feet separated Camp Four from the summit; at much lower altitudes, one could hustle up in two hours. Here, where every step requires four or five deep breaths, sometimes even while breathing bottled oxygen, it might take ten hours.

The weather improved and the entire Hall group (eight clients, three guides, four Sherpas) prepared to leave just before midnight on May 9. And it was at this point that Krakauer admits one of the key negative aspects of high-altitude mountaineering, something that never occurs consistently in any other human endeavor, and which is partially responsible for many tragedies: For two days, he had eaten almost nothing, and he had not slept at all; he was also wracked with severe pain. Thus, he began one of the most difficult tasks a human being can undertake malnourished and necessarily tired (even if his adrenaline fooled him). Fisher's fifteen Mountain Madness people (including Boukreev, Charlotte Fox, and Sandy Pittman) followed thirty minutes later.

Krakauer was surprisingly strong and therefore fast, but was held back, and often had to sit in the cold, because Hall did not want his people to separate. At one point, as he waited, he noticed that someone was being short-roped, pulled by another climber up the slope. This was the unfairly infamous Sandy Pittman (who did not request this service), a very wealthy women who was here completing the Seven Summits. Because Pittman brought vast quantities of electronic equipment, such as a satellite dish, as well as other unnecessary stuff, along on her climbs, all of which burdened the Sherpas or porters, she annoyed some of her peers, and because the press she relished and received may have painted a picture of a spoiled rich girl, she was often disparaged. But some of her fellow climbers had good things to say about her, and if she was not the strongest climber on the mountain, this Park Avenue socialite was here (once again), working hard and risking her life. She struggled and suffered like everyone else to accomplish her goals. She was dramatically different than some other truly uncooperative, selfish climbers who refused simple requests for help, which may have cost lives.

One of the early problems that impeded progress was that the highest fixed lines were not in place when the first climbers arrived at a point where they were required. (This is not entirely unusual, but nevertheless, it hinders progress and can result in great harm.) Krakauer helped three guides (not Sherpas) set these in place. At this point, three of Hall's clients, accompanied by two Sherpas, decided to retreat. Krakauer, however, persevered, and reached the summit too tired and too worried about his diminishing oxygen supply and the descent to feel elated. He stayed for just a few minutes and then headed down. At the top of the famous Hillary Step, he was stymied by the many ascending climbers. While waiting, he asked someone to turn his oxygen valve off, but the person accidentally turned it to full and this quickly depleted whatever supply of oxygen was left. An hour later, he finally was able to continue, but in a dizzy, fearful state. He desperately needed to reach his new oxygen tank just below. At 27,600 feet, he discovered that Beck Weathers had been waiting for hours to descend. He was almost completely snow blind, and he had promised Hall he would wait for him to return from the summit. Weathers could have descended with others, including Krakauer, but chose to keep his promise. This was a tragic mistake. Krakauer struggled downward on difficult terrain and in stormy, windy, and cold conditions, exacerbated by his diminishing mental and physical abilities. Finally, he reached the safety of Camp Four, exhausted and incapable of any further movement. He rested. At the same time, nineteen climbers were still descending in a vicious storm, trapped above in the open, unable to reach the safety of the tents.

The reason for this dismal occurrence was that neither Hall nor Fisher stuck to his turn-around time. No one insisted that clients and guides turn back at a reasonable hour, say, 1:00 or 2:00 p.m. Instead, people were still ascending after 4:00 p.m. And then many of these exhausted people were often incapable of descending safely on their own: Pittman was very tired and required an injection, Weathers was snow blind, and Yasuko Namba had to be dragged. These folks and others, comprising a large group, reached a point a mere 200 vertical feet above camp, and fifteen minutes behind Krakauer, who had just arrived. But the storm intensified and they lost their way. These eleven people wandered around for two hours in a potent whiteout, often on the edge of sheer drop-offs, unable to locate the nearby tents. The windchill was so intense (100-plus below zero) that they decided to huddle up and wait for a break. Charlotte Fox noted, "The cold was so painful. I didn't think I could endure it anymore. I just curled up in a ball and hoped death would come quickly." Another Hall client, Stuart Hutchinson, tried to rouse Krakauer, but he was too tired to help, so Hutchinson went out into the raging storm six times, but could not go far from the tents because of the cold and his desire not to get lost.

After many hours of suffering, Neal Beidleman, one of the Mountain Madness guides, noticed that the sky was clearing; this revealed Everest and Lhotse, which allowed them to figure out which way to go. Six people headed for the tents, which they reached just after midnight. Five stayed behind, waiting to be rescued. Earlier, at 7:30 p.m., Boukreev had tried to ascend in order to locate and help those who were lost, but he had been turned back by the fierce storm. Ironically, the missing were already wandering on the col near the tents. Once the survivors arrived and told Boukreev where the others were, he went out alone again (he could not find anyone willing to accompany him), but was unsuccessful; after an hour he returned, got better directions, and then tried again. Finally, he located Tim Madsen, who had stayed to protect Fox, who was his girlfriend, Pittman, Weathers, and Namba—all four of whom were in dismal shape. Boukreev led Fox back, returned, and brought Pittman in, with Madsen following behind. It was now 4:30 a.m., May 11. They gave up on Weathers and Namba, who seemed to be dead. At 9:30 a.m., two Sherpas attempted to climb 3,000 feet to rescue Hall; they were soon followed by three others, who were to rescue Fisher and Makalu Gau, the Taiwanese expedition leader, who was the only one brought down from that expedition.

Weathers and Namba were said to be dead. Krakauer and others needed oxygen, but none was available. The guides were dead or incapacitated, and so Stuart Hutchison, a physician, went out to check on the bodies. He discovered that both climbers were still breathing, but extremely close to death; there was nothing he and the Sherpas could do. Some climbers then descended, but others remained at Camp Four.

Pete Athans, the well-known climber, and Todd Burleson arrived with oxygen and offered canisters to those who needed it. Shortly thereafter, Burleson was outside and observed a climber approaching the tents. The man walked in a strange way, and his uncovered hand was frozen in place. It was Weathers, who somehow had survived, gotten up—despite his ice-encrusted face, virtual blindness, low pulse, and the many hours spent in the cold in a comatose state—and located the camp, astonishing everyone.

The next day, just before heading down, Krakauer visited Weathers and discovered that he had been in real misery all night, unable to breathe or do anything with his badly frozen hands. When Hall's group had ascended, there were eleven members. Now, upon descent, only six remained. At Camp Two, Krakauer learned that Weathers, whom he was certain was about to die, was able to descend under his own power, aided by Athans and Burleson. This resurrection must stand as one of the most amazing recoveries in the annals of human calamity. The title of Weathers's memoir, *Left for Dead*, perfectly epitomizes his plight.

Gau and Weathers were helicoptered to a hospital in Kathmandu. Gau lived to climb again. Weathers also survived but paid a terrible price, losing a hand, fingers, and his nose. He continued practicing as a pathologist and began to present lectures on his experience. His retelling of the 1996 climb is an extraordinary tale because it concentrates not only on the physicality of the expedition and his climbing generally, but also offers insights into how loved ones, in this case, his wife and children, must cope when an adventurer goes off and leaves family behind. Sometimes the adventurer comes back, shattered; sometimes, he does not return at all. One can only imagine his family's emotional reactions when they were informed that he was dead (confirmed by two doctors), only to receive another call shortly thereafter indicating that he was alive (Weathers, passim).

Hall was healthy and strong but insisted on waiting for his clients at 29,000 feet; he then ran out of energy. He lingered rather than forcing himself to descend, until it was too late. Fisher had been ill and weak for some time; he too ran out of energy and simply could not proceed. They both died high on Everest's flanks, Hall after a tear-inducing talk with his pregnant wife, who was back in New Zealand. Guides, clients, friends, relatives, and especially the Sherpas, who were very close to these two extraordinary men, were extremely devastated by their deaths, which, naturally, were exacerbated by the mutilation and sometimes unnecessary deaths of the many other climbers, including three on the north side of the mountain, for a total of twelve during the awful 1996 season. A Japanese climber who failed to help some Indians here later explained: "Above 8,000 meters is not a place where people can afford morality." This type of attitude has resulted in many catastrophes. Some of the people who perished might have been saved if attitudes had been different. Even sadder is Krakauer's supposition that had the blizzard held off for just two more hours, everyone could have made it to safety.

Matt Dickinson's *Other Side of Everest* never gained the cachet that Krakauer's bestseller did, but it provides an excellent overview of the tribulations of an amateur climber/filmmaker's personal life in relation to his sport and work, as well as a vivid account of what occurred on the other side of the mountain, which was almost as devastating, since four men died (Dickinson, x). Dickinson went to Everest to direct a film; he had no intention of climbing high. Nevertheless, following the difficult Mallory/Irvine route, he summited and survived (Dickinson, vii, xx). The goal of the movie was to film the out-of-shape, physically gigantic, and obsessed actor, Brian Blessed, on his third and hoped-for final attempt on the mountain (Dickinson, 19). Somehow Blessed had previously managed to reach almost 25,000 feet, which David Breashears vividly captured on film (Dickinson, 24–25). His next "astonishing" attempt brought him above 27,000 feet, which strongly suggested that he might be able to reach the summit, something that was very important to Dickinson as the film's director; he did not want to merely echo what Breashears had recorded (Dickinson, 26).

Dickinson was a competent documentarian but his climbing experience was minimal, and he admitted that he was careless. He was clumsy and uncoordinated, often dropped and lost things, and had even set a tent on fire (Dickinson, 30–31, 51). None of this augured well for a serious Himalayan climb. His group underwent the usual trials as they traveled in to base camp: The food was bad, people got ill, the roads were dangerous, the altitude was enervating, but it was all apparently worth the suffering, because the view of Everest on the north side is more powerful than what one sees in the south. It took nine days to travel from Kathmandu to base camp, where they arrived on April 11. They were surrounded by many small and larger national expeditions (Dickinson, 68, 70). Four days later, they headed up to Camp Three (Advance Base Camp), located just above 21,000 feet. Even though it was situated high up on the East Rongbuk Glacier, yaks were able ascend and transport supplies (Dickinson, 77). They continued to acclimatize by descending and then reascending.

Finally, the summit push arrived. The nine men split into two teams: Blessed and the film crew were to try first; then the remaining four would have their chance (Dickinson, 108). Once again, they reached Advance Base Camp (ABC), where more than thirty climbers awaited better weather. May 10 presented an ostensibly perfect day, crystal clear, but those in charge were put off by some distant clouds. They decided to wait, while other expeditions moved up (Dickinson, 116–17). They were right: By afternoon, the weather had changed, and the horrific storm inundated the mountain (Dickinson, 118). Three members of the Indian expedition had indicated that they had summited, but they had been mistaken, confused by whiteout conditions (Dickinson, 120, 143). Like the climbers on the south side, they were caught in the open and were unable to descend. As they lay dying, members of the Japanese team passed them twice, but were unable or unwilling to render help (Dickinson, 140).

The Dickinson group waited at ABC for a total of seven days, and then on May 15, they left for the summit, with intermediate stops at three higher camps. They were rather debilitated (Dickinson had lost 22 pounds), and extremely angry to discover that some other climbers had ransacked their tents at Camp Four (Dickinson, 145, 148, 149, 151). Further on, some of the men were unable to continue, and so they returned to Four, and then just Dickinson and Al Hinkes, an excellent mountaineer, tried again. This obviously altered the nature of the film, substituting Hinkes for Blessed in a quest for the summit. Because three members of the team had retreated, there was an abundant supply of oxygen, and they began to use it at about 25,000 feet. They also met up with their Sherpas, who had been waiting for them (Dickinson, 160, 162, 169–71). They arose at midnight and climbed tough snow and then steep rock, including the difficult first, second, and third steps in crampons, which made rock work hazardous. They encountered the dead Indians, but despite their importance to the film, Dickinson was loath to videotape them out of respect for their families (Dickinson, 187, 191, 199, 200). They pressed on in the cold and wind, reaching the summit without any liquid nourishment, because their juice bottles had frozen solid, and tired, because Dickinson had not slept in thirty hours. The descent, naturally, was more onerous and dangerous than the climb. The film was a success (Dickinson, 213, 218, 231).

Dickinson noted that an Austrian's imminent death had little effect on him because he was emotionally hardened, and later, when Hinkes lagged behind, he insisted that he had simply ignored his friends' potential plight in his compulsive quest to reach the summit (Dickinson, 182, 210). We think that he is unnecessarily hard on himself here. In both cases, there was really nothing he could have done. So, bad things occurred simultaneously on both the north and south routes.

JA read *Into Thin Air* shortly after it was published. Everything seemed clear, and although Krakauer indicated some culpability, it seemed unwarranted. It was Boukreev who appeared to be the villain—for refusing to use oxygen when guiding, and because he retreated to his tent long before his clients descended. Then Boukreev's *Climb* came out. Here Boukreev presented his side of the story and clarified and explained so that he came off as a hero rather than a slacker. (Krakauer had given him full credit for his courageous rescues.) And so matters stood. In 1999, two years after the original publication of *Into Thin Air*, the ongoing altercation between Boukreev and especially his coauthor, G. Weston

DeWalt, on the one hand, and Krakauer, on the other, had reached such a fevered pitch that Krakauer decided to break his avowed silence on their petty disagreements and published a defense in a postscript to a more-recent edition.

Here he scrupulously countered points that DeWalt made, some of which are apparently patently false. Especially noteworthy is the fact that DeWalt impugned his journalistic integrity; Krakauer pointed out errors in *The Climb*, but its publisher did not correct them in a subsequent edition; DeWalt did not interview apposite people; Sherpas blamed Boukreev for the debacle; and a lost ice ax was not located where DeWalt had it. Krakauer sums matters up when he admonishes that, "Sadly, some of the errors in *The Climb* do not appear to be the product of mere carelessness, but rather to be deliberate distortions of the truth intended to discredit my reporting." David Breashears, the IMAX film director, who happened to be on Everest at the time of the disaster, insists that Boukreev was irresponsible for not using oxygen and should have stayed with his clients. This is seconded by Reinhold Messner, probably the greatest mountaineer of all time. JA now, once again, believes that despite his heroic rescues, Boukreev neither acted honorably on Everest nor, along with DeWalt, produced an honest account. This is especially sad because he can no longer defend himself: On December 25, 1997, he died in an avalanche on Annapurna.

Although this would seem to be the end of the controversy, it is not. Two years after Boukreev died, the publisher issued a new paperback edition of *The Climb*, appended to which is a thirty-eight-page DeWalt rebuttal (which also appears to have validity) to Krakauer's defense. All of these claims and counter remarks whip the uninvolved reader back and forth so that the truth is hard to ascertain. Let Weathers, an involved expedition member, have the last word: "That day, Anatoli [Boukreev] had forsaken his duty as a guide. While everyone was struggling up and down the ridge to the summit, or stacked up like cordwood at the Hillary Step, Anatoli climbed for himself, by himself, without oxygen. He just went straight up, tagged the summit, and came straight back down. Because he lacked oxygen, he couldn't persist in the cold, and was forced to retreat to the shelter of his tent" (Weathers, 45).

NOTES

1 The extreme stupidity manifested by arrogant climbers is epitomized in the following anecdote. JA, standing at the top of the Aiguille du Midi in Chamonix, France, observed a group returning from a climb. The leader was showing off for an audience, some of whose members had probably never even set foot on a glacier. He furled his long rope, began to clamber over a barrier, and then purposely slipped to entertain the gawkers. It was a dangerous and pathetic performance.

2 On at least two occasions, JA was appalled by the way in which human evacuation is handled. On Orizaba, the 18,800-foot volcano near Mexico City, the many hundreds of climbers from all over the world can sleep in a large refuge that holds thirty people, but has no toilet facilities; as a result, excrement and toilet paper are everywhere. On France's Aiguille du Tour, the refuge's toilet empties directly onto the sloping rocks below. This would be inconceivable (and illegal) anywhere in the United States.

SOURCES

The primary source for this chapter is Krakauer's book. This is supplemented by other material duly noted in the text.

Boukreev, Anatoli, with G. Weston DeWalt. *The Climb: Tragic Ambitions on Everest.* New York: St. Martin's Griffin, 1999.

Dickinson, Matt. *The Other Side of Everest: Climbing the Treacherous North Face Through the Killer Storm.* New York: Times Books, 1999.

Krakauer, Jon. *Into Thin Air: A Personal Account of the Mount Everest Disaster.* New York: Anchor, 1999.

Weathers, Beck, with Stephen G. Michaud. *Left for Dead: My Journey Home from Everest.* New York: Villard, 2000.

Section Six:
Siula Grande (20,814 feet)

CHAPTER 9

Siula Grande, 1985:
Joe Simpson's Escape

THE STORY THAT JOE SIMPSON TELLS IN *TOUCHING THE VOID*, AND WHICH is recast in the superb cinematic version, is one of the finest articulations of a harrowing ordeal and escape in the history of adventuring, comparable to the incredible events in Ernest Shackleton's *South* or Yossi Ghinsberg's *Jungle*. Additionally, his narrative is beautifully and lyrically articulated, also an extraordinary feat, since he had never written anything prior to this. Simpson, who it turns out is extremely accident-prone,[1] manifests all of the extraordinary character traits that allow humans to prosper, to fully contravene Rilke's apothem—"Who speaks of victory? Survival is everything."[2] (The same may be said of Aron Ralston's experience, detailed below.) We are more than the sum of our parts and experiences; we do more than merely endure, even in exigent situations such as inhuman concentration camps or gulags. We sometimes, even often, truly triumph in a way that synecdochically affirms all that is good in human beings.

In 1985, Joe Simpson and his climbing partner, Simon Yates, decided to try Siula Grande, an unsummited Peruvian peak set off far from civilization. On the way to their base camp, they picked up Richard, a young American whose job it would be to guard the tent and supplies until the men returned from their climb. Things went well, and as the men ascended they took many photographs. The early part of the account covers the rock, snow, and ice climb, which was often extremely difficult and dangerous, with excruciating exposure and on surfaces including bad ice and soft snow, where protection was very difficult to implement. Simpson offers a series of very precise descriptions of what they encountered and how they proceeded.[3]

After some minor nearby explorations, they began the climb and encountered these ongoing problems: rocks, including a deadly large boulder that almost hit Yates cascaded down; bad ice and soft powder on steep slopes; very low temperatures (between minus-20 and minus-40 windchill); extreme and frightening exposure; falls, fear, and trembling. The descent turned out to be as horrific as the climb. The narrow upper ridge was fractured and corniced, and they were both afraid of a disaster. At one point, Simpson, trailing 150 feet behind, thought that if Yates fell, he might be able to counter it if he jumped off the opposite side of the ridge, thus balancing the falling weight. If Simpson fell, Yates, leading, would not have enough time to react. It was, as climbing often is, extremely stressful. Matters deteriorated as darkness fell. As they had done on the ascent, they bivouacked in a snow hole. The following day, they continued down with difficulty. A poor placement of one of Simpson's ice tools allowed it to pull out and he fell. He hit hard and badly hurt his right knee: "It wasn't just broken, it was ruptured, twisted, crushed." The excruciating pain was unbearable. Yates arrived and realized that the situation was life-threatening. The climb and early descent were extremely difficult when the men were fit and whole; now it seemed that it would be almost impossible for Simpson to get down.

It is at this point in the account that the author or his editor had a brilliant idea: Simpson would shift voices and offer Yates's directly articulated thoughts. The appropriate narrative voice is made clear by italicizing Yates's passages or chapters. This ingenious device allows the reader to listen in on what is happening (physically and mentally) to each of the players, in his own words.[4] Yates's passages are intercalated, but the effect is mellifluous and cohesive. The reader is entranced as Yates silently rearticulates some of what is already known, as well as his fear as he was forced to re-climb a portion to free the rope on corniced snow, which allowed him to break through into open space: This "was the hardest and most dangerous thing I'd ever done," he wrote. Although Yates was discouraged and thought it impossible for Simpson to get down, he did not share this with his partner, who began hopping along a highly exposed slope. Ironically, Simpson thought that Yates would fall as he attempted to retrieve the rope. Intermittently, they would indicate their emotional states: "I was shaking and so strung out" (Yates). "I felt small and useless" (Simpson).

They decided to allow Simpson to rappel (lower) down, but since they had no pickets (snow stakes), they had to come up with a way to hold his weight. They laboriously dug bucket seats in which Yates could sit and slowly play out the rope as Simpson descended. All of this took time, and Yates became understandably impatient and cold, so he played out the rope as quickly as possible, which made things unbearable for Simpson, who had a hard time controlling his descent and too often hit his injured leg, resulting in ongoing horrific pain. He made this clear—"Howling and screaming for Simon to stop achieved nothing"; "I had barely ceased sobbing before my boot snagged again"—but it is impossible for even an empathetic reader to truly experience this excruciating and unrelenting torture, especially if one has never had a bad injury or illness.

They both suffered from the cold and incipient frostbite, which resulted in hands that could barely grip or manipulate. When Simpson reached a new stance, he would begin to dig out the seat while Yates descended. They repeated this difficult business over and over again. To increase efficiency and to decrease the number of seats that had to be dug, they tied two ropes together. This 300-foot line allowed for a very long lowering, but at the halfway point, Yates had to slip the knot around the belay plate, and this could only be done if Simpson somehow held his own weight. Since they were far apart, it was very difficult to communicate, and it is this, in part, that eventually resulted in the final debacle.[5] In the early stages, however, Simpson was elated that the system worked and that he was descending quickly, whereas shortly before he had been despondent, thinking he would not be capable of escaping a most unpleasant fate.

They had managed two rappels and eight lowerings, which covered just about 3,000 feet; this should have brought them down to the glacier, a stunning and seemingly impossible achievement. But on the final lowering, the slope steepened and Simpson dropped off into space. He hung there about 100 feet above the glacier; he could not reach the ice wall, six feet away, hold himself, and thereby take his weight off the rope. He tried to install Prusik knots, which would have allowed him to climb upward on the rope, but did not fully succeed. Additionally, he could not communicate with Yates, who did not know what had occurred, and who was slowly beginning to lose his stance (Simpson realized this too). The dead weight was pulling him out of his seat and he now had only two choices: He could be pulled off and then plummet down, which would obviously release Simpson (who also would fall), or he could do the unthinkable: cut the rope—which he did.[6]

Yates spent the night in a snow cave, and in the morning began his dangerous descent down the slope. He did not think he would make it back to the tents. When he reached the crevasse, he shouted to Simpson, but there was no response. Unable to recall the route through the complex crevasse field, he struggled downward, haunted by the probability that his partner had fallen in and had died. He had a very hard time, was extremely thirsty, and was additionally overcome by the fact that he had cut the rope and would have to admit it when he returned to civilization. He briefly considered not telling anyone. Eventually he reached the tents, presented a truthful account to Richard, and then another small miracle occurred. Normally, after summiting (or failing) and returning to camp, mountaineers want to leave camp immediately, move on to the next adventure (after recuperating, perhaps at a tea house or motel), or go home. Filth, hunger, thirst, and the desire for the comforts of civilization, after sleeping on boulders, drive people out very quickly. But Yates and Richard were too dismayed (depressed) to take any action. They lingered, day after day. Had they left, all of Simpson's struggles would have been in vain (although it is not impossible that some little shepherd children might have found him alive).

To this point, Simpson tells a typical if remarkable mountaineering tale, one in which adventurers discover that they have undertaken more than they can handle and pay a price (loss, extreme emotional trauma, physical injury, death). But now a unique unfolding occurs. Naturally, there have been similar astounding triumphs, e.g., Doug Scott's descent off the Ogre with two broken legs, or Aron Ralston's amputation and escape (both with some help), but none, as far as we know, in which a badly injured individual miraculously rescues himself from the depths of a crevasse and then crawls 6 miles without food, water, or any help.

Simpson hung on the rope for a long time, the cold causing him to lose all sensation in his arms and legs. Suddenly, he began to fall, accelerated, and stopped. Amazingly, he had landed on a tiny ledge deep within the crevasse. Despite the excruciating pain, and his precarious slippery position in the darkness, he immediately managed to pound in an ice screw for protection against falling. With his flashlight, he could see at least 100 feet of emptiness below him, and a 20-foot gap between the walls of his icy grave. He did not think he could climb back out. He pulled on the rope, hoping it would tighten, which would allow him to climb up; instead, it came completely down and he discovered that it had been cut. He was dismayed, cried, and fell asleep. He awoke and attempted to climb straight up the ice wall, but failed. He then decided to lower himself into the abyss, hoping for a miracle.

It is very difficult to fully comprehend both the physical layout of Simpson's ice-bridge ledge and the abyss below, on the one hand, and the decision to rappel down (in order to go up) on the other. Gravity pulled him down the slope but he simultaneously wanted to stop. He continued, and suddenly the slope became vertical and he found himself dangling. He had purposely not knotted the rope, so if and when he reached the end, he knew he would fall off into space. As he described his progress, he continually alluded to his emotional state: "I felt paralyzed, incapable of thinking, as waves of panic swept through me." He then thought that he had reached the crevasse's bottom, but it was just another ledge, a tenuous snow floor. But the configuration here was very different: Another slope headed upward, and, astonishingly, a beam of sunlight penetrated the darkness. This allowed him to hope that he could somehow climb out. His dejection turned to optimism, and he now knew that he would escape.

Simpson first had to cross a gap between his snow ledge and the beginning of the slope that would lead to freedom. It took ten minutes of careful crawling in order to avoid crashing through the precarious snow floor. Once at the foot of the slope, he discovered that it was long and steep, and he wondered whether he would succeed. He was still tied to the secured rappel rope, but if he misstepped on the slope, he would fall, crash through the bridge, and pendulum across the abyss. He knew that would be the end of his escape possibilities.

He began to climb the 45-degree slope, which steepened near the top, and which he estimated to be about 130 feet long. The routine he worked out included digging two steps, planting his axes, and then hopping from the lower to the higher step. More than two hours of suffering exertion brought him to the steeper portion. He almost fell twice, but he caught himself, crying and cursing, which embarrassed him. He was sweating from the exertion, but cold as well. His rope had followed him in a long crescent, but a fall would have carried him a very long way down and across. He continued for more than two additional hours (a total of five), which brought him just below the hole that would take him out of the crevasse. The slope was now extremely steep, his pain constant, and his strength much diminished. Nevertheless, he managed the last 10 feet, crawled out, and was stunned by the spectacular beauty of the clear sky and surrounding mountains: "the most stupendous view I had ever seen." He rested.

Lamentably, his relief soon evaporated when he realized that he still had to descend 200 feet to the glacier and then travel 6 miles back to camp. (It did not occur to him that Yates and Richard might have left.) He descended, fell, and suffered mightily. He then noticed Yates's meandering, down-flowing footprints. He followed them, crawling, halting in the oppressive heat (despite which his fingers were frostbitten), and thus making very slow progress. But a voice urged him onward and he obeyed, automatically attempting to reach a specific, preordained point, and then starting the cycle again.[7] Much of the time, he was in a daze, seeing figures in the cliff's ice. As the day drew to an end, he found himself enveloped in a storm, which buried the prints (which he needed to guide him around crevasses, but also to connect him with another person), and this frightened him. Despite the snow, wind, and darkness, he continued. But finally, he dug a snow cave, laboriously and painfully removed his crampons, and got into his sleeping bag. He slept.

He awoke the next day in pain and panic. He had no way to quench his unbearable thirst, since eating snow does not do the job. He crawled, wary of the complex series of crevasses; finally, he managed to circumvent them and reach the moraine. There the onset of snow blindness scared him. He dozed and awoke often but continued downward. Eventually, crawling became impossible, so he fashioned a splint so that he could hop across or around the rocks and boulders. Hopping, however, often resulted in falling and getting hurt. After many hours, he discovered a trickle of water and drank just a bit before it ran out. Night fell and he slept once again. The next morning, he was in very bad shape, weak, lethargic, barely able to move; and now on the third day of his excruciating escape, it suddenly occurred to him that Yates might have decamped. Nevertheless, he soldiered on, hopping, falling, suffering, and then repeating the actions again, even though he often thought he could not move; but he did, like a Beckettian character who cannot go on, but does. Finally, he located a good source of water and drank until his stomach hurt. This reinvigorated him both physically and mentally, but soon thereafter he weakened again and hallucinated. Now all he could do was crawl. He knew that he was moving extremely slowly, but what mattered was that he was moving. Close to the tents, he tried screaming for Yates, but there was no answering call. Much later, he discovered that he was crawling through their bathroom area, which was very near to the tents. At the end of his tether, he howled "SIIIIMMMmoonnnn." He saw a light and then heard a reply: "Joe! Is that you? JOE!"

Simpson was in extremely bad shape, almost paralyzed, and Yates was emotionally devastated; he hardly knew what he was saying: "Joe! God! Oh my God! Fucking hell, fuck, look at you. Shit, Richard, hold him. Lift him, lift him, you stupid bastard! God Joe, how? How?"

He and Richard brought him into the tent and plied him with tea and many different drugs. They talked. When they removed his pants to look at the leg, they were stunned, shocked: "Bloody hell!" "God! It's worse than I thought." It was a multicolored stump; the thigh and ankle were the same size; the knee was a lump. He also had a broken heel and frozen fingers. Yates realized that they must get out immediately, but Simpson did not feel able to leave yet. Yates insisted, since it would take three days to reach a hospital, and the leg could get infected. Simpson was about to fall asleep when he said, "You saved my life, you know. It must have been terrible for you that night. I don't blame you. You had no choice. . . . Thanks for getting me down."

They left on donkeys and a mule, even though Simpson could hardly stay awake or stand. He suffered a great deal as they wended their way back to civilization and a hospital in Lima, where doctors operated on his leg, much against his wishes. Eventually, he went home and had five more surgeries. Ten weeks after the last one found him climbing again in the Karakoram! Yates also returned immediately to mountaineering, and a few weeks after returning from Peru, he ascended the Eiger's north face (Yates).

This magnificent tale is, as the great Chris Bonington observes in the foreword, "one of the most incredible stories of survival that I have ever read"—perhaps the single finest, most emotionally draining mountaineering account ever written. Despite the fact that Simpson had never done anything like this and was very unsure of himself when it was suggested that he write a book, *Touching the Void* won the 1988 Boardman Tasker award for the best book of mountain literature, among other encomiums. No prize was ever more deserved.

People who have encountered Simpson for the first time through *Touching the Void* will not realize that this was but one of the earliest of many catastrophic debacles he has experienced: He slept in a dug hole on a cornice; purposely sledded off a ski jump; partially dropped a boot high on a wall; walked unroped among crevasses (his partner fell in); was pulled off, fell 500 feet, and was very seriously injured and lowered once again, soon after which he climbed to 20,500 feet on crutches; and hung from a tenuous piton for twelve hours, as described in the first note below, among many others. Almost as astonishing as his Peruvian adventure, and more impossible to fathom, is his escape from an enormous avalanche that caught him as he began to descend Les Courtes near Chamonix, France, after climbing the Austrian route on its north face. The descent took place in the northeast on a broader slope, one newly covered with loose, unconsolidated snow that had not yet adhered to an older base. The sun beat down, further diminishing adhesion. After just 100 feet, Simpson knew that an avalanche was imminent, but he and his partner were impatient to descend. Nevertheless, he was just about to retrace his steps, when the snow came pouring down and engulfed him. He screamed to his partner to follow his fall so that he would be able to dig him out. Down he went, tumbling, flailing, and swimming, as one is told to do. The snow got into his mouth and nose, he banged his head on a rock, then was thrown through the air, and finally landed on the glacier, buried only up to his waist. It took an hour for his partner to reach him and then dig him out. Simpson was dazed with a concussion, had holes in his forehead and cheek, bruises on his face, and his speech was slurred. After reaching a refuge, a lovely Italian woman kindly gave him some hot chocolate, but he was shaking so badly that the scalding liquid ended up on his legs.

Many people are caught in avalanches. Some survive; others do not. What is beyond belief here is that Simpson was carried for 2,000 feet on a very steep slope (perhaps 80 degrees near the top). He rolled along with the snow among and over rocks and across a 30-foot *Bergschrund*, but survived. He got away with what must be considered minor injuries (Simpson, *This Game*, 289 ff, 103–09, passim).

NOTES

1 For example, he mentions in passing a preceding attempt, on the Bonatti Pillar, where he and a partner lost the ledge on which they were resting (because it broke away and fell off the mountain). They were belayed to a strung rope whose anchors were more than tenuous. They hung on there for twelve hours until rescued by a helicopter.

2 Rainer Maria Rilke: "*Wer spricht von Siegen? Überstehen ist alles.*" (Trans. by the authors.)

3 Readers unfamiliar with long-distance hiking, climbing, or mountaineering will be understandably skeptical that an adventurer who may have climbed a specific mountain ten or twenty or even one hundred times can recall precise individual climbs in great detail and differentiate among them even many years later, but JA knows from experience that this is hardly unusual.

4 Faulkner, in *The Sound and the Fury*, manages a similar feat. He had originally wanted the publisher to use different-color inks to differentiate among characters.

5 Things would have unfolded very differently had these men carried radios, walkie-talkies, air horns, and/or ascenders. But one must make choices to keep equipment at a reasonable weight, and these items would certainly have seemed expendable when packing. In this case, even avalanche beacons and probes would probably have been left behind. At any rate, the trend today, thirty years after the events described here took place, is toward lighter equipment and smaller backpacks. JA once met a young woman on a mountaintop. Commenting on her pack, he discovered that it contained both tent and sleeping bag, which was almost impossible to believe, since it looked as if it weighed 10 pounds. She explained that they were miniaturized versions of traditional camping equipment, each weighing just a few ounces!

6 This may appear to have been a selfish act of self-preservation, but in reality it was the reasonable thing to do, shown by Simpson's first coherent words offered to his partner: "Thanks, Simon . . . You did right." Had he not cut the rope, they both would have fallen and perhaps hit each other; it is also possible that their combined weight would have broken the snow ledge that saved Simpson. It is important to point out that this was not an unprecedented act: In 1931, on Kangchenjunga, Tsin Norbu cut a rope and two men died (Neale, 121).

7 This method—noting a distant point and allowing oneself a specific amount of time or number of breaths to reach it—often used by mountaineers, can be very effective in exigent situations.

SOURCES

The primary source for this chapter is Simpson's 1988 book. Others are cited in the text.

Neale, Jonathan. *Tigers of the Snow: How One Fateful Climb Made the Sherpas Mountaineering Legends*. New York: Thomas Dunne Books, 2002.

Simpson, Joe. *This Game of Ghosts*. Seattle: The Mountaineers, 1993.

Simpson, Joe. *Touching the Void*. New York: Harper & Row, 1988.

Touching the Void. (Film). Kevin MacDonald, Dir. IFC/MGM, 2004.

Yates, Simon. "Mountaineering: The Legacy of Touching the Void T[elegraph] Travel." April 19, 2013. Accessed September 22, 2014. www.telegraph.co.uk/travel/activity andadventure/9997685/Mountaineering-The-legacy-of-Touching-the-Void.html.

Section Seven:
Nanga Parbat (26,660 feet)

CHAPTER 10

Nanga Parbat, 1934:
A German Tragedy

NANGA PARBAT, THE "GERMAN MOUNTAIN," THE ONE THE GERMANS desperately craved for a first ascent, is, like the thirteen other 8,000-meter peaks, a real killer. Indeed, it is called the "killer mountain" because some seventy people have lost their lives there. And, sadly, in 2013, it was the location at which terrorists murdered eleven innocent climbers. (See "Terrorism" below.) The Germans attempted Nanga Parbat in 1932 on an expedition led by Willy Merkl that included the great Fritz Wiessner, but there were many problems with porters, and they failed. Since they were not allowed to visit Everest, the "British mountain," they were back again in 1934. Once again, Merkl, with ten additional climbers, was the expedition leader, but he made some errors: He moved too quickly, because, as Jonathan Neale[1] points out, he felt pressure from the new Nazi regime (cf., its later sponsorship of the expedition that, with Heinrich Harrer, soon thereafter conquered the terrifying Eiger North Face). And he apparently did not fully understand the need to acclimatize, or the potentially tragic results of a failure to do so.

They hired some fifteen Sherpas and twenty Tibetans from Darjeeling to act as high-altitude porters and an additional six hundred Kashmiri men (supplemented by substitutes) to carry loads to base camp. The Sirdar was a man named Lewa. There was much bickering among these people. Nevertheless, they eventually reached base camp and then moved up the mountain. The first death occurred because, not fully appreciating the deadly effect of altitude on someone who begins to suffer from AMS, they did not immediately evacuate Alfred Drexel, who remained on high where a doctor and oxygen, impeded by storms, were slowly brought up to him rather than taking him as low as possible. He suffered and quickly died. After some major disagreements (which seem to occur frequently on these large expeditions), they were ready to try for the upper camps and the summit. Neale makes very clear why a major catastrophe was imminent:

> *Almost all the ingredients of the tragedy that would follow were now in place. Merkl was under personal pressure and leading a divided expedition. He had chosen the politics of iron determination. And the route to a summit would mean many days on a long ridge at an altitude whose effects Merkl and his companions did not understand.*

Fritz Bechtold, in *Deutsche am Nanga Parbat* (translated as *Nanga Parbat Adventure*), the beautifully and fully illustrated, semiofficial expedition account, fails to address these and other negative aspects of the men, the leadership, or the expedition. This is perhaps one reason why Neale accuses Bechtold of being deceptive. This is reminiscent of Maurice Herzog's glossing over troubles and problems in *Annapurna* (see below).

Of course, the men were unaware of all of these subtleties, and slowly worked their way up the mountain, setting camp after camp. They reached the sixth of these on the ridge, slept, and then all of the climbers and porters heading for the summit continued. In 2000, Neale interviewed Ang Tsering, the ninety-six-year-old Sherpa who was the last man alive from the expedition. From him he learned many things, some that contradict what Bechtold presented. Neale insisted that Bechtold was deceptive because he was ashamed of what had occurred. Tsering is more reliable, and Neale corrected the record. Tsering stated that not dividing the men into groups and having only some proceed is what led to the tragedy, because they did not have any higher camps in place that were stocked with food and help; everyone was marching along together. They set up an unsupplied Camp Seven at 23,570 feet. In the morning, two Sherpas were ill, and Bechtold accompanied them down; they had a very hard time descending, but finally made it to Four, and help. This left five climbers and an astonishing eleven porters at Camp Seven, sixteen men trapped at a temporary (unsupplied) camp, near the death zone.

It started to snow. The wind howled, blowing at 100 miles per hour. In the morning, conditions were horrible. Nevertheless, Peter Aschenbrenner and Erwin Schneider[2] decided to descend. Three Sherpas accompanied them. Pasang Picture was okay, but the other Sherpas were ill and incapacitated. All five men were tied into one rope. They had a long way to go in a very bad blizzard, and they had problems: The route was hard to follow, and two men could hardly walk. Suddenly, the wind picked up Nima Dorje and he floated around, held nearby by the extended rope. They had a very difficult time; finally, two men managed to grab him and haul him in.

It is at this point that a unique development occurred. Ang Tsering claimed that the two Austrian climbers unroped and put on their skis. There is no controversy concerning the fact that the Europeans left the Sherpas, but Maurice Isserman and Stewart Weaver do not believe that they skied away (Isserman, 471, nt. 18). They quickly left the three Sherpas, only one of whom was well, alone on the dangerous upper slopes of Nanga Parbat. The skiers eventually reached Four and their friends. Neale offers some of the imaginings of the Sherpas, but although what he narrates is probable, there is no real evidence for their thoughts (for example, that the Germans left the Sherpas to die). Neale also says that as Pasang took over, he became a leader, not a mere coolie,[3] the first time that this ever occurred. They started down but it was very hard to see. They decided to dig in and wait for better weather.

Aschenbrenner and Schneider had left the three Sherpas along the way, but they had also left weaker fellow climbers and Sherpas above. Later, they were harshly criticized for their actions. These eleven men started down soon after the first group; they too ran into trouble and decided to bivouac. They had three sleeping bags, which could accommodate just six men. Some did not have protective clothing, but nevertheless, they had to sleep on the snow. By the next day, one Sherpa had died and three, who were ill, could not continue. The others descended. Simultaneously, Bechtold mounted a rescue; in a moment of clarity, the rescuers saw men coming down, but they were still very high above them.

The rescuers returned to Four. When the large group reached Seven, the Europeans took the single tent and sent the Sherpas to Six. They did not reach it, but spent the night in the open. It continued to snow. They were extremely hungry and thirsty when they began the descent again. Suddenly they came upon the remnant of the first group, led by Pasang Picture. They made some rope adjustments and then they all crossed the dangerous traverse, with frostbitten hands and feet. At the fixed lines, they had no means of attaching themselves and they were not wearing crampons. Things went very slowly and carefully. One man simply died; then another. When they finally got to the tents, they found that another had passed away. They continued to Four, whence a rescue party went up to meet them. In camp, the four remaining men were massaged and cared for. But there were still three Sherpas bivouacked above Seven, and two more at the camp.

Ang Tsering, snow-blind, and his two fellow Sherpas stayed put in their open bivouac for three nights. Then Tsering and another man went down, but Dakshi was unable to continue, so they left him. On the way, Tsering stumbled across Uli Wieland, dead in the snow. He had died just above the tent in which the other two climbers, Merkl and Willo Welzenbach, were lying, too frail to rid the tent of snow. Tsering had a hard time communicating with Merkl, who knew little English. Tsering wanted to go down; he was afraid that the men at Four would leave, thinking those above were all dead. But he stayed because fellow Sherpa Gaylay, who had been left above, now arrived at Seven.

The next day they could see six men coming up from a distant Four. They reached Five, but had to turn back. Then Welzenbach died and there was no reason to stay at Seven any longer, and so the following day, Tsering, Gaylay, and Merkl finally headed down. Neale makes it clear that this was the "sixth day without water, the eighth day without food." He also continues to emphasize the horrible class differences that existed between Westerners (in this case, Germans) and the indigenous peoples who acted as porters. For example, even in this extreme, life-threatening situation, the climbers slept in the tent, the others, unprotected, on the snow.

The descent was a struggle because Merkl was in very bad shape. They all probably were frostbitten. From Four below, Aschenbrenner, Schneider, and others could see them descending, but they were too weak to go up to help. Tsering and the Sherpas almost reached Six, but were forced to bivouac, "the sixth night of their retreat," and they continued to eat ice. Neale claims that this was and is a unique act of Himalayan endurance. In the morning, Tsering went for help, leaving Merkl and Gaylay. He struggled, especially to pass a body hanging on the fixed rope. The Sherpa people are very chary of even looking at the dead, let alone touching them; this must have been extremely trying for him. He found no one at Five, and so continued to Four, where his shouts were heard and the doctor and others came to him with tea. He recuperated. The next morning, shouts were heard and they tried to go up but failed. Merkl and Gaylay never made it. In 1938, Bechtold returned and found them dead and frozen.

Various men made rescue attempts, but none got anywhere near those high above. Tsering was carried out, had his toes amputated, and spent six months in the hospital. Of the sixteen men on the ridge when the storm struck, nine perished. It was a very large price to pay because of some small errors.

But this was not the end of the quest. The Germans were not deterred, and tried again in 1937 (when an avalanche buried camp under 10 feet of snow, and took the lives of sixteen men); in 1938; in 1939 (an exploration of the Diamir Face, with Heinrich Harrer); and again in 1953, when Karl Herligkoffer decided to mount an expedition. This was very strange because he was not really a climber; rather, he wanted to honor Willy Merkl, his half brother. Amazingly, he managed to convince Aschenbrenner (now in his fifties) to participate. They attacked Nanga Parbat in the usual way, and eventually two men were ready for the summit, the great Hermann Buhl[4] and Otto Kempter. But Aschenbrenner told them from below that they should descend; they reasonably refused. They argued a lot, over the radio, but finally they received permission to continue. Buhl left a bit before Kempter, who never caught up; eventually he turned back. Buhl continued for seventeen hours. By the time he returned to his comrades he had been out for forty-one hours, including a bivouac, and had covered 8,000 vertical feet (round-trip). He was the first person to reach the summit of an 8,000-meter peak alone, and did it without oxygen.

So, the French had the first ascent of Annapurna (with some dissension); the British, Everest (honorably); the Germans, their coveted Nanga Parbat (heroically); and soon, the Italians, K2 (deceptively). (With the exception of Everest, all of these problematic triumphs are covered in this book.) In 1936, Frank Leberecht directed *Nanga Parbat—Das Schicksal deutscher Helden*, a documentary that features the 1934 climbers.

Notes

1 Neale's *Tigers of the Snow* is similar to Zuckerman and Padoan's *Buried in the Sky* (see chapter 6 in this volume). Both books place the Sherpas at the forefront and narrate the story from their point of view, giving them the full credit that is often elided in mountaineering accounts.

2 In 1964–1965 (that is, thirty years later), JA studied at the University of Innsbruck. One of his roommates was Seppl Manhart, whose stepfather was Erwin Schneider (born in 1906). Manhart and JA would sometimes talk about mountaineering, and especially, Norman Dyhrenfurth, whose father Oskar was very close to Schneider.

3 It is certainly true that in the early days of mountaineering, the Europeans mistreated porters and even climbing Sherpas. Germans and Austrians are very formal peoples. The British are aristocratic. They all condescended to their help in a most egregious fashion, e.g., some men kissed the Europeans' feet.

4 Buhl came from Innsbruck and probably skied and climbed on the *Nordkette*, where JA did some years later.

Sources

The primary source for this account is the Neale study. Others are cited in the text.

Bechtold, Fritz. *Nanga Parbat Adventure: A Himalayan Expedition*, tr. H. E. G. Tyndale. London: John Murray, 1935.

Isserman, Maurice, and Stewart Weaver. *Fallen Giants: A History of Himalayan Mountaineering from the Age of Empire to the Age of Extremes*. New Haven: Yale University Press, 2008.

Neale, Jonathan. *Tigers of the Snow: How One Fateful Climb Made the Sherpas Mountaineering Legends*. New York: Thomas Dunne Books, 2002.

CHAPTER 11

Nanga Parbat, 1970:
Günther Messner's Death

DEATH AND REBIRTH ON NANGA PARBAT

*I remember, years later, his describing to me the effect of the sudden
view you get of Nanga Parbat from one of those Kashmir valleys; you
have been riding for hours among quiet richly wooded scenery, wind-
ing up along the side of some kind of gorge, with nothing very big to
look at, just lush, leafy, pussy-cat country of steep hillsides and waterfalls; then suddenly you come round a corner where the view opens up
the valley, and you are almost struck senseless by the blinding splen-
dour of that vast face of ice-hung precipices and soaring ridges, sixteen
thousand feet from top to toe, filling a whole quarter of the heavens at
a distance of, I suppose, only a dozen miles. And now, whenever I call
to mind my first sight of Lessingham in that little daleside church so
many years ago, I think of Nanga Parbat.*

—E. R. EDDISON

FEW MOUNTAINS IN THE WORLD COMBINE THE HAUNTING BEAUTY, PROM-
inence, and extreme climbing lines of Nanga Parbat, literally, the Naked
Mountain, in Urdu. At 8,126 meters (26,660 feet), this soaring peak is
the ninth-highest mountain in the world, one of only fourteen summits
above 8,000 meters (26,247 feet), over 5 vertical miles in elevation, and the
crown jewel of a series of national parks in the Jammu and Kashmir region,

perennially contested by Pakistan and India: Lulusar-Dudipatsar, Deosai, and Shandur, on the Pakistani side, where the regal mountain resides; Dachigam, Kishtwar, and Hemis, on the Indian side. "The Nanga Parbat massif forces the Indus to change course and head off at 90 degrees to the south on its 2,000-kilometer journey from Mount Kailas to the Indian Ocean," observed Hermann Schäfer in his book, *Die weisse Kathedrale: Abenteuer Nanga Parbat (The White Cathedral: Adventure Nanga Parbat)*.

A world away, in the Dolomites of Südtirol, or Tirolo in Italian, a medieval castle is now the home of the world's foremost mountaineer, Reinhold Messner. Disparate as they may seem, these two areas share far more than idyllic pastures filled with the fragrance of wild alpine flowers, sweet cedars, and balmy pines; névés and rock towers under preternaturally blue skies; the poetry of little things, mushrooms, frogs, lichen, insects, moss, salamanders, or fern; the feeling of adventure in the high realm of glaciers, precipices, and glorious summits: They share a profound human tragedy between two brothers, climbing companions, and explorers of human endurance in the dangerous playground of mind and mountain.

Reinhold Messner is often recognized as the greatest mountaineer of our time. It bears mentioning that he has had an amazing career as a climber, alpinist, author, explorer, and advocate for ethical, fair-means climbing. To properly understand the magnitude of Günther Messner's death on Nanga Parbat, and its devastating effects on Reinhold, it is necessary and enlightening to read about their childhood and formative years, in the Dolomites, where they formed the bond that was so tragically severed high on the Diamir flank of the Naked Mountain. The first chapters of Reinhold's book, *Free Spirit*, describe this enchanted period, punctuated by thrilling rock climbs, magnificent winter scenes, and a simple family life with eight siblings. Reinhold was born in 1949, and spent his childhood near Santa Magdalena, in the Italian South Tyrol. Nearby peaks like the Geislerspitze, a dolomitic wall of limestone towers, including the Furchetta and Sass Rigais, frame the postcard landscape of northern Italy.

In the company of his parents and brother Helmut, at the tender age of five, Reinhold climbed his first summit, the Sass Rigais, 3,025 meters

(9,925 feet). They ascended a series of rock ledges with solid hand- and footholds, and gained the top of the mountain, where Reinhold's world expanded to a horizon bounded by the magnificent jagged peaks of the Dolomites and the soaring summits of the Ötztal Alps. Later on, Reinhold and his father, who had climbed extensively in the Dolomites, ascended the east face of the Kleine Fermeda; this was his first venture on Class III rock. The whole family often took hikes and scrambles in the region immediately surrounding the Villnöss valley; most of the Messner children grew up with a keen interest in travel and rambling.

Reinhold and Günther's first climb as a team was the 800-meter (2,600-foot) north face of the Sass Rigais. Beyond the technical difficulties this climb presented, route-finding was also part of the challenge: As the climb progressed, they discovered that the face looked completely different from its aspect from below, and the brothers overshot the correct line, continuing instead across a slanting traverse to a point where no further progress seemed possible. They regained the route proper, which leads to the headwall and a series of cracks toward the summit. With only two rudimentary pitons for protection, they climbed gingerly, beyond the highest point their father had reached on this very route, all the way to the top, where they recorded their ascent. "Then and there I became what I am today," notes Reinhold; the brothers' enduring team was shaped and tempered in the vertical world of the Südtirol Dolomites.

In *The Naked Mountain*, Reinhold briefly mentions the brothers' relationship with one another and with their father:

> *Meanwhile, two young lads who had grown up in a large family in the South Tyrol were forging a partnership. They were brothers but otherwise had little in common. I was thirteen, my brother Günther, twelve years old. "As children we did not like each other. Reinhold and I were so different," Günther later recalled. At the end of June 1957, however, this was all to change when a cruel injustice threw us together as accomplices united against the rest of the world. At home in South Tyrol, I found my younger brother Günther cowering in a dog kennel. Our father, during one of his fits of rage, had thrashed Günther so badly with the dog whip that he could no longer walk. On that day*

we not only became friends; Günther also became my climbing part-
ner, and soon he was climbing just as well as I was. We began to talk
about trips together and started to view our climbs as little escapes. We
wanted to get away, away from our authoritarian father and away
from the injustices of this world. Our climbing soon took on a new
dimension.

This is contrasted with their ties to their mother; for example, at base camp, on Nanga Parbat, Reinhold relates that, "The next day Günther wrote a letter to our mother, with whom we both had a particularly intimate relationship. After all, it was she who was the calming influence in our big family. If anyone understood us, it was she, and in spite of feeling anxiety about what we were doing she shared our enthusiasm."

Numerous climbs followed these formative adventures—first, within the circle of the Dolomites; next, in the Alps; and finally, worldwide. The brothers repeated very difficult climbs, opened new routes, and broadened their technique from pure rock to mixed terrain, and very steep ice. They also encountered dangerous route conditions, terrible weather, and objective dangers, including avalanches, seracs and rockfalls, hidden crevasses, enormous *bergschrunds*, *rimayes*, and *randklufts*, hanging glaciers, black ice, hoarfrost, and rime. In just a few years they became prominent all-around mountaineers.

The first solo climb performed by Reinhold on difficult rock began with his father, on the Fermeda Towers, between the Kleine Fermeda and the Seceda-Kamm tower, on the Castiglioni route. After the steep approach, Reinhold's father let his son take the lead on the first difficult pitch; he then decided that the climb would be too difficult altogether and asked Reinhold to rappel down. After some back-and-forth, the pair agreed that Reinhold would continue solo, while his father would meet him on the normal route, which is also the logical way down the mountain. And so it was that Reinhold soloed his first technical route, a feat he would reprise on the highest peaks on Earth.

In the summer of 1963, Reinhold, eighteen years old, ascended the Tissi route on the first Sella Tower, his first Grade VI climb. He also began to work on steep ice, with the north face of the Similaun, 3,606 meters (11,831 feet), in the Ötztal Alps, which is most famous for being the mountain where Helmut Simon and Erika Simon discovered Ötzi the Iceman in 1991. This beautiful climb is followed by a traverse of the Ortler, 3,905 meters (12,812 feet), Zebrù and Königspitze, which involves altitude, hanging glaciers, and lovely ridges; the trio is known as *das Dreigestirn* ("the three heavenly bodies"). The next summer was followed by another round of ice climbs: the north face of the Königspitze, with Heindl Messner, a distant cousin; then, with Günther, a series of north faces; Vertain, Hochfeiler, and Ortler via the hanging glacier; followed by a variation of the Solleder route on the Furchetta.

In 1965, the brothers were intent on ascending the north face of the Hochferner. A first attempt in April was aborted due to a snowstorm; a few weeks later, the pair was back in the region to climb the north face of the Griessferner. This is a serious ice climb, on difficult terrain involving seracs, numerous crevasses, and ice towers, including a 20-meter vertical ice wall, above which the slope eases toward the summit. The two mountaineers also opened a new, Grade V+, 600-meter route on the north face of the Grosse Fermeda, and traveled to the Pennine Alps to climb the direct north face route of the Courtes, as well as the north face of the Aiguille du Triolet, both very difficult ice climbs on the Glacier d'Argentière, near Chamonix.

The most epic climb of the season for the brothers was on Mount Pelmo, with the north face as their objective. Even in perfect weather, this climb is extremely severe, and requires commitment, since rappelling down the nearly vertical face would be very tedious and dangerous. The ascent comprises some 850 meters of mostly vertical rock, with a complex structure, over a broad limestone wall. As it turned out, three powerful storms struck the mountain that day—indeed, the whole region—and numerous areas in northern Italy were devastated by the rapid succession of these cyclonic weather events. On the mountain, the situation was dire: rockfalls exploding everywhere, water cascading down every gully, slippery rock and melting ice—a veritable carnage. Climbing down or abseiling became nearly impossible and horrendously hazardous; they had no choice but to battle the elements with all their strength and wits, and escape the death trap via the summit. The succession of torrential rain, howling winds, and dark clouds quickly brought about hypothermia, a debilitating condition that can quickly prove fatal; add to this an extremely challenging climb on vertical cliffs. Reinhold and Günther were in dire straits. Somehow they made the top and survived what was arguably their most hazardous climb to date.

Reinhold went on to perform a series of extreme climbs on the Civetta, including the infamous Livanos dihedral and the 900-meter (2,950-foot) Philipp-Flamm route, along with first winter climbs, including the Furchetta and the Agnèr ridge. Winter climbs are typically defined in terms of calendar, although exceptional conditions in the fall or spring may qualify specific climbs as performed under "winter conditions." In the Dolomites, where routes are mostly rock lines, the ice and snow provide an additional technical challenge, while the shorter days, more-hostile weather conditions, and cold further conspire to redefine the character of the climbs to a new level—a truly epic scale. Reinhold performed most of these climbs with a small group of friends, including Sepp Mayerl, Heini Holzer, and Heindl Messner.

In 1967, Reinhold and Günther were at the Dirupi di Larsec, intent on repeating a line that involves a very large, prominent yellow overhang; their ascent would be the second on this extremely difficult, highly exposed, vertiginous route. They partnered with a second rope comprising their cousin, Heindl, and Heini Holzer. They had already climbed fairly extensively using artificial means: Numerous dolomitic walls are known to overhang from bottom to summit; one could drop a stone, and it would never bounce until it reached the typical limestone debris cone, under the face proper. Good examples of such gravity-defying climbs can be found in the Tre Cime di Lavaredo group (the Drei Zinnen, in German). For this type of artificial climb, étriers are de rigueur; these are like portable, adjustable ladder rungs that one hangs from a piton or a bolt, to provide foot support. In such a manner, one can follow a bolt ladder on a perfectly smooth, vertical, or overhanging slab, or even traverse a roof. The key skills required are sheer physical strength, concentration, situation awareness, and good rope management, but no specific climbing capabilities, since artificial climbing aid is designed to completely replace rock features. Typically, the pure free climber will avoid routes comprising artificial climbs, unless a compelling line contains a minimum of short pitches requiring that type of equipment and technique. It should also be pointed out that artificial climbing is also possible on ice, to surmount overhanging ice formations, such as seracs, or those found on hanging glaciers, or frozen waterfalls (for example, tapering stalactites). Finally, it is worth mentioning that some overhangs, including roofs of great magnitudes, projecting many tens of feet from the wall, can be (and have been) climbed free, only using the natural holds offered by the mountain.

Artificial climbing can be tedious, as the Messner brothers reflected: "Günther punched me in the arm and said, 'This artificial climbing is a joke,' and then, 'When you've done it once, the fun goes out of it, it's always the same after that.'" This is particularly true if the line is mostly artificial; the climb then becomes almost automatic, gymnastics without aim. One of the great joys of climbing is the immediate problem-solving aspect of the sport: the mountain and its terrain, the minute details of a rock slab that may offer solutions to upward progress to the astute climber. This is true at all levels; there is a great deal of satisfaction derived from surmounting an obstacle that is difficult for you, but may be trivial for a stronger, more-experienced climber. As one hones one's technique and fitness, more difficult challenges can be tackled. Difficulties span an enormous range of varieties: exposure, commitment, altitude, weather, rock or ice conditions, route-finding, terrain, season, remoteness, and so on.

The group of friends quickly reached the crux of their intended climb: the 8-meter overhang, 400 meters up the face, riddled with bolts. A difficult pitch, to be sure, very exposed, yet, unsatisfactory to Reinhold in many ways—an empty exercise in strength: "This was the day we decided to carry on from where we had been a year before, on the great free climbs. Silently I decided never in my life to place a bolt, never to take one with me."

In this spirit, they turned to the southeast face of the Cima Scotoni, a famed climb including an extreme traverse requiring a pendulum, and a crux pitch where the rock was nearly featureless. The first climb required thirty-eight hours and 140 pitons! Reinhold and Sepp Mayerl were able to perform the third ascent using only free climbing, and far fewer pitons for protection; in the process, they had to perform slight deviations from the original route, perhaps a less direct line, but ethically perfect. The Civetta direttissima, and the Via Ideale on the Marmolada d'Ombretta, both at the very edge of climbing technique in 1967, pushed Reinhold further into his quest for the most difficult free lines in the Dolomites, and the Alps.

In the fall of that year, the brothers were on the Kreuzkofel Wall, ascending a huge dihedral, with poor-quality loose rock, on a route opened by Livanos. Protection was minimal because the pitons would barely hold in the fissured rock, and this made for slow, protracted progress. Three overhangs barred the way above the Conca, a large ledge up the wall; rock quality appeared as appallingly bad as it had been below. They set up a bivouac, after a draining day; the night was bitterly cold, but the weather remained good. Farther up, as they made their way the next day, the rock became better, but featureless. They managed the roofs using slings and small fissures, to find beautiful terrain above; extremely challenging, quality free climbing.

The year 1968 saw the focus of Reinhold captured by north faces, those coldest, iciest walls in the Alps, including the famous trio: Grandes Jorasses, Matterhorn, and Eiger. These faces are very tall, 1,200 to over 1,800 meters (3,950 to 5,905 feet); the climbs are mixed and very steep. They were the last problems in the Alps for many years, and the progress of alpinism has often been gauged against these benchmark climbs: first ascent, first winter ascent, first solo ascent, combination (*enchaînement*, in French), speed ascent, etc. The Agnèr-Wand winter first was Messner's prime objective; he accomplished this perilous feat with Sepp Mayerl and Heindl Messner. With Günther, he performed the first free climb of the north face direct of the Peitlerkofel, 2,875 meters (9,432 feet), also known as the Sass de Putia in Italian. This lovely, isolated peak with typical dolomitic vertical lines has now become a classic.

They then went to the Bernese Oberland, to ascend the north face of the Gletscherhorn, 3,983 meters (13,068 feet). This glaciated peak forms the eastern edge of the Lauterbrunnen Wall (en.wikipedia.org/wiki/Lauterbrunnen_Wall), south of the Jungfrau (en.wikipedia.org/wiki/Jungfrau). The north face is over 1,000 meters in amplitude, with a rather severe angle in some portions above the *bergschrund*. In order to better protect the climb, the brothers used rock islands interspersed along the slope, where possible. This type of climb, albeit at a considerably lower altitude, did present some of the difficulties they were going to battle on a much grander scale later on Nanga Parbat. A sudden change of weather, preceded by the rise of a glacial mist, forced the brothers to finish the climb hurriedly, to escape on the Ebnefluh, 3,962 meters (12,999 feet), and descend via its less-steep north face.

Sometime later, in the same year, Toni Hiebeler, a famous climber and editor of the German mountaineering magazine *Alpinismus*, contacted the Messner brothers to invite them to attempt a new route on the Eiger. While the proposed climb did not match the degree of difficulty of some of the most notorious lines on the 1,800-meter-tall *Eigerwand*, it did offer an interesting path through mixed terrain, on a poorly defined buttress, between the Lauper route and the concave north wall itself. One of the big advantages of the path was that it was not exposed to rockfall, a definite and acute danger on the *Eigerwand*. The *Nordwand* of the Eiger is particularly famous for the long saga of attempted first climbs, some of them ending in shattering catastrophe. It was finally first climbed on July 24, 1938, by Anderl Heckmair, Ludwig Vörg, Heinrich Harrer, and Fritz Kasparek, a group formed by German and Austrian climbers. The team had originally consisted of two independent, competing parties; Heckmair and Vörg, who had used the fixed rope that the first team had left across the crux Hinterstoisser Traverse, caught up with Harrer and Kasparek on the vertiginous face. The new team, led by their most experienced member, Anderl Heckmair, worked together on some of the most extreme pitches in the upper part of the *Nordwand*, and decided to finish the climb and summit roped as a single party.

Reinhold had originally estimated their intended route as Grade IV, but the ice conditions they met after a first bivouac made the climb far more difficult, and progress rather slow; the rock was also icy, covered with verglas in some spots, while the character of the snow varied considerably, from firn to an icy aggregate akin to black ice, but softer and more friable. During the second bivouac, snow slides ran down the route, indicating deteriorating or unstable conditions, with increasing avalanche danger. No freeze came overnight to consolidate the rock, ice, and snow, and the weather continued to be oppressive, with clouds building up, and wet, unreliable snow all around. Snow came a bit later, and the disparate party of four was moving unreasonably slowly, at least from Reinhold's viewpoint. They finally reached the ice field below the summit, and the Mittegli ridge in the waning diffuse light of late afternoon, in snow flurries.

Later that year, Reinhold and Günther paired up again for a climb of the north face of the second Sella Tower, a short 200-meter climb, back in their stomping ground of Südtirol. They started very late, seemingly underestimating the severity of the difficulties lying ahead. Günther recounts his irritation at his brother for misrepresenting the amplitude of the climb: not a few hours, but a whole day! To his surprise, Günther realized that the key difficulties on this extreme climb were no match for Reinhold's honed technique; indeed, the entire series of vertical slabs was climbed in a few hours, to Günther's delight: "My irritation had long since passed away. It was a joy to see how Reinhold climbed toward the evening sky!" The brothers' team was now capable of climbing the most esoteric lines on rock, mixed terrain, and ice; they were at the forefront of alpinism, in the literal and geographical sense of the word.

An expedition to the Andes was one of the highlights of 1969. During this trip, Reinhold discovered higher mountains, with entirely different weather and climbing conditions; he also found a new rope partner, with whom he would perform ascents that would stay forever in the annals of mountaineering, and acquire legendary status: Peter Habeler. The expedition was organized by climbers from Innsbruck, and called the Tyrol 1969 Expedition to the Andes. The main objective was the east face of Yerupajá, the highest peak of the Waywash mountain range in west central Peru. At 6,635 meters (21,768 feet), it is the second-highest peak in Peru. The summit is the highest point in the Amazon River watershed, and was first ascended in 1950 by Jim Maxwell and Dave Harrah; the northern peak (Yerupajá Norte) was first climbed in 1968 by Roger Bates and Graeme Dingle. The east face of the mountain is a formidable climbing objective: The start of the climb involves very steep rock and mixed terrain, followed by an extraordinary steep ice field, above which a hanging glacier holds miraculously, seemingly defying gravity.

As is often the case near the equator, deep columnar structures form in the ice and snow due to the near-vertical sun rays; on glaciers, near the terminus, the same effect produces the phantasmagoric *penitentes*: conical ice towers that look like the hoods worn in Spain and other Hispanic countries during religious festivals. The ice formations high on Yerupajá are rather fragile, and deadly ice- and rockfalls were known to devastate the lower part of the face with blunt force; the concave structure of the face did not offer protection, and further funneled the deadly projectiles in horrid salvos. Only the cold of the mineral night offered a modicum of safety, as the ice and rocks were temporarily locked into precarious piles by frost and verglas; therefore, timing and speed were paramount for a successful ascent.

Reinhold and Peter Habeler left the relative comfort of high camp, located near the base of the face at approximately 5,300 meters (17,390 feet), an hour after dark; theirs was going to be a rapid night climb, followed by a series of rappels down the oriental fluted mirror face of Yerupajá Grande. They climbed very fast: 200 meters (650 feet) per hour, an amazing pace on 60- to 75-degree ice and serious rock cliffs of high grade. "As the first rays of sun reached the face it came alive around us," remembered Reinhold; at that point they were in the ever-steepening upper portion of the ice face, near the deeply fluted cornices hanging under the summit ridge. They gained the arête, only to discover that the combination of extreme overhanging cornices and what Reinhold refers to as "detritus" rocks would make access to the summit proper extremely dangerous and tedious. Since their altimeter read 6,612 meters (21,693 feet), they decided to abseil down, after having completed their main objective: the east face of Yerupajá. Before heading back home, they also climbed Yerupajá Chico, 6,121 meters (20,082 feet), a hard climb in its own right.

The École Nationale de Ski et d'Alpinisme (ENSA), in Chamonix, holds international climbers' meetings on a regular basis, and Reinhold was invited to participate in the summer of 1969. This was a welcome return to the Western Alps and the Mont Blanc range, a wonderful playground for hikers, climbers, and alpinists alike, offering all degrees of difficulty, and ranging in amplitude from day hikes and rock scrambles to very committed, multiday climbs on some of the world's best granite. Altitude is moderate, but above 4,000 meters (13,123 feet), it can still pose a real challenge, especially when combined with difficult, sustained mixed terrain on long routes. What would Reinhold climb? He settled for a solo ascent of the Droites, 4,000 meters, one of the hardest mountaineering routes in the Mont Blanc massif: Smooth rock bulges, polished by the Argentière Glacier, reach vertical inclination at the bottom of the 1,000-meter-tall north face; these are followed by extremely steep ice, alternating with short pitches of mixed cliffs, with an overall sustained slope of 65 to 75 degrees. The climb is severe and austere, in the great basin of the Argentière Glacier, surrounded by a series of magnificent peaks forming an uninterrupted, nearly vertical wall, over 2,800 feet tall over a few miles on the northern boundary of the cirque. This wall is anchored by the Aiguille Verte, 4,121 meters (13,520 feet), thus named after the beautiful coloration of the hanging glacier at the top of the peak, and the Aiguille du Triolet. The south aspect includes the Tour Noir, the Aiguille d'Argentière, 3,900 meters (12,795 feet), and the Chardonnet. Few glacial cirques in the Alps are as grandiose and oppressive as the Argentière basin; in France, the north faces of the Glacier Noir, in Oisans, provide a similar feeling of entering a sanctuary of nature, a sacred place larger than man, where beauty and danger mirror one another in an eternal embrace.

Reinhold found the climb impressive: "As I stood under the *bergschrund*, the day dawned. The vertical part was extremely difficult"; then, "There was only a thin layer of ice on the rock slabs that soared up alarmingly steeply above me." This was to be the fourth climb of the face, and its first solo ascent. Soon, the difficulties began: "The alarmingly steep gully above me was blank." Conditions were good, however, and he made steady progress by climbing the gully using a technique somewhat akin to ascending a dihedral. Like Yerupajá, the climb required speed and focus, as rockfalls and ice slides swept the face constantly during the warm hours. A number of pitches along the route were nearly excessively hard; he notes: "This crack cost me a lot of time and concentration. It was more than a rope-length long and extremely difficult. Five times I climbed back down and up again, before I reached the top." After seven hours of upward struggle, alone, he gained the summit; he quickly set off to descend on the Talèfre side, where he could rest in the climbing hut. Reflecting on his solo climb, Reinhold describes his mind-set: "Once more strong emotion gripped me. If someone had come across from the hut now, I would have had to avoid him. I had not wept for many years. Now, pushing my rucksack under my head as a pillow, suddenly my defenses were down and the tears flowed freely. I had the feeling of being free of something. I thought of nothing more. I sensed, however, that these tears had given me a clearer understanding of myself." Such can be the emotional power of a climb, surrounded by a cathedral of nature, a marvel of colors, hues, proportions, and perspectives, in the perfect stillness of dawn at altitude, where time is measured only by the progress of immense shadows over the pearly, iridescent pink glow of the ice fields.

A series of what Reinhold refers to as "crazy solos" rounded off 1969; most of these climbs were first solo ascents of some of the most difficult routes in the Dolomites, including the line on the Civetta first climbed by Walter Philipp and Dieter Flamm in 1957. He also soloed the south face direct of the Marmolada di Rocca. The Marmolada is a mountain located east of Trento in northeastern Italy, and the highest peak of the Dolomites, at 3,343 meters (10,968 feet). Situated approximately 60 miles north-northwest of Venice, the massive mountain can be seen from the Adriatic coast on a clear day. It consists of a ridge running west to east; toward the south it breaks suddenly into sheer cliffs, forming a rock face several miles long. On the north side lies a comparatively flat glacier, the only substantial glacier in the Dolomites, called the Ghiacciaio della Marmolada. The ridge is composed of several summits, decreasing in altitude from west to east: Punta Penia (3,343 meters), Punta Rocca (3,309 meters), Punta Ombretta (3,230 meters), Monte Serauta (3,069 meters), and Pizzo Serauta (3,035 meters). Finally, he performed a solo climb of the Soldà route on the north face of the Langkofel. The Langkofel, also called Saslonch in Ladin, and Sassolungo in Italian, reaches 3,181 meters (10,436 feet); it is the highest mountain of the Langkofel Group in the Dolomites in South Tyrol, and soars over the Ladin community of Val Gardena.

By 1970, Reinhold was ready to climb beyond the Alps, having exhaustively ascended far and wide throughout the range, and performed extreme alpinism in all its forms: rock, mixed terrain, and ice; sheer cliffs, long ridges, dangerous hanging glaciers, haunting couloirs, perfect north faces of glistening ice; climbs during any season, under vastly different weather conditions; first climbs, new variations, winter climbs, free climbs, and solo ascents. Dr. Karl Maria Herrligkoffer, a noted expedition leader, but not a climber himself, had contacted Reinhold in the fall of 1969, and invited him to join the Siegi Löw Memorial Expedition to Nanga Parbat. In *Free Spirit*, Reinhold reflects that he had no particular inclination to climb in the Himalaya and Karakoram, as he judged the routes "too flat"; he "did not want snow-plodding."

Interestingly, this can be contrasted with his more-enthusiastic views on the world's highest range, expressed in *The Naked Mountain*; here, he indicated that both he and Günther had been keenly aware of and excited about climbing in the Himalaya and Karakoram, especially on Nanga Parbat: "After the death of Hermann Buhl we both dreamed the same dreams: of Buhl's first ascent, of his style, of a life far, faraway. And of Nanga Parbat, too. We had grown to detest authority in any form, loathed injustice and found middle-class life a torment. The distant mountains became a means of fleeing to an as yet unknown future." This passage also shows the rebellious aspects of youth, reinforced by the strict upbringing of the Messner brothers. He continues in a sublimated tone: "It is really not surprising that the heroic saga of Nanga Parbat gave wings to our pre-pubescent imaginations. While my fellow pupils were summoning the courage to make their first tentative approaches to girls, I was dreaming of Himalayan peaks. And I secretly hoped that one day I would go to Nanga Parbat."

The goal of the expedition was precisely Nanga Parbat, where Hermann Buhl had performed a legendary, solo first climb, and the route to be attempted directly attacked one of the steepest, most direct lines on the Rupal Face. In fact, Buhl himself had estimated that the Rupal Face was unclimbable: "The South Face is a mountain wall seamed with vertical cliffs. Even to attempt it would be suicide." This was a challenge that, in the end, Reinhold could not resist. Günther was invited later, around Christmas, after Peter Habeler and Sepp Mayerl had canceled their participation. In fact, it was Reinhold, who was now communicating with Herrligkoffer, who suggested Günther as a replacement when he was asked about potential candidates to replace the two defections. Reinhold put Herrligkoffer's telegram accepting Günther in the expedition as a gift to his brother under the Christmas tree. So it was that the Messner brothers were anticipating their first foray into the world's highest peaks, in that mysterious zone above 7,000 meters, on a soaring mountain with a nearly unequaled reputation for its beauty, vertiginous lines of ascent, and lethality. In his *Nanga Parbat Pilgrimage*, Hermann Buhl eloquently sums up the state of affairs and perception of the Naked Mountain in 1953: "Nanga Parbat—a symbol to conjure with in the world of mountaineers and for millions, elsewhere, too. That peak of many names—sometimes called the Fateful Peak, or the Mountain of Terror; that cloud-piercing giant which had already devoured thirty-one victims; that pitiless domain demanding its holocaust and giving nothing in return, luring men into its thrall, never to set them free again."

From a European viewpoint, Nanga Parbat was discovered in 1856 by Adolf Schlagintweit, a German botanist and explorer, who was assassinated in Kashgar shortly thereafter. In 1934, another Municher, Richard Finsterwalder, a professor, reconnoitered and surveyed the entire Nanga Parbat massif; he was followed by alpinist, explorer, and geologist Günter Oskar Dyhrenfurth, who was interested in the rock formations in the range, as well as its mountaineering possibilities, including climbing the summit proper. The accounts from these three outstanding pioneers contributed compellingly to the perception and mystique surrounding Nanga Parbat.

The climbing history of the mountain reads like a series of tragedies, punctuated by utter disasters. Climbing attempts started very early: In 1895 Albert F. Mummery, a famous British mountaineer, known for numerous first climbs in the Alps during the golden age of alpinism, led an expedition to the peak and reached almost 7,000 meters (23,000 feet) on the Diamir flank. During the same trip, Mummery and two Gurkha cohorts died while reconnoitering the Rakhiot flank, presumably becoming the first climbing casualties on the mountain.

In the 1930s, Nanga Parbat became the focus of German interest in the Himalaya. At the time, Mount Everest was exclusively within British domain, because they were the only foreigners allowed into Tibet; the Nepali side of the mountain had not yet been identified as a viable point of approach, with the great Khumbu Icefall protecting the sanctuary of the Western Cwm. Kanchenjunga thus became the initial focus of German efforts, with Paul Bauer leading two expeditions there, in 1930 and 1931. Kanchenjunga appeared more difficult than Everest, with steep slopes and ridges extending over tremendous distances; as a result, little progress was made toward climbing the world's third-highest mountain. Little was known about K2, because of its extremely remote location deep in the Karakoram, and the general wisdom was that it would probably be the hardest 8,000-meter peak to ascend, with challenging logistical support, numerous difficult and dangerous river crossings, hazardous trails, and a complete lack of civilized outposts for hundreds of miles. Some of the other highest peaks were largely or entirely unexplored, but Nanga Parbat was a known geographical entity, and was deemed a possible climb by the mountaineering community at the time. It also had a reasonable approach.

In 1932, Willy Merkl led the first German expedition to Nanga Parbat; the climbing party also included Rand Herron, an American, and Fritz Wiessner, who would become an American citizen in 1935. Wiessner established an impressive list of first ascents across North America in climbing areas, including Ragged Mountain (Connecticut); Cannon Mountain (New Hampshire); Wallface Mountain (New York), in the Adirondacks; and Mount Rushmore (South Dakota). He also performed the first free ascent of Devils Tower (Wyoming), and climbed Mount Waddington, 4,019 meters (13,186 feet), a remote peak in the wild Coast Ranges of British Columbia. Wiessner had also made the first ascent of the Fleischbank, 2,187 meters (7,175 feet) in the Wilder Kaiser range of the Northern Limestone Alps in Tyrol, reputedly among the hardest rock climbs at the time.

While the team comprised very strong climbers, none had Himalayan experience, where altitude, prominence, and remoteness form a triple threat; adding to these, weather and snow conditions are quite different from those found in the Alps, or even the Andes. Logistically, the climb was poorly planned; in particular, the number of porters was inadequate, slowing down the supply line between different camps on the mountain. Bad weather prevented the team from progressing beyond the Rakhiot Peak, which was reached by Austrian Peter Aschenbrenner and German Herbert Kunigk. However, the feasibility of a route on the Rakhiot flank, up to the Silbersattel (Silver Saddle) and the main ridge, was established.

In 1934, drawing on his experience, Merkl led a second, better-prepared expedition, which was financed with the full backing of the new Nazi government. Early in the expedition Alfred Drexel died, probably of high-altitude pulmonary edema. On July 6, Tyrolean climbers Peter Aschenbrenner and Erwin Schneider reached an estimated altitude of 7,895 meters (25,900 feet), but were forced to return because of worsening weather conditions. The next day saw the beginning of a blizzard that lasted for nine days. When it finally dissipated, three famous German mountaineers, Uli Wieland, Willo Welzenbach, and Merkl himself, along with six Sherpa folks, all trapped by the storm at 7,480 meters (24,540 feet), were dead. It is apparent that their deaths had been slow and extremely arduous, caused by extended exposure to cold and starvation. Merkl's frozen body, and those of several of his team members, was discovered in 1938 after another German expedition stumbled upon the snow cave in which they had taken refuge. The last survivor to reach safety, Ang Tsering, did so after having spent seven days battling through the storm. It has been said that the disaster "for sheer protracted agony, has no parallel in climbing annals."

After this terrible catastrophe, Herrligkoffer, who was Willy Merkl's half brother, decided to publish Merkl's diaries, and took the achievement of the first ascent of Nanga Parbat as his personal duty, although he was not a strong climber himself, partly because of medical limitations. Therefore, he would act as expedition leader and gather the necessary funding, manage the logistics, decide on climbing strategies, and handle public relations. Herrligkoffer was dedicated to this role, for the memory of Willy Merkl; he wrote: "'The crowning glory and the ultimate aspiration of the mountaineer's wistful yearning!' That was how Willy Merkl described the high peaks of the Himalaya. His whole life had been geared towards achieving this objective, yet shortly before he could taste victory an unimaginable destiny had snatched that crown from his grasp."

Herrligkoffer also reminisced, somewhat lyrically: "For him, the mountain was the highest of holy shrines, a lifetime objective. The mountain, with its myriad rapturous joys, with its bright golden adventures, its many struggles, and austere mortal dangers. It is not for us to cast doubt or to despair of the legitimacy of his actions, to weigh the pros and cons of this bold deed. Heroic greatness lies in the willingness to dedicate oneself body and soul, even unto the end. The value of playing for the highest stakes of all—one's life—lies not in success but in the deed itself." Clearly, Herrligkoffer's longing for the mountains, unrequited, was sublimated into a somewhat Wagnerian struggle, whence heroes would be forged and tempered by the most hostile forces of nature, conjured by the highest mountains, in full majesty. The German magazine, *Der Spiegel*, quoted Herrligkoffer thus: "The sight of an eight-thousander is described by the Munich doctor as 'probably the strongest of all purely male experiences.'"

In 1937, Karl Wien led another attempt on the mountain, following the route established during the previous Merkl expeditions. Slow progress was made, due to heavy snowfall. Around June 14, seven Germans and nine Sherpas, most of the climbing team, were at Camp IV below Rakhiot Peak, when a massive avalanche destroyed and leveled the entire area. All sixteen men died instantly in what remains the worst single disaster to occur on an 8,000-meter peak.

The Germans returned in 1938, under the leadership of Paul Bauer, but the expedition was plagued by bad weather; Bauer, mindful of the previous disasters, ordered the party down before the Silbersattel, halfway between Rakhiot Peak and Nanga Parbat summit, was reached. The following year a small four-man expedition, including Heinrich Harrer, explored the Diamir Face with the aim of finding an easier route. They concluded that the face was viable, but World War II intervened, and the four men were interned in India. Harrer's escape and subsequent travels became the subject of his book, *Seven Years in Tibet*.

Austrian climber Hermann Buhl, a member of a German-Austrian team, first climbed Nanga Parbat on July 3, 1953; the ascent was performed via the Rakhiot flank of the mountain, connecting with the East Ridge near the Rakhiot Peak, up the Silbersattel, to the summit. Karl Herrligkoffer organized the expedition, and the technical expedition leader was Peter Aschenbrenner, from Innsbruck, who was familiar with the mountain, having participated to the 1932 and 1934 attempts. Thirty-one people had already died on the mountain by the time of this expedition. The final push for the summit was extraordinarily dramatic, truly legendary, as beautifully told by Buhl himself in his *Nanga Parbat Pilgrimage*. Buhl climbed the last 1,300 vertical meters (4,265 feet) alone: one of his companions stayed at Camp V, while the other began climbing much later than Buhl, and moving considerably slower, decided to return to camp.

Meanwhile, under the potent influence of the amphetamines Pervitin[1] and Padutin[2] and tea from coca leaves, he reached the summit dangerously late, at 7:00 p.m., the climbing far harder and more time-consuming than he had anticipated. His descent was slowed when he lost a crampon; caught by darkness, he was forced to bivouac standing upright on a narrow ledge, holding a small handhold with one hand. Exhausted, he dozed occasionally, but managed to maintain his balance. He was also very fortunate to have a calm night, so he was not subjected to windchill. He finally reached his high camp at 7:00 p.m. the next day, forty hours after setting out. The ascent was made without supplemental oxygen, and Buhl is the only man to have performed the first ascent of an 8,000-meter peak solo.

Unfortunately, controversy followed this magnificent first climb: A number of people began questioning the veracity of Buhl's account, including expedition leader, Herrligkoffer. This may be due, in part, to the astounding, almost incredible, sustained effort by Buhl in the death zone to reach the summit.

In *The Naked Mountain*, Reinhold recounted Buhl's first ascent:

> *Hermann Buhl finally succeeded in making the first ascent of the mountain, against the express wishes of Herrligkoffer. Pepped up by the drug Pervitin, he managed 1,300 meters of ascent in a single day, reaching the summit alone on the evening of July 3, 1953. After surviving a night out in the open, he managed to descend safely. With his last ounces of strength he reached the camp below the Silver Saddle, where the colleagues who had supported him on his summit bid were*

waiting. Herrligkoffer, however, was in an emotional quandary. His feelings wavered between joy at success and disappointment in the manner in which it was achieved. He felt he had been betrayed by the three men, who had acted against his instructions, outshone by Buhl, who had acted selfishly on his own account, and passed over by the world media. Perhaps he also felt cheated of the "unconditional" ascent that the voice of his dead brother demanded of him?

Of course, 1953 was the year that saw the first ascent of the world's highest peak, Mount Everest, by Sir Edmund Hillary and Tenzing Norgay, and media attention was sharply focused on that most important mountaineering achievement.

Reinhold's account is quite indicative of his own perception of Herrligkoffer's micromanaging, authoritarian style. "Back in Europe, doubts arose as to the validity of Buhl's summit bid. Herrligkoffer even initiated legal proceedings against the 'victorious summiteer' at a later date. In Herrligkoffer's eyes, Buhl remained until his death the 'defiler of the pure ideal.'" When Buhl died on Chogolisa—after performing the first ascent of Broad Peak, 8,051 meters (26,414 feet), in the Karakoram, and thus becoming one of very few men to have made the first ascent of two 8,000-meter peaks—Herrligkoffer eulogized him by comparing him to his half brother: "Hermann Buhl, who has stood on the summit of two eight-thousanders, found a mountaineer's grave on the ice face of Chogolisa . . . a grave such as my brother Willy Merkl had found at the Moor's Head on Nanga Parbat in 1934. But the battle for eight-thousanders goes on."

It is quite interesting to contrast these views with Buhl's own account, as he related in the last two chapters of his wonderful *Nanga Parbat Pilgrimage*. At the highest camp, located at 22,640 feet, on his summit push, he tried to get Otto Kempter to join him: "I heard a mumble come from his sleeping-bag: 'Not me—I ain't got none.' That settled it for me. I packed my little storm-rucksack with things for an attempt on my own. I put in bacon, Dextro, Ovosport, and a few cuts of Neapolitan; I added warm clothing, my own Agfa Karat camera—the Expedition unfortunately didn't supply me with a Leica as supplementary equipment—then the little flask with Ertl's precious coca tea, which he had brought all the way from Bolivia, and my crampons." Kempter seemed to be waking up as Buhl was leaving: "You'll catch up with me somewhere." Little did they know that their reunion would happen under far more dramatic circumstances. For now, Buhl was alone; "[T]he sky above my head was brilliant with stars, but it was dreadfully cold. The slender crescent of the waning moon threw its ghostly light on the sharp snow-crest tilting to the Silbersattel. The curved ice-edge between the dark heads of the Silberzacken hung like a shining crescent of purest silver." As he slowly made his way on crusted snow using ski poles for balance, he became aware of the immense shadow projected by a huge corniced ridge, and reflected: "There, in bygone years, fourteen first-class Sherpas had been in position, with another group of eleven up above, on the Silbersattel; and that expedition of outstanding mountaineers had nonetheless ended in shattering tragedy. A sense of desolation swept over me. But you mustn't think of death or indulge in thoughts of horror when you are on your own."

Buhl gained the ridge, where he found firm snow, requiring crampons; he made good progress, sheltering from the wind blowing from the Rupal Face by making his way on the north side and traversing steep slopes under rock towers, leading to the Silbersattel. Over the Karakoram, the sun rose; around 5:00 a.m., he was very close to the Silberzacken. Buhl's next objective was the Silbersattel itself, a large, trapezoidal ice field leading to the final part of the climb, to the south, under the summit. He estimated that, at his current pace of taking two breaths for each stride, some thirty minutes would suffice. He then noted: "What about my half-hour now? I had been climbing for a full hour [since then] and the Silbersattel seemed just as far away as ever. The thin air robs one of every means of measurements, makes a mockery of all one's assessments." This last statement would turn out to be fatefully true for the Messner brothers, when ascending the upper sections of the Merkl couloir, on the Rupal Face of the mountain.

Some two hours later, after careful progress on the difficult, steep slopes leading upward, Buhl entered the sacred realm of the Silbersattel, where blue ice lay, striated by wind drifts. He stood on the lower lip of the Silver Saddle, at an elevation of 24,443 feet, with an astonishing view. "Beyond the furrow of the Indus, the Hindu Kush and Karakoram peaks ranged far and wide; indeed, I could see further still—those mountains in the distance must be the Pamirs, in Russia!" At that point, Buhl, who was climbing without supplemental oxygen, was moving far slower: five breaths per stride. The sun was merciless; instead of bringing some warmth, it was burning hot, parching the throat, amplifying the desiccating effect of the dry, thin air. Food was all but impossible to ingest, thirst intense and unquenchable.

At 10:00 a.m., Buhl was poised to climb the summit ridge. Below him, the Silbersattel spread out to the north; he noticed a small dot, probably Kempter after a late start from Camp V. Between him and the Bazhin Gap, the terrain was quite dangerous: to the left, the Rupal Face fell more than 4,500 meters to the Bazhin Glacier cirque; the north might work better at the very top of the Diamir flank, but real climbing was involved, and Buhl decided to leave his small backpack behind for his final push into the ether; it was not really heavy, "but up here every extra ounce was an affliction."

After checking on Kempter's progress and realizing that the dot stood motionless, Buhl was ready for the most draining, exhilarating, harrowing, and foreboding mile in his life. From where he stood to the summit, the elevation gain was approximately 1,000 feet. Access to the gap via the upper Diamir slopes and gullies proved extremely hard—better, perhaps, than the extremely exposed Rupal Face, but still an incredible, epic climbing feat in the rarefied atmosphere above 25,000 feet. Buhl was tempted to use Pervitin, but knowing the adverse side effects, "I thought I could get as far as the Bazhin Gap without drugs."

At 2:00 p.m., Buhl was at the Bazhin Gap, with agonizing hunger and obscene thirst distressing every fiber of his tormented body. At that point, he took two tablets of the amphetamine for a possible boost out of the crippling lethargy of high altitude. A steep climb to the fore summit lay in front; between the Scylla and Charybdis of the extremely steep Rupal ice couloirs and the Diamir treacherous terrain, there was no easy way up: "I stood on the sharp-crested snow right at the foot of the rock-ridge and looked out over my boots at the abysmal deeps of the Rupal Nullah, 17,000 feet below." Upward progress was most difficult on the summit pyramid: unprotected mixed climbing on very steep terrain, now above 8,000 meters, with numerous rock protrusions, including a 60-meter gendarme, followed by a small tower of poor rock; "It was climbing of the severest order."

The last shoulder was gained at 6:00 p.m.: "The realization of that gave me a horrid fright." Buhl took a last drink from his flask of coca tea; the combination of this with the amphetamines, altitude, and the extraordinary metabolic conditions of hunger, thirst, and exhaustion may well have finished a lesser athlete: "I moved forward in a kind of self-induced hypnosis." He reached the summit at 7:00 p.m., seventeen hours after setting off.

Using his small Agfa camera, Buhl documented his achievement in the fading light. As soon as the sun dipped below the jagged western horizon, the temperature plummeted; it was far beyond time to climb down! Buhl left his ice ax on the summit, as proof of his ascent, it was to be recovered forty-six years later, in 1999, and is now part of the Messner museum's collection. Buhl quickly realized that the difficult climb up would be insurmountable in the twilight, on the way down, unroped. Desperate times call for desperate measures; Buhl decided to stay away from the yawning abyss of the Rupal Face, and climbed down on the Diamir side, a rock face serrated with steep gullies. He started on a steep ice slope, hoping to reach the Bazhin Gap before nightfall, perhaps crossing the Silbersattel under the moonlight, and reaching Camp V. The first near disaster came under the guise of a crampon strap coming off and falling into the unknown below. With no way to fix his left crampon, Buhl decided to gain rocky terrain as quickly as possible, where crampons would not be indispensable. This involved a very dangerous traverse on icy, mixed terrain, with a single crampon. Meanwhile, as darkness fell upon the mountain, Buhl was now on a 50- to 60-degree rock face. A small break in the cliff allowed for Buhl to stand on firm ground, but the platform was too small to even sit on. Yet, this precarious ledge was going to be his location for a bivouac at 8,000 meters: "I almost faced that night at 26,000 feet with complete equanimity."

Buhl writing on his bivouac oscillates between the harsh reality of his feet slowly becoming frozen, and simple poetry: "I was caught up again in the immensity of the night . . . in the glory of the starlit sky stretched overhead."

The amazing weather held and offered a still night, which Buhl survived. He continued down at first light, the warmth of the sun a welcome contrast to the frigid, mineral night. His feet felt like blocks of wood, and there still remained so much walking and downclimbing. He proceeded gingerly down gullies and short rock ridges, on and on.

Like Messner, Buhl experienced the presence of an ethereal companion in the lethal zone, perhaps an avatar of sorts, summoned by an oxygen-starved brain: "During those hours of extreme tension I had an extraordinary feeling that I was not alone. I had a partner with me, looking after me, taking care of me, belaying me. I knew it was imagination; but the feeling persisted." And, "Here I climbed back again and wanted to put my gloves on once more. I couldn't find them. Horrified, I asked my mysterious companion: 'Have you seen my gloves?' I heard the answer quite clearly: 'You have lost them.'" After an agonizingly slow descent to the Silbersattel, Buhl felt he was near death: "I was no longer myself; I was only a shadow—a shadow behind a shadow." His last chance was another dose of Pervitin, three tablets this time. His throat was parched and bloody, and taking the medicine was torture; yet he gained enough strength to make it farther down. Forty-one splendid and miserable hours later, Buhl was back at Camp V.

Buhl's own account of reuniting with Herrligkoffer at base camp is quite laconic: "When I went to meet the Leader of the Expedition, he greeted me with: 'Well, how did it go?' and later 'How are you?'" He found that Herrligkoffer was keen on hurrying away to Gilgit, in order to catch the next ship to Europe. This was bad news for Buhl and his high-camp companions, who were in dire need of rest and recuperation. Most of the food and equipment were already packed and gone; even medical supplies were no longer available. To quote Buhl: "A very peculiar atmosphere descended on Base Camp." In particular, Peter Aschenbrenner, who had been on Merkl's disastrous expedition, had left immediately upon learning of Buhl's success. A toast to the great success from Albert Bitterling was received with an "oppressive silence."

A few excerpts from Buhl's epilogue are telling; first: "The storm died away. It was a storm raised by men, to whirl up a hideous cloud of dust, which for a time obscured even the shining magic of the Mountain.

During those unpleasant days breath was scarcer than at great heights, vision was obscured, the right relationship with men and things—even with oneself—was lost." And: "My memories are still too fresh to have been purged of recollection's tricky play; the humdrum is still the humdrum; the petty, petty; the ugly, ugly." Finally: "You cannot climb a great mountain, least of all a 26,000-foot peak like Nanga Parbat, without personal risk. The leaders of the 1953 Expedition would not face this truth or the responsibility underlying it."

In *The Naked Mountain*, Reinhold recounts the climbing history of Nanga Parbat in detail, beginning with Mummery's attempt on the Diamir flank; Hermann Buhl's first ascent and subsequent falling-out with Herrligkoffer is also discussed at length. Messner cites Buhl: "We thought there was something a bit odd about all the complicated legal clauses in the expedition contract we were asked to sign, but our expedition leader reassured us that it was a mere formality; that the whole enterprise rested on comradeship, and that the exclusive aim of the expedition was to fulfill a sacred legacy."

In fact, Herrligkoffer used this document to firmly reassert control of all public communications; when he announced the successful climb, he strongly emphasized that this was a team victory, belonging to no one in particular. Buhl's role became a side story, not worthy of public interest. Buhl was also barred from participating in Herrligkoffer's next ventures, including a trip to Broad Peak. The schism was so deep that when the German ambassador welcomed the team, and the conversation turned to the summit ascent, Buhl was not even allowed to amend an error in Herrligkoffer's retelling of the feat! As astutely noted by Messner, Herrligkoffer used the rhetorical "we" at an alarming rate, when he lectured and recounted the climb that he had witnessed in the relative comfort of base camp; at the same time, he continually minimized Buhl's achievement, labeling him as selfish, egotistical, unreliable, and irrelevant.

It took nine years before the second ascent of Nanga Parbat occurred: In 1962, Germans Toni Kinshofer, Siegfried "Siegi" Löw, and A. Mannhardt climbed the peak via the Diamir Face. The Kinshofer route, as it is now known, does not ascend the middle of the Diamir Face, which is threatened by avalanches from massive hanging glaciers; instead, it follows a prominent buttress on the left side. Eight years later, we find the Messner brothers on their way to the Naked Mountain, their very first trip to the Himalaya, under the watchful stewardship of Dr. Karl Maria Herrligkoffer. Their harrowing saga has been laconically summarized: "In 1970 the brothers Günther and Reinhold Messner made the third ascent of the mountain and the first ascent of the Rupal Face. They were unable to descend by their original route, and instead descended by the Diamir Face, making the first traverse of the mountain. Unfortunately Günther was killed in an avalanche on the Diamir Face. (Reinhold's account of this incident has been disputed. In 2005, Günther's remains were found on the Diamir Face.) In 1978, Reinhold returned to the Diamir Face and achieved the first completely solo ascent (i.e., always solo above base camp) of an 8,000-meter peak (Nanga Parbat).

For a deeper gauge and understanding of the tragic adventure of the Messner brothers, the extreme conditions of high-altitude climbing, and the immensity of the mountain and its many perils, the internal dynamics of the Siegi Löw Memorial Expedition and its personalities must be examined, as well as the character of the local folks who played two very important roles—as Sherpa climbing porters on the Naked Mountain, and as rescuers of a distraught Reinhold Messner.

At high altitude, the sun is schizophrenic: On the one hand, it is your friend, providing warmth against the bitter cold; on the other hand, it is a deadly enemy that parches your throat and burns your lips and any exposed skin. The snow and ice conspire to reflect the ultraviolet light, and Phoebus blazes you from above and below. The air can be completely still, or howling with the full force of the jet stream; a distant gathering of clouds becomes a raging storm within minutes; the air you try to breathe barely fills your lungs with every gasping, rasping inhalation. This is the death zone, on a good day. Deathly fatigue, extreme lack of oxygen, nauseated hunger, and profound and overwhelming thirst haunt your every step, throbbing thoughts return to your hypoxia-bound brain, like a mantra repeated ad nauseam.

Yet, your will burns deep, pushing you ever higher, toward the summit. Your body literally eats itself: Your metabolism is now burning muscle tissue, after all the precious fat is gone; emaciation is another cruel foe awaiting you along the corniced ridge. Around you are astoundingly beautiful vistas: peak after unknown peak, Shangri-las waiting to be discovered, distant to the point of poignancy. A small green patch reminds you of the living world, far below the mineral realm that you are violating. And pay you will: If you survive the ordeal, and can extract yourself from the powerful grip of the mountains, from the thousand icy traps of crevasses, from the torrents of gigantic avalanches, from the ongoing titanic forces reshaping glaciers and icefalls every minute of every century, you will be a shadow of your former self, barely able to walk, hurt and bruised and cut. This will be the happiest day of your life, for you will have reached the summit of your dreams, and safely walked back down to tell your tale.

Reinhold, the premier all-around mountaineer of his generation, the Michael Jordan of alpinism, the first man to ever climb all 8,000-meter (26,247-foot) peaks without supplemental oxygen, would have dreamed of such a story, shared with his brother Günther, on Nanga Parbat. A glorious climb, on one of the most technical, sustained routes ever contemplated, especially on such a gigantic mountain: extremely steep ice and snow, well above 21,000 feet, into the lethal zone. No oxygen; pure will and talent.

It was not to be. One of the main protagonists of the terrible ordeal to come was the lofty, ethereal mountain itself, certainly one of the mightiest massifs to be found anywhere on Earth, one of the greatest peaks, even by Himalayan standards. The Nanga Parbat massif forms the western anchor of the Himalayas, around which the Indus River skirts through deep gorges, canyons, and chasms, before entering the northern plains of Pakistan. It is located in the Gilgit-Baltistan region, and is locally known as Deo Mir. Nanga Parbat is one of fourteen peaks above 8,000 meters, found exclusively in the Himalaya and Karakoram ranges. An immense, dramatic peak rising far above its surrounding terrain, Nanga Parbat is also a notoriously difficult climb, with extremely difficult and challenging routes. Numerous mountaineering deaths in the mid- and early twentieth century lent it the nickname "Killer Mountain." Along with K2, it has the distinction of never having been climbed in winter.

Nanga Parbat is the westernmost 8,000-meter peak. It lies just south of the Indus River in the Diamir District of Gilgit-Baltistan in Pakistan.

Some 50 to 60 miles to the north are Rakaposhi, 7,788 meters (25,551 feet), also known as Dumani, or "Mother of Mist," and Malubiting, 7,458 meters (24,469 feet), both located at the western end of the Karakoram Range. Among its most notable features, Nanga Parbat has enormous vertical relief over local terrain in all directions; its prominence is unparalleled. To the south, Nanga Parbat boasts what is often referred to as the highest mountain face in the world. The Rupal Face rises very steeply, over 4,600 meters (15,090 feet) above its base. To the north, the complex, somewhat more gently sloped Rakhiot Flank rises 7,000 meters (22,966 feet) from the Indus River valley to the summit in just 25 kilometers (16 miles), one of the ten greatest elevation gains in so short a distance on Earth. The view of the mountain from Fairy Meadows is truly exceptionally lovely.

There are only two peaks that rank in both the twenty highest and most prominent mountains in the world: Nanga Parbat, ranking ninth and fourteenth, respectively, and Mount Everest, which tops both lists. The Himalaya ranges from Nanga Parbat to the west, to Namcha Barwa, 7,782 meters (25,531 feet) on the Tibetan Plateau, to the east.

The core of Nanga Parbat is a 9-kilometer-long ridge trending southwest–northeast, an enormous bulk of ice and rock. It begins with a prominent peak at 6,840 meters, at the western start of the Mazeno Ridge, and ends with a double summit at 6,760 meters to the northeast. The entire spine is well above 6,000 meters in elevation. The Nanga Parbat massif has three main flanks: Diamir and Rakhiot, defining the northwest and northern aspects of the mountain, and the Rupal Face. The latter has sustained slopes with angles varying between 50 and 70 degrees, reaching up to 8,000 meters. The southwestern portion of this major ridge is known as the Mazeno Wall, and has a number of subsidiary peaks, reaching above 7,000 meters. In the other direction, the main ridge arcs northeast at Rakhiot Peak, 7,070 meters (23,196 feet). The powerful Rupal Face dominates the south-southeast aspect of the mountain. The north and northwest sides of the mountain, leading to the Indus, are far more complex. They are split into the Diamir and Rakhiot flanks by a long ridge projecting to the north, comprising a number of subsidiary summits, including the Nordgipfel (North Peak), 7,816 meters (25,643 feet), approximately 3 kilometers north of the main summit. The other outstanding feature of Nanga Parbat is the huge trapezoidal summit plateau sloping upward toward the main peak, with elevations ranging from 7,450 to 7,850 meters, known as the Silbersattel, or Silver Saddle. The Silbersattel, over a mile long and some three-quarters of a mile at its widest, is encircled by the Silberzacken, or East Peak, 7,597 meters (24,925 feet), the aforementioned Nordgipfel, or North Peak, and the Vorgibfel, which leads to the Bazhin Gap and an *antécime*, or fore-summit, at 8,070 meters (26,476 feet), due north of the true summit.

Among the protagonists, the local mountain folks, Urdu and Kashmiris, played an important role, saving the life of Reinhold, as he came down the mountain alone, distraught, and very nearly delirious. The simple farmers and goat herders of the Diamir region helped him get sufficiently well so that he could start the long trek to the bottom of the Rupal Face, where he would reunite with the expedition, with devastating news. These people living in the areas surrounding Nanga Parbat are extremely poor, and live a harsh everyday life; political unrest in the contested Jammu and Kashmir territories, and the Taliban presence in Pakistan, add death and oppression to an already-difficult subsistence. Yet, these folks saved Reinhold, and Hunza porters have been indispensable to many expeditions—first, to carry loads to base camp, and next, up the mountain, where the best mountaineers of the lot would help find routes, establish camps, set fixed ropes, equip difficult pitches, and so on. These people are progressively being better recognized, but it ought to be realized that they really are equal in their strength, moral and physical, to the best Western mountaineers, as exemplified by Tenzing Norgay, who teamed up with Sir Edmund Hillary and performed the first climb of Mount Everest. The Sherpa people also assume risks that are deemed unacceptable by others, for very low pay, and are often at the center of tragedies (for example, the sixteen deaths in the Khumbu Icefall avalanche of 2014).

The Kashmiri people are a Dardic ethnolinguistic group living in, or originating from, the Kashmir Valley, which is located in the Indian state of Jammu and Kashmir, currently under dispute with neighboring Pakistan. There are both Hindu and Muslim Kashmiris. Other ethnic groups living in the area include Gujjars, Bakarwals, Dogras, Punjabis, and Gaddis.

According to language research conducted by the International Institute at UCLA, the Kashmiri language is "a Northwestern Dardic language of the Indo-Aryan branch of the Indo-Iranian subfamily of the Indo-European language family." There is, however, no universally agreed-upon genetic basis for the language. UCLA estimates the number of speakers at approximately 4.4 million, with preponderance in the Kashmir Valley, whereas the 2001 census of India recorded 5,362,349 throughout India, effectively excluding speakers in the non-Indian Kashmiri areas. The people living in Azad Kashmir speak the Pothohari dialect, also known as Pahari language, which is also spoken in neighboring regions. There are approximately 4.6 million people living within Pakistani-administered Azad Kashmir; this does not include the population living in Gilgit-Baltistan, which would increase that number to 6.4 million people. Many of these people speak languages differing from Kashmiri, and are not ethnic Kashmiris, since they do not trace their origins to the Kashmir valley proper. There are around 105,000 Kashmiris in Pakistan; most of them migrated from the Kashmir Valley after the partition from India; in addition a few reside in the border villages of the Neelum district.

Islam arrived to Kashmir after the Ghorids expansion, starting with the conversion of Rincana, the first king of a new dynasty from Ladakh, in 1323, at the hands of the saint, Bulbul Sha. After conversion to Islam he called himself Malik Sadur-ud-Din and was the first Muslim ruler of Kashmir. The Kashmiris subsequently killed him. Since the arrival of invaders and the start of religious conflicts, before the partition of British India, many Kashmir Hindus and Buddhists migrated to other regions. At the same time, some people from India, Pakistan, and Afghanistan settled in Kashmir. Nowadays, most Kashmiris practice Islam, but a sizable Hindu community also exists.

In 1780, after the death of Ranjit Deo, the Raja of Jammu, the kingdom of Jammu, which lies to the south of the Kashmir valley, was also captured by the Sikhs and afterwards, until 1846, became a tributary to Sikh power. Ranjit Deo's grandnephew, Gulab Singh, subsequently sought service at the court of Ranjit Singh, distinguished himself in later campaigns, especially the annexation of the Kashmir valley, and, for his services, was appointed governor of Jammu in 1820. With the help of his officer, Zorawar Singh, Gulab Singh soon captured for the Sikhs the lands of Ladakh and Baltistan to the east and northeast, respectively, of Jammu.

In 1819, the Kashmir valley passed from the control of the Durrani Empire of Afghanistan, after four centuries of Muslim rule under the Mughals and the Afghans, to the conquering armies of the Sikhs under Ranjit Singh of Lahore. As the Kashmiris had suffered under the Afghans, they initially welcomed the new Sikh rulers. However, the Sikh governors turned out to be hard taskmasters, and the local Sikh rule was generally considered oppressive, protected perhaps by the remoteness of Kashmir from the capital of the Sikh empire in Lahore. The Sikhs enacted a number of anti-Muslim laws, which included handing out death sentences for cow slaughter, closing down the Jamia Masjid in Srinagar, and banning the *azaan*, the public Muslim call to prayer. Kashmir had also now begun to attract European visitors, several of whom wrote of the abject poverty of the vast Muslim peasantry and of the exorbitant taxes under the Sikhs. High taxes, according to some contemporary accounts, had depopulated large tracts of the countryside, allowing only one-sixteenth of the cultivable land to be cultivated.

During the year 1800, a severe drought swept across Kashmir, which caused many in the region to migrate out of the Kashmir Valley, and south of the Jhelum River into Punjab. Those who migrated entered mainly into agriculture, and by the 1820s, after the drought passed, many of the Kashmiri immigrants returned to the Kashmir Valley. Many, however, remained in Punjab, as they had settled comfortably. Some chose to continue migrating southwards. After a famine in 1832, the Sikhs reduced the land tax to half the produce of the land and also began to offer interest-free loans to farmers; Kashmir became the second-highest revenue earner for the Sikh empire. During this time Kashmiri shawls became known worldwide, attracting many buyers, especially in the West.

The social structure is based on extended families; however, the wider kinship network of *biraderi*, and its impact on relations and mobilization, is equally important. The extended family is of fundamental importance as a unit of decision-making and with respect to the relations of its members with the wider society. The institution of *biraderi*, which loosely translates as "brotherhood," provides a useful collective framework for promoting mutual well-being. It is based on the notion of caste, prevalent both in Muslim and Hindu societies. This is achieved through help and cooperation in social, economic, and political spheres, and reinforces a sense of belonging and collective self-assurance. Historically, Kashmiri Muslim women of high descent were strictly forbidden to pierce their noses. This practice had an archaic origin in an unusual tradition that is still followed by certain Kashmiris up to this day, particularly those settled in Punjab.

The first major endeavor of the Siegi Löw Memorial Expedition was to travel from Europe to base camp. Günther traveled by truck, along with the first group of the expedition. This was a lengthy and time-consuming endeavor, unthinkable nowadays. Such a trip today would involve crossing many areas that are now in great unrest, including the Near East, Middle East, Afghanistan, and Pakistan. He sent letters back home, describing the bazaars of the Orient, Ankara and Tehran, the dust and filth of Kabul, the thrill of crossing the Khyber Pass, and the different customs and lifestyles.

Reinhold flew with the rest of the crew and met up with his brother in Rawalpindi; from there, they flew the 250 miles north to Gilgit. Base camp, located in the Rupal valley at an elevation of 3,600 meters (11,800 feet), was reached by four-wheel drive and trekking; the equipment for the climb was carried by some three hundred Hunza porters. The "siege mentality" approach to climbing the highest peaks still prevailed in the Himalaya at the time.

The team comprised top-notch German-speaking climbers, veterans of past Herrligkoffer expeditions, support personnel, and a couple of interlopers: Herrligkoffer, the expedition leader, needs no introduction; Reinhold qualified him as "taciturn and reserved"; Felix Kuen, a Municher, was also an army mountain guide, "a predestined 'summit victor,'" in Messner's estimation, but also a man who combined grim determination with a lack of self-assurance, an ominous combination in the theater of the Naked Mountain. Werner Haim had a similar background, but a pleasant, warm personality; Peter Scholz was also from Munich, and a well-respected veteran of Nanga Parbat from the 1968 Rupal Face attempt. Baron Max von Kienlin followed the expedition as an experienced trekker, and as an amateur of climbing history. Gerhard Baur was the expedition filmmaker, also an enthusiastic climber. Jürgen Winkler was also part of the expedition, both to document and to climb; he was a well-known mountain photographer with an anchored, stabilizing personality.

Hans Saler was an adventurer from Munich, who "[found] it impossible to come to terms with routine middle-class life," remarked Reinhold. Hermann Kühn was the team scientist, who also loved mountains; Reinhold respectfully called him "[a] great man." Günther Kroh, nicknamed Gine, was a gifted rock climber from Swabia, with an impish, playful sense of humor. Both Peter Vogler and Gerhard "Gerd" Mändl were qualified by Reinhold as "subordinate"; however, the latter was a strong mountaineer, while Vogler was a much younger man, prone to sickness.

Logistics fell under the stewardship of Elmar Raab, helpful, with keen organizational skills. Wolfgang "Wolfi" Bitterling was the son of Albert Bitterling, one of the 1953 expedition members favorable to Hermann Buhl; according to Reinhold, he was an excellent cook. Alice von Hobe, nicknamed Alex, was Herrligkoffer's assistant, and the only woman in the team. Michl Anderl was a veteran with much experience, but lacking in leadership skills, according to Reinhold. Finally, Captain Saqi was the official liaison officer, as was customary on many expeditions in the Himalaya and Karakoram. Fifteen Hunza porters, the "Tigers," complemented the team for operations above base camp; these were tough climbers, experienced at high altitude, and tireless.

Günther's attitude toward Nanga Parbat was encapsulated in his own words: "With Nanga Parbat as our objective, our secret kingdom that we had founded on our first independent climbs together received a new dimension. Although we knew that the mountain had been climbed, the myth lived on, particularly on the Rupal Face. This myth had an astonishing power, and we were quite prepared to leave all the logistics to the expedition leadership. We would have gone with the devil himself to Nanga Parbat."

After choosing a protected site for base camp, and setting it up, cataloging loads ferried by the porters, organizing the mess tent, distributing supplies, and verifying the condition of technical equipment, the first forays to the mountain were eagerly anticipated. The team had established base camp far ahead of the beginning of the monsoon season, which would lock the mountain up in a deep shell of impenetrable snow, with avalanches roaring down all flanks and unleashing the fury of white death.

At an altitude of 4,700 meters (15,400 feet), Camp I was located near the site chosen during the unsuccessful 1968 expedition, which had turned around farther up near the crux of the route, the Merkl Ice Field. The camp sat some 1,000 meters above base camp, in a somewhat-protected area offering amazing views of the surrounding mountains, as well as the climb above, where difficulties loomed in the great couloirs and seracs of the upper Rupal Face. Access to Camp I was via a steep gully, which required fixed ropes; Reinhold and Günther fixed those ropes—with the help of Mändl, Saler, and two Hunza porters, including the best of the Tigers, Sepp. Herrligkoffer, who had not been consulted, was upset, and decided that Reinhold and Günther should no longer climb as a team, an order that Reinhold contested.

On May 17, 1970, around 2:00 a.m., the Messner brothers set off to further establish Camp I with Haim and Scholz. They climbed the steep gully with 55-pound loads and quickly reached the campsite, where they dug a large snow platform and set up a kitchen and four tent spaces, with the help of three Hunza porters. This was hard work at that altitude, and the following night they fell into a deep sleep. Despite the altitude, the sun baked Camp I: "Midday. We are lying in the tent. The heat is murderous. The water drips from the overhangs run like quicksilver over the tent flysheet. Like lizards crawling across the sky." The nights, however, were very cold, well below freezing. The tent, the boredom, the pounding sun, chocolate tasting like plaster, the whispers and cries of the wind at night, hours spent melting snow of dubious provenance—all these are part and parcel of the climb, an oscillation between the mundane and excessive fear, adrenaline rushing through, hypoxia on the prowl.

Camp II was now on the minds of the climbers, and the ascent to the campsite followed steep terrain that had to be equipped with fixed ropes to organize the ferrying of the heavy loads required to stock the camp. They found a protected site under a 100-foot-tall vertical ice wall at the edge of a stable serac; K2 and Broad Peak loomed in the east. Avalanches funneled around the bulging seracs and ice towers. Above, the difficult

Wieland Rocks and Glacier were already being fixed with ropes for a push to establish Camp III. Thus far, the weather had held, with sunny days and frigid nights.

On May 20, snow began falling in the afternoon; the wind of the morning brought bad weather, and a half-foot of fresh snow quickly accumulated at Camp II, which was only minimally stocked with food. They knew this could become an issue should the bad weather persist. On May 21, the climb to the site of Camp III proved difficult, with a tricky *bergschrund* below the ice wall leading upward. These were the first major technical problems on the route, following the exposed but easier terrain below. As the storm abated, they climbed down to base camp. Reinhold took only fifty minutes to drop some 2,000 meters (6,560 feet)! There, he spent a leisurely day, washing clothes, equipment, and himself, after a week up on the Rupal Face. At base camp, Günther and Reinhold wrote letters to their mother and little brother Hubert, respectively; Reinhold described the climb thus far: "The face is every bit as steep as the steepest walls in the Western Alps and sections of it are bloody difficult."

On May 26, they climbed back to Camp II; it required three and a half hours to ascend 2,000 meters! Fresh snow had accumulated, and the trail had to be broken, a hard task anywhere, especially above 5,000 meters. They established cables to ferry loads between Camps II and III. Although demanding, the ascent to Camp II could be done with heavy loads, thanks to the fixed ropes. The ice cliff below Camp III would simply be too difficult for such transport. Camp III would function as an advance base camp, where food and equipment could be stocked in preparation for further progress with the lighter packs demanded by altitude and technical difficulties.

The exact location of Camp III was found by sheer chance. Reinhold, looking for a site that would be appropriate—with sufficient space for a platform accommodating two or three tents, away from avalanches and rockfalls—poked through the ice into a hidden crevasse, whereupon he discovered a hidden ice cave large enough for Camp III. That location was also in close proximity to "winch camp," at the upper end of the cables set to ferry loads from Camp II. The elevation of Camp III, also referred to as "Ice Dome," was 6,000 meters (19,685 feet), almost a vertical mile and a half above base camp, but hardly at the halfway point on the Rupal Face. Above the Ice Dome still lay the most difficult climbing, first to the Welzenbach ice field.

After a few days of acclimatization at Camp III, the climbers started attacking the vertiginous landscape leading toward the lower Welzenbach névé. The Messner brothers installed 200 meters of fixed lines. In the middle part of the Welzenbach ice field the terrain changed from a very steep névé to ice cliffs leading to a severe couloir. On June 1, Reinhold and Günther made it up to approximately 100 meters below the planned location of Camp IV, but had to turn around because it was late: "We abseiled off: 700 meters of terrain similar to the Ortler and the north face of the Matterhorn. Very exposed!" This represents some 2,300 feet of dangerous mixed terrain, interspersed with near-vertical cliffs, with an average slope far in excess of 65 degrees. Below, the mountain was still quite steep, with gullies funneling slab avalanches and serac falls, with the Hange-Gletscher far below, to the left-hand side of the climbers on their way up, and the infinite Mazeno Ridge with rock towers, spires, and gendarmes punctuating the top of mighty mile-tall granite and gneiss spurs.

June 2 was a rest day at Ice Dome, during which they recuperated from the potent mix of hard work, difficult climbing, and altitude. The next day, June 3, they set off at 5:00 a.m. for Camp IV in good weather. The first 400 meters went relatively quickly, when snow began falling softly, silently covering the ice cliffs. They reached the last vertical 100 meters where the ice was bulging significantly, and become even steeper; that section still had to be equipped with fixed rope. They reached the intended site of Camp IV, identical to that of 1968, in gale-force winds. The snow was now falling fast and furiously and accumulating at an alarmingly fast rate. Loads were dumped in a hurry, and they descended over 800 meters back to Camp III and the cover of the Ice Dome. The ice was now much harder as the temperature plummeted.

By June 4, it became evident that the weather deterioration was going to be an event of significant duration: A full meter of snow had fallen, well over 3 feet. This kept the crew at Camp III busy digging out tents and equipment, while the excess snow avalanched away, to the great depth below. On June 5, another 3.5 feet of snow had accumulated, slowly taking the Ice Dome in its icy grip: "The roof of the tent is full of ice crystals that glisten in the candlelight. Strange Nirvana." Avalanches crashed down the tremendous slopes at regular intervals, roaring a violent scream, followed by the rush of air back into the partial vacuum trailing the immense loads of snow and ice; at these times, man felt like the tiniest of specks hanging for dear life in the frigid maelstrom of the angry winds.

June 6 brought more snow. Peter Scholz and Felix Kuen decided to retreat down to base camp; the Messner brothers, hoping for better weather soon, stayed in the Ice Dome to keep Camp III functional. They noted that the temperature kept getting lower, with nights at minus-20 degrees Celsius, and days below freezing. The snow became extremely light and powdery, sliding continually, while raging spindrifts danced angrily on the ridges up near the stratosphere.

On June 8, the sun appeared for half an hour in the morning, while a biting cold night followed with more snow; the spindrifts became so intense that they buried the tent under the Ice Dome! The same day, at base camp, Herrligkoffer and his lieutenants discussed their plan of attack for a summit bid, once the weather cleared. Two summit teams were debated and settled as follows: Reinhold and Peter Scholz would form the first rope, while Felix Kuen and Gerd Mändl would follow immediately, along with Gerhard Baur for filming and documenting. Further teams would then be allowed to attempt the summit after either party had first climbed Nanga Parbat via the Rupal Face. The Messner brothers, sitting a vertical mile and a half above, were not included in the debate, as they were to discover a day later.

On June 9, six days after the storm began, the weather was improving; Felix Kuen arrived at Camp III around noon, bringing with him the plan devised by Herrligkoffer, after consultation with the climbers present at base camp. Reinhold recalls: "I had read some time earlier that Karl Herrligkoffer did not hold the principles of leadership in very high regards. Then this plan arrived, which I was supposed to approve. According to the plan, Peter Scholz and I were to have been the first team to go for the summit, with Felix Kuen, Gerd Mändl, and Gerhard as the second. My brother Günther and Hans Saler, with Werner Haim, were meant to spend three consecutive days fixing the Merkl Couloir. It would not only be three days of hard labour in the Death Zone, it would actually be more strenuous than going for the summit."

Indeed, the Merkl Couloir was the undisputed crux of the climb, the point where the 1968 team had given up: extremely difficult terrain, at very high altitude, between the high camp, Camp V, and the summit. This couloir was the key to gaining the summit ridge after a traverse under the Merkl Gap. Logically, three different teams could have prepared the couloir with sections of fixed rope, thus dividing the strenuous task more evenly, and providing a higher probability of success; instead, the three climbers designated to lead and open that section were essentially "sacrificed" for a higher cause.

This is the point in the climb that could potentially be identified as a root cause of events that were to follow: The Messner brothers, reacting honestly to what they viewed as an unjust directive, began to envision a different course: "'Karl has obviously only spoken to part of the team. Now he's relying on you approving his plan. He hasn't even asked me. He doesn't like it when anyone interferes with his plans,' Günther remarked after he had finished reading. 'Him down there, he thinks a bit like a field marshal before the battle,' I agreed angrily. 'But since our field marshal is unwell, the battle plan is a sick one, too.' I shared Günther's irony. If an expedition leader stipulates that one man spends three consecutive days fixing the Merkl Couloir so the well-rested summit team can go up fixed ropes to the top and the guy simply decides to go for the summit first, then no one can criticize him. If he gives unreasonable orders, he has no right to expect reasonable reactions." The very word *unreasonable* is a dangerous term in the mountains, for it is only reason and rational thought that give the climber his final, decisive edge against the forces of nature: A single mistake can be lethal; poor judgment can lead to utter disaster.

The weather window closed almost as fast as it had opened; snow began falling again. This did not help to ease the tensions that were developing between the Messner brothers and Felix Kuen, whom they regarded as a military man, with what Reinhold described as an "apathy that bordered on subservience," when it came to Herrligkoffer's summit strategy. Continued bad weather forced most of the team down, back to base camp. This could have been an opportunity for all to regroup as a cohesive team;

instead, negative opinions had already germinated, and a poisonous sap was forming. For Reinhold and Günther, though, this was also a welcome break, after many idle, uncomfortable, boring days spent waiting out the storm at 6,000 meters. The air at 3,700 meters felt hyperoxygenated, as they had acclimatized up to 6,800 meters. They cleaned, bathed, and ate to their hearts' content; they talked, wrote letters to their loved ones, and played chess. Soon, they hoped, a weather window would liberate their pent-up energies, and they would climb back to the higher camps, rested and ready for the Merkl Couloir, the last traverse on 70-degree ice under the Merkl Gap, and the final climb on a difficult fortress of mixed terrain and vertiginous gullies to the summit of their dreams.

On June 15, the entire team was at base camp, the weather still variable, with intermittent showers; most climbers were in good physical shape, except for Vogler, who was suffering from pleurisy, an inflammation of the pleura, a membrane that surrounds the lungs. The next day presented better weather, and Reinhold, Günther, and von Kienlin decided to climb Heran Peak, approximately 5,950 meters (19,520 feet) high. They had an enjoyable time on this excursion, took photographs, and even had a good look at Nanga Parbat, when the clouds parted for a moment. Still, upon return to base camp and the Tap Alp, they felt as if they had committed some unspoken transgression. Herrligkoffer, a taciturn-minded, somewhat enigmatic, and tragic character, kept to himself most of the time; however, Reinhold recounted that "There were some evenings when Herrligkoffer really livened up. When he came into the mess tent, pulled up a crate, opened a can of beer, and played cards, it was as if he really did belong to the team. Sometimes he would come out of his shell and tell stories about earlier expeditions, and every time he looked at me I had a strange mixture of feelings: sympathy for his illness and high esteem for his single-mindedness. Suppressed anger gave way to understanding—perhaps he wasn't really as bad as he seemed, perhaps he was just incapable of being any different."

Incomplete or unachieved sublimation of his love of the high peaks, frustrated by his sickness, which prevented him from living the life of a top mountaineer, was the defining contradiction for Herrligkoffer, who longed to join his fellow climbers at the front lines of their hand-to-hand combat with the mountain, only to be condemned to insignificant hikes and scrambles around base camp, a burden that may well have affected his decision-making. Apposite to this Tantalus-like melancholy fate, the Messner brothers also brewed an admixture of unusual feelings, full of restless, undisciplined youth, yet aware of the ghosts of Herrligkoffer's past, admiring and refusing his stance all at once. How could they communicate within such strong emotive circumstances? Would each faction push the other closer to the lethal edge of folly on the Naked Mountain?

Because of the uncertain weather, a feeling of impending failure permeated base camp, igniting a multitude of trivial incidents, even with those members of the expedition who were generally even-keeled. For example, Jürgen Winkler was tasked with taking advertising shots for various products used during the expedition. A useless argument erupted when Herrligkoffer criticized him for actually eating the applesauce that was used as a prop in a series of photos. In fact, it was the climbers who had eaten the compote, not the photographer, who felt angry for being singled out for such a trivial trespass.

A few climbers, however, were still harboring a modicum of enthusiasm for a summit attempt, including Reinhold, who was invited to a consultation with the expedition leader on June 18. When asked about his views, he suggested that they should climb up to Camp III despite the weather conditions, if only to make sure that important pieces of equipment, including cameras and a radio, were not left on the mountain. He also argued that this would provide additional time for the weather to clear. Herrligkoffer agreed, further indicating that their climbing permit would expire on July 7, but could be extended if required.

The conversation then turned to the personnel who would be involved: twelve Hunza porters, and whoever was able and willing among the climbers. That would include Günther, Haim, and Raab, according to Reinhold. The exchange left him with mixed feelings: "As I left his tent I felt relieved and suspicious at the same time. I felt suddenly constrained by responsibility." On the same evening, the four climbers proposed by Reinhold left base camp, with a dual mission: climbing at least as far as Camp III and securing equipment, while hoping for better weather, which might lead to a window for a summit assault, a last bid. They arrived at Camp I shortly after sunset, and enjoyed a clear, short night under the starlight. At 1:00 a.m., the four climbers and the altitude porters left Camp I and made their way up above the Wieland rocks, where they dropped their loads because of the depth of powder snow that had accumulated earlier. The sun rose as they arrived back at camp.

As they resumed progress toward Camp II, they discovered that part of their loads had been swept down by some avalanching, unconsolidated snow. They continued on, and Reinhold, who had assumed leadership for the time being, instructed three of the porters to help clear the snow off the Wieland Glacier. After a fairly rapid ascent, they found Camp II buried under snow; digging the tents out was their next task. Meanwhile, the weather held and seemed to be improving slightly. With Camp II fixed and usable, the plan was now to continue on to the Ice Dome, Camp III, as soon as the next morning; at the same time, Kuen and Scholz had arrived at Camp II, and would closely follow the foursome.

The difficult sections leading to Camp III turned out to be in excellent condition, especially with good ice on the steepest pitches, but any flat area was buried in flaky powder snow, and proved extremely draining physically. Camp III was in no better shape than the lower sections, and a lot of hard work was required to make it habitable again. The weather was definitely improving: On that evening, the cloud cover was gone, and the wind calm; a summit bid might be possible, after all! Another good sign was that the night was frigid.

Before dawn, Reinhold and Günther, Kuen, Scholz, and Mändl woke up, melted snow and made breakfast, put on crampons, and finally set off beyond Camp III, to some of the hardest climbing on the Rupal Face. Kuen led the climb, and worked very hard ascending on the fixed ropes, breaking a deep trail in the powdery, icy snow. After some 100 vertical meters, Reinhold took the lead, and shortly thereafter, Günther overtook Kuen, who had used a lot of energy in his initial snow plodding. As the face steepened, hard ice appeared; fortunately, the fixed ropes were in good order, offering protection on the bluish surface. The sublime Rupal Face, covered in green ice, presented itself in full vertiginous glory, tremendous exposure over unfathomable lines falling aesthetically down untold precipices. Huge serac cliffs now barred the way; the equipment put in place was gone, stolen by the elements. The altitude was 6,600 meters (21,650 feet), higher than Denali. Belayed by Günther, Reinhold reopened the pitch of vertical ice, perhaps the most technically difficult section on the entire climb. The gates to Camp IV had been pushed ajar.

At first, Camp IV was set in two separate locations: Scholz and Kuen used the same spot as the 1968 expedition, while the Messner brothers pushed on higher to the *bergschrund* of the Merkl Ice Field, which they found to be better protected. On June 23, they were at Camp IV, 6,600 meters above sea level. At 7:00 a.m. on June 24, after an extremely cold night, Haim, Saler, and Mändl arrived from the Ice Dome camp with supplies; the effort to stock Camp IV for a summit bid had begun. Scholz and Kuen consolidated their tent and equipment in the safer spot found by Reinhold and Günther. On June 25, the brothers made their way up the Merkl Ice Field, all the way to the beginning of the Merkl Couloir, to locate a possible site for the last camp, Camp V. A small platform, protected by a rocky ridge and big enough to pitch a small tent on, was dug into the hard ice. Above, the Merkl Couloir led to the gullies and cliffs under the South Shoulder. Back down at Camp IV, new loads had arrived, carried by Saler, Mändl, and Haim over the very difficult slopes above the Ice Dome. On their way up the Merkl Ice Field, Kühn and Baur also carried huge loads under the unbearable, ultraviolet heat of the day. All camps below were now stocked and occupied, the very situation prescribed by Herrligkoffer in his previous plan for a final push to the summit.

Camp IV had now grown to three tents, accommodating the Messner brothers, Baur, as well as Kuen and Scholz. On June 26, Kuen and Scholz climbed all the way to the small platform chopped in the ice by the Messner brothers and established Camp V, at 7,350 meters (24,114 feet), by pitching a small tent and dropping 200 meters of rope to fix the Merkl Couloir. On their way back to Camp IV, they noticed a change in weather, with large cloud formations in the south. This observation brought back the doubts and tension that had plagued relations at base camp. At the same time, plans seemed to be changing: Kuen and Scholz now thought that the Messner brothers and Baur would go to the three-man tent at Camp V, and work from there on the Couloir, establishing fixed ropes that would presumably facilitate a summit assault by Kuen and Scholz. In fact, the plan went further: Another 300 meters of fixed ropes would be set up on the upper portion of the Couloir by Baur and Günther, now supplemented by Mändl, Saler, and Haim, who would then wait for Kuen, Scholz, and Reinhold, as they attempted to reach the summit. This approach incorporated some elements of the original Herrligkoffer plan, but also deviated substantially from it. For example, both Mändl and Baur had been eliminated from the summit push, perhaps because Camp V could only accommodate three climbers. Reinhold commented on the situation: "It was a bit like the Tower of Babel up there, a place where misunderstanding and confusion were rife. Maybe it was the altitude."

Is it possible that after the mighty effort of setting up Camp V, Kuen considered that he could give orders? Were there additional consultations with Herrligkoffer that Reinhold did not know about? In any event, at the time of the climb, the new plan and its logistical details seemed somewhat incongruous to the Messner brothers, who were to proceed by ignoring Kuen's commands. These considerations should be considerably amplified in view of the altitude factor, and because of the fact that the climbing team had reached terra incognita: The Merkl Couloir was an unknown quantity; they were higher than the highest point that the 1968 expedition had attained. One thing is certain: In Reinhold's mind, there was no plan for the summit bid. The original plan was weeks old, and much had changed since then; Kuen's strategy issued from no clear authority, and was therefore null and void.

That same fateful day, June 26, Reinhold contacted base camp by radio from Camp IV. He talked to Herrligkoffer about logistics, supplies, food, and supplemental oxygen. Most importantly, they discussed the weather conditions, and devised a simple plan to communicate the forecast trend from base camp to the climbers above 7,000 meters: A red rocket would indicate that the 8:00 p.m. weather report forecasted bad weather, while a blue one would stand for continued good conditions. In turn, two subordinate strategies would follow: In case of bad weather, Reinhold would go as high as possible, perhaps to the summit, alone; the blue rocket would mean that the team had time to further equip the Couloir with fixed ropes, in stages, for a more-systematic summit attempt.

In case of an unclear forecast, a red and a blue rocket would be fired in close succession; the summit climbers were then free to decide on which approach to follow.

Reinhold was quite clear about this crucial exchange: "The colours of the rockets and their meanings were repeated several times. There was no doubt in my mind about our arrangement."

Baur, Günther, and Reinhold left Camp IV for Camp V. At precisely 8:00 p.m., while on the Merkl Ice Field, they saw a red glare originating from the Tab Alpe: the agreed-upon signal for a bad-weather forecast. The night was extremely cold, minus-30 degrees C; they were cramped and uncomfortable; above, 775 vertical meters of unknown climbing, 2,545 feet of ice, gullies, and mixed terrain; and finally, the lonely, lofty summit. Reinhold began preparations for his final push into the ether around 2:00 a.m.; he was already fully clothed, and took only a few items, including a camera and a photograph of the upper Rupal Face for orienting. The cold had pushed all the water vapor down, and the sky was profoundly dark, adorned with a tapestry of twinkling stars.

Anxiety, a sense of destiny, a feeling of insignificance rushed adrenaline through Reinhold's body, under the preternatural moonshine. His solo summit bid was under way, crampons barely biting into the hardened ice. He reckoned that the terrain, although steep and enormous in amplitude, was perhaps Grade IV, from a technical standpoint. He established a slow, methodical climbing rhythm in the rarefied air, and reached the first step, a rocky section far more difficult than the preceding terrain. It required his complete focus. The more-even climbing resumed, in the thin, frigid air; the effort kept him warm, and he was making steady progress, as the Couloir became narrower. Farther up, however, an overhanging bulge, impossible to climb alone, especially at that altitude, barred the line of ascent. He had gone too far up the gully and now needed to climb back down, in order to locate an escape route that would lead to a more-favorable line toward the summit. This took a while; he was not only concerned about surmounting the obstacles, but also about the descent, which is always harder, absent fixed ropes or a rappel. After trying different possibilities, the solution presented itself in the form of a two-pitch long-hidden upward ramp, traversing to the right of the Couloir into easier terrain, and leading above the bulge blocking the gully. Now at about 7,800 meters, Reinhold recalled, "I felt very calm."

The gully now led to the Merkl Notch, followed by a traverse to the South Shoulder, on to the summit. The blinding sun was shining mercilessly, and the heat became oppressive in the rarefied air; the considerable efforts of the very early dawn had drawn his reserves down, and he was making slower progress up into the lonely death zone.

Günther appeared, as in a dream: A small spot, far down the couloir, he was now closing and catching up with Reinhold. What was he doing up here? Wasn't he supposed to equip the lower part of the Couloir with fixed ropes? In *Free Spirit*, Messner described the reunion: "I waited and soon he was standing next to me. I did not ask him why he had followed me. His voice sounded normal, not tired, not hoarse—just cheerful. Had he brought a rope? For six weeks we had climbed on this huge face together, had slept next to each other, and had cooked for each other. For fifteen years we had climbed as a rope in the mountains. It was clear that we would go on together."

In contradistinction, in *The Naked Mountain*, Reinhold recounted the reunion as follows: "I looked down again and watched him, a little irritated, then decided to wait. The next thing I knew, Günther was standing beside me, breathing hard. 'How did you find the route?' I asked. 'Your tracks. The route is logical anyway.' 'And what about the bit where the gully closes up?' 'Up the ramp. No other possibility.' 'Were you roped up?' 'Only to begin with.' We did not talk much. Günther had climbed the whole of the Merkl Couloir in less than four hours—almost 600 meters of vertical height, at this altitude! There was no longer any question: We would carry on together. We belonged together, and we would soon be on the summit, I thought."

These two passages do complement one another, but they also clearly show different emotional contexts. In the first one, the summary begins in a fairly neutral tone, and ends up with a note of brotherly love; in the longer version, emotions range from irritation to admiration, with a similar brotherly bonding at the conclusion. The irritation may simply be due to the fact that Günther did not follow the agreed-upon plan; at the same time, there is no question that Günther's climb, catching up to Reinhold, is a veritable tour de force at such elevation—although it would come at a very high price. The one advantage Günther had was the trailblazing effort of Reinhold: Günther did not have to seek a path forward. As for the other discrepancies, they may well be due to the extreme altitude where these events took place. In fact, the very tone Reinhold used to convey the rest of the climb to the summit is quite reminiscent of Buhl's account on the other side of the mountain: the torturous affliction of rest breaks becoming more and more frequent, progress ever slower, a process of limits, which one hopes will converge on the summit, like the infinite series of halved steps of Zeno's Paradox. Here is thirst deeper than bears description, ineffable tiredness, the slow drowning in the stratospheric air, hallucinations, and temporal lapses, yet, an unshakable will to climb, to terminate the suffering by setting foot on the highest point, beyond which all dreams dissolve into the ultraviolet skies.

The big traverse was now ahead, slanting up to a small notch in the ridge, the top of the Rupal Face. Very close, the splendid summit beckoned: "My first impressions on emerging onto the ridge from the South Face was [sic] for me the most powerful moment of the entire Nanga Parbat Expedition. Everything seemed so unreal, so quiet. And there was Günther, right next to me." Indeed, after weeks within the same surroundings and landmarks, the ridge marked the beginning of a brand-new world, whose lofty gates hovered some 5 vertical miles into the sky!

In *Free Spirit*, Reinhold remembers: "The arrival on the ridge was exciting. Everything was spread out before us: the summit, the plateau, the Silver Saddle, Rakhiot Peak. Günther and I were impressed." The South Shoulder looked like the prow of a great ship in the mist, as small clouds of spindrift flew by; inch by inch, the brothers made their way up the mixed terrain. Above the Shoulder, a gentle snowfield led to the highest point: "Time and space have no real meaning at such altitudes. Here, nothing is the same; none of the usual rules apply. We drift along; floating high above the valleys, yet feel so heavy. So far away from the world, and so far away from ourselves."

These impressions closely resemble Buhl's feelings on the Silbersattel, where seemingly close landmarks appear to recede away, taking far more time to reach than first anticipated. Altitude, no doubt, plays a major role in this strange world of misperceptions; perhaps the lack of scale for comparison also contributes to the illusion. Everything is so much bigger than man in these immense mountains. The summiting is often anticlimactic, falling short of expectations, as reality not living up to the dream.

They spent a while taking photographs, gasping for air; Reinhold left a pair of extra mittens under a rock, as a marker of their passage. In *Free Spirit*, Reinhold recounts: "Only a few more minutes, I thought. These minutes seem like hours. At last a snow dome; it was the summit of Nanga Parbat! Günther, who had photographed my ascent, followed slowly. Now he was here, beside me. He took off his gloves and stretched out his hand to me. I looked into his eyes, for we had taken off our goggles; I don't know why."

The relieved elation of reaching the summit gave way to the realization that they had to descend, climbing down quickly to avoid a dangerous bivouac. Alas, they were exhausted; Günther was now paying the price of his astonishing dash up the Merkl Couloir, and became quite weary during the descent, especially in the treacherous and difficult section they had overcome that morning. This led to a fateful decision: They would reach the Merkl Gap and bivouac there. Along the way, Günther started insisting that they should go down using an easier route than the Merkl Couloir; Reinhold began to suspect that Günther might well be suffering from altitude sickness, especially now that Günther requested that they go down the Diamir flank. This was impossible. There were no camps or any shelters there, no food, no liquid, and they would end up tens of miles away from base camp, with no way to communicate with the rest of the team; this was madness!

Nevertheless, Günther was in no state to go down the steep Merkl Couloir; the only choice was to bivouac and hope for help the next day. Surviving a bivouac at such extreme altitude is a matter of strength and luck; Buhl had done it, but on a singular night, devoid of any wind. Would the Messner brothers be able to repeat the impossible? In their spent state, the easier Diamir flank looked more and more promising. They compromised and decided to drop on that side of the mountain, below the ridge they had reached in the morning, to make their way to the notch where the Merkl Couloir abuts and terminates, and to spend the night in the immediate vicinity. Reinhold also remembered the red rocket and its implications for bad weather; this was powerful motivation to lose altitude as quickly as possible. All of these decisions concatenated into a dangerous admixture.

Night and darkness forced them into a hideous bivouac, with temperatures plummeting well below minus-30 degrees C; they had no tent, no covers, and very little protection, except the damp clothing they had worn all day. They spent a wretched night. At some point, Günther asked for a blanket: "'What blanket?' 'The one on the ground there.' 'There is no blanket.' Günther was hallucinating." The conversation then turned to their toes, which had gone beyond numbness in the minus-40 degree C cryogenic air. This was dangerous frostbite, a stealthy enemy: numbness, followed by a tingling rush, nearly unbearable, as extremities may return from a dangerously close encounter with frostbite, freezing, tissue death, gangrene, and amputation. Maurice Herzog, after his harrowing climb of Annapurna, was treated with live maggots, which clean the rotten flesh, thus avoiding infection and preparing for a proper amputation! Reinhold would lose a few toes, when amputation became unavoidable.

At dawn, Günther became agitated, and, quite suddenly, stood up and started to walk in a gyre, mumbling and groaning; this behavior was quite alarming. Around 6:00 a.m., Reinhold, having checked again on his brother's deteriorating state, decided to try and call for help. The only possibility was to leave Günther behind, at their bivouac site, and to proceed toward the top of the Merkl Couloir, the link to the lower camps, and the logical escape route, hard as the descent would be. He reached a notch in the ridge, from which he could plainly see the upper sections of the Couloir; he desperately needed a rope that could be used to help Günther descend the difficult terrain above Camp V. The mixed terrain below was "plumb vertical," yet that was the shortest path to the route they had climbed the day before, tantalizingly close: approximately 100 meters (300 feet) below. He returned to Günther, very nearly hopeless, and clearly hypoxic: "I realized with a mixture of curiosity and shock that I was also losing the ability to reason properly, too."

After a short time with Günther, Reinhold made his way back to the edge where, for two hours, he called for help and asked desperately for a rope. Tired beyond the pale, he once more made his way back to the bivouac where Günther was steadily deteriorating. For the third time, Reinhold trudged heavily, wearily to the precipice; this time he saw two specks, moving slowly upward: "Help!" The two climbers were still quite far away, so he went back to Günther, this time with good news: "Günther, they're coming!" This time Günther seemed to understand: "At last!" he said, before standing up with difficulty, his balance now almost completely gone.

It was 10:00 a.m., and Reinhold could now recognize the climbing rope: Kuen and Scholz were reaching the upper sections of the Merkl Couloir, with Kuen leading. This time, his shouts for help were heard, as Felix looked up. He was now convinced that the pair was coming to rescue them from their horrendous predicament. The wind made it difficult, perhaps impossible to understand the back-and-forth shouting. Messner indicated that they were descending, and the only words he clearly understood from Kuen were: "Were you on the summit?" which he answered in the affirmative. He also answered Kuen's question, "Are you both okay?" in the affirmative: "Yes! Everything's okay, Felix." The precise meaning of this single word, *okay*, would come to haunt Reinhold for years to come. The whole scene took place above 7,900 meters (25,918 feet), where the air pressure is approximately a third of that at sea level; as a result, sound propagates quite differently, and the constant strong winds issuing from the jet stream muffle and distort vocal communications. Finally, the desiccating dry air makes voices hoarse and feeble, all of which contributed to this fateful episode. In the end, with hypoxia setting in, it was the drive of each party that self-convinced them: The climbing team was summit-bound at nearly all costs, while the Messner brothers believed they were being rescued. Kuen and Scholz continued up, leaving the distraught brothers in utter shock. Additionally, the physical state of even the best mountaineer at such altitudes is barely sufficient for them to function at a minimal level; under these circumstances, a rescue is impossible, and would simply endanger the would-be rescuers, potentially resulting in more injuries or fatalities. Kuen and Scholz were climbing in the death zone, which was also an incommunicado region, as the only radio was at Camp IV, thousands of vertical feet below. This was a drama played by the deaf and mute, in the lethal theater of the upper reaches of the Rupal Face. Tragedy would ensue.

Later on, Kuen indicated that he had gathered that everything was okay, that he had no reason to think otherwise; he also was exhausted and took some Pervitin to help him continue toward the summit. In the end, he and Scholz were simply following the agreed-upon plan. Reinhold wrote:

> *After Felix and Peter had disappeared and I knew they were going to the summit, I traversed back despairingly to the bivouac to explain everything to Günther. I stumbled, fell a few times, and hurt my hand. Then I went back again to the Couloir. The sun slanted across me. For a moment a great uneasiness arose in me. It was as if I had gone mad. My thoughts eddied through each other. I plunged away and looked at my ax and myself, as from without. I wept without knowing why. Günther caught me up and said, "Now it's you who has lost his head." His voice drew me up short. The moment of crisis was past; for a short time I had lost control of myself. Now decisions must be taken. Günther insisted on descending at once. No second bivouac at this height! Perhaps alone I could have gone down the Merkl Couloir to fetch help? But then Günther would have been alone all night. No, no splitting up!*

This meant that they would continue descending on the immense Diamir flank of the mountain, perhaps to reach the route that Mummery had partially pioneered, and which was far easier technically than the Rupal Face. Climbing down an unknown mountain face is difficult, because route-finding is even harder than when ascending: One cannot know if a gentle glacier ends up in a terrific cliff of giant, impassable seracs; the difficulties barring the way cannot always be seen from above, and there is considerable risk of having to double back in search of a practical itinerary leading to safety. They were trading the Scylla of the Rupal Face for the Charybdis lurking on the Diamir flank. Yet, this was their only hope, given their physical and mental states.

The Mummery spur, a distinct rock ridge cleaving the giant Diamir flank was their goal and guide. Around 11:00 a.m., they set out, down the Bazhin basin on easy snow slopes, and found a way across towering seracs leading lower to the northwest. The weather alternated between wind and thunderstorms lower down; it even softly hailed. Günther's energy appeared to have picked up, now that they were going down. Neither brother had drunk anything for forty hours; Reinhold was able to use vitamin-drink powder and make a few precious ounces of liquid that helped Günther further recover enough strength to go down, zombie-like, but on his own. Each foot down would bring thicker air, a small, nearly insignificant victory, but it would keep them going for a long time.

The sheer amplitude of the task ahead seemingly did not fully register with the brothers. Assuming that they escaped from the treacherous Diamir flank, they had no food, nor equipment, not even a map; how would they survive? How would they reconnect with the expedition, tens of miles away, through unknown territory? True, they had studied maps and photographs back at home, but how could they rely on memory, when hypoxia and exhaustion had robbed them of elementary logic? For Reinhold, these thoughts permeated his mind as an amorphous feeling of fear and impending doom; the risks were very great, but the sole alternative was a terrible death, like so many before them, on that fateful mountain: Willy Merkl, Gaylay, Siegi Löw, all the others. The terrible fatigue and desperate concentration, as he attempted to find the easiest ground to travel down in the maze of seracs and ice towers sprinkled across the upper Diamir face, in order to spare Günther having to climb back up, and continually finding new detours, were starting to have a strange effect on Reinhold's mind. He became convinced that a third climber followed their every move, shadowing them on their quest for life. This figment was silent, but his presence strong and benevolent.

As night came, they found an unprotected bivouac site "somewhere on the top of the Mummery Spur," at an elevation probably around 6,500 meters. The site was dangerously exposed to avalanching from the serac fields above, but Günther was exhausted, and barely coherent; he needed some rest. The moon rose above the fantastic landscape of titanic glaciers, glistening ice fields bearing the darker bluish hue of angry seracs, serrated rock ribs, unfathomable crevasses, and vertical cliffs. They did not wait for a dawn that would surely bring down murderous icefall; they went down in the moonlight, over exposed terrain, tripping and sliding, staying alive by hook or by crook. Down was life itself: Melting ice and snow meant water; then patches of grass, flowers, perhaps small animals; farther down, people, food, rest; ultimately, salvation.

As they progressed, Reinhold began experiencing strong déjà-vu: "'I've climbed this thing before,' I said to Günther. 'You can't have done.' 'This bit exactly. I know where every hold is.' 'Impossible.'" Sometime after this weird episode, they reached a relatively easy gully near the termination of the upper part of the Mummery Spur; this marked the boundary between the more-difficult high-altitude terrain and the lower slopes, leading to the Diamir glacier. It was approximately 8:00 a.m. when they reached the last slopes at the foot of the face. With renewed hope, they descended faster on the "hard firn slopes, crampons biting nicely and all the crevasses clearly visible." Reinhold also noted that "Günther seemed much fresher than yesterday; obviously he had recovered [a] little." Further down, they each chose a path, on the wide open, concave face leading to the glacier below; this was comparatively easy terrain, requiring some attention for crevasses and the occasional serac, but the navigation was now far simpler, with a clear objective in sight. The main worry at this point was the danger of avalanches when the sun would warm up the face; Reinhold wanted to increase the pace again.

"Are we going to head down there to the right, between the seracs?" asked Günther; "Yes. It will be the fastest way down." "We'll wait for each other at the first spring." In *Free Spirit*, Reinhold's recollection is a bit different: "Slowly we climbed down, one after the other, first a rock barrier, then a big snow face. Tacitly we agreed to meet at the first spring; there one would wait for the other." This difference is of some import, because in the first version, the two are climbing down separately, although they regroup at some point and have a brief conversation, while in the abbreviated version, their agreement is unspoken, but they walk down in unison. What happened next is the very crux of their entire saga; again, it is instructive to compare and contrast the two versions provided by Reinhold in *The Naked Mountain* and *Free Spirit*, the abbreviated version.

In the short recounting of these fateful moments at the foot of the Diamir flank of Nanga Parbat, Reinhold notes that, at the bottom of the last big snow slope, "where the glacier forms a terrace," he decided to bear left and move quickly down an avalanche cone leading to melting ice and water, where he drank profusely; absent Günther, he continued down to the debris-strewn glacier: "Suddenly I saw people. They were coming toward me at the edge of the glacier, a horseman among them. I heard voices and waved." The constant noises of an active glacier—grinding, water rushing down below, seracs breaking apart, the wind whooshing past—all of these could well conspire to confuse the wrecked mind of a climber lost in the immensity of the Naked Mountain. The strange shapes of rock piles along the glacier and lateral moraines could be misperceived in the blinding sun, assuming the desired sight of other humans. "I could hear Günther. But there was no Günther, no one at all. I kept feeling that Günther was behind me but when I looked round for him he had vanished.

"'This is like a motorway,' I thought as I started out across an avalanche chute to the left. I instinctively knew that descending the avalanche debris would be less strenuous." Sometime later, "Rays of sunlight strafed the Mazeno Ridge as the first avalanches began to thunder down the faces." Finally, "The glacier began to flow with rivulets of water. I chopped a small hollow in the ice, lay down, and drank without stopping. I was insatiable."

Now Reinhold was making his way on what he calls the "dead glacier," the less-active part of the glacier that is covered with debris, slowly churning its way down to its terminus. On that terrain, the ice is hard and dirty, and the crevasses are plainly visible; the general slope is very gentle, and progress is generally quite easy, but Reinhold "was moving hunched over like an old man." He was not overly worried about Günther, who had presumably taken a slightly different path; in any event, there were no actual springs yet, so the rendezvous point would be farther below. "Then I sat on a rock. I was dead tired. I thought I could hear voices. One voice calling my name and others talking to me in whole sentences, although I could only understand fragments of what they were saying." "So many voices!" and "My mother's voice was also there. The voices babbled along like a stream, like trickles of meltwater.

"My brain registered everything that happened in exact detail—the external and the emotional, the physical and the mental processes—as if there were intervals or spaces between the feeling, the realization, and the storing of information." In view of the extreme ordeal he suffered, including an unusually long span of time in the lethal zone and a bivouac at 8,000 meters, this statement sounds eerily symptomatic of either a trance state, at the very edge of catatonia, or a series of mini-strokes, perhaps due to cerebral edema: "Although in the final instance these mental leaps were concentrated purely on the human organism's instinct to preserve life—slowed down, perhaps by the imminent possibility of dying and the lack of oxygen—their effect on my conscious mind was similar to a state of schizophrenia, as perceptions and emotions faced each other like images of the sun and moon."

In his beautifully poignant narrative, *The Naked Mountain*, he uses the literary device of shifting his storytelling perspective from the first to the third person, in order to emphasize the shifting mental states he experienced at high altitude, under constant stress, punishing conditions, and culminating with the inexplicable, shattering, lethal disappearance of his brother, so close to safer ground, yet so far away from home.

"Reinhold!" Nobody? No, the third climber was there; not Günther. "The voices were silent for a while, but as I reached the edge of the moraine they were back again. And there were people, too, waiting for me—no doubt about it. Further left, I could see a horse; yes, a horse." Here, the visual hallucinations are completely similar; only the horseman is now a horse. He continues only to discover that "The horse turned out to be a crevasse, the people just clumps of bushes and stones." Again, given the astonishing exertion, anguish, thirst, hunger, and altitude of the past hundred hours, it is no surprise that, after days in the mineral desert of high altitude, smaller, human-scale objects would be confused for desired images by a tortured brain at the ragged edge between reality and madness.

Finally, Reinhold finds an actual freshwater spring: "I took a drink and had another look around, feeling suddenly uneasy. Where was Günther?" An anguished panic began to cruelly pang at his soul; he had recovered some feeble strength, and began looking for his brother like an aimless madman. He retraced his way, but the sun had melted any clues of his passage; the only possibility was to go back where they had last been together, somewhere on that terminal slope, below which Reinhold had veered left onto the avalanche debris cone. Perhaps Günther had chosen the path to the right? Reinhold tried to follow that route: "Where [were] those footprints? An avalanche! It filled me with horror." These are the succinct findings reported in *Free Spirit*; in *The Naked Mountain*, he elaborates: "All of a sudden I stumbled across the debris from an avalanche: a chaotic jumble of lumps of ice and powder snow. Huge blocks of ice, some the size of cupboards, lay scattered and piled beneath a vertical band of tottering seracs. A little shaken at first, I just stood and stared at the sheer quantity of ice that had fallen. Then the shock and disbelief set in."

At that point, for the first time, he conceives of the possibility that Günther might be gone, but he relates it as a negative: "I simply could not believe that Günther might be lying buried beneath the debris, that he might be dead." He then describes the frantic hours he spent going back and forth at the base of the titanic cirque that is the Diamir flank. Night came: "The whole world was suddenly in a state of suspended animation. Everything was dead, the stones frozen to the ice." Death's presence was becoming more real, but he could not go home without Günther, so he searched, almost aimlessly. By morning, back at the spring, he saw the devastating avalanches come down all over the Diamir flank, tens of avalanches roaring and thundering. "'Günther!' I shouted. It was the anguished cry of a lost animal."

By now, Messner was in a wretched state: vomit, excrement, blood, sweat, and tears; the metallic taste of blood in his mouth.

Another night came. "I knew now that Günther was dead—yet I waited for him." Sleeping in fits and starts, every moment awake a reminder of the horrible reality, only to doze back into dreams and nightmares; that morning, he woke up different, almost emotionless. The third climber's role was now clear: Reinhold would simply follow him, wherever he went. "As if in a trance, I watched the third man as he made his descent, stumbling along." The third man looks like Reinhold: "The skin hung in tatters from his nose. His lips and eyes were badly swollen. He seemed to move automatically, without thinking." In moments when his internal monologue took over, he remembers, "I felt ready to die." "Still with no answers to the questions that Günther had posed during the night, I began to die." How could he possibly return home to their mother without Günther?

In *Free Spirit*, before he had invented the third man and the literary device of shifting his storytelling perspective from the first to the third person, he talks more prosaically of dragging himself down, of discovering that his feet were frozen blue, of the slow, painful swelling that made it harder and harder to walk, and of the desperate glacier crossing to a moraine above the Diamir Gah, the mountain stream birthed by the glacier: "I fell asleep. I was finished." A lesser death, perhaps. Taking his clothes off, he remarked that, "They smelled of sweat and grit and death and ice." "When I awoke, it was late afternoon, the sun low"; "I slept a few hours and when I awoke the sun was high in the sky." That fourth night out, he slept very little, "falling into a death-like state of unconsciousness." He was extremely weak and extraordinarily hungry; his feet were in very bad shape, and it was only a question of time before he could simply no longer walk. If that happened before he met any people, he would slowly die, of hunger and exposure. Somehow, he made it through the night: "I watched the blades of grass before my eyes as they shivered in the chill early morning breeze. It got colder and I sat up. A bright new morning was dawning over the mountain. I was still alive." Rebirth and deep sadness: "The third climber and I had become one and the same person."

Down the Diamir glacier lies the tiny community of Ser, then Jil; a few miles to the west, the Karakoram Highway is the main thoroughfare in the region. To the south, the Mazeno Ridge forms a long wall preventing access back to the Rupal Face; the only shortcut would be a pass at 5,300 meters. Messner, in his current state, could never make it back to base camp.

When he had gathered enough feeble energy to be on the move again, he decided to leave a small piece of clothing behind, a sign of sorts; a piece of red legging, a red nylon gaiter, would do. He weighted it with a couple of stones, on top of the rock that had stood over his bivouac. Then Reinhold and his avatar walked and stumbled down the jumbled terrain, with a longing and empty soul. Along some 6 miles of glacier, covered with stones and debris, they slowly worked their way down the valley where life was unfolding: green pastures and alps, lovely streams running from the glaciers above, flowers, and butterflies. He was in horrific shape; his frozen feet would not carry him anymore. He had to crawl. His parched throat was filled with mucous, the sun burning every inch of exposed skin. As he stopped by a small water puddle to cool his burning feet, he clearly evaluated the severity of his wounds, understanding the imminent danger of infection and gangrene. As time passed in a series of images separated by nothingness or sadness or deep melancholy, the first signs of human life appeared in the form of deserted ruins, with perhaps a couple of shacks remaining. At that point, he began to think that death would bring sweet relief; yet he went on among a purgatory of rock and dust, seeking escape down the valley where men lived.

The atrocity of his predicament was mercifully softened by the state of shock triggered by sheer exhaustion, altitude sickness, hunger, trauma, and the terrible, unknowable fate of Günther. Deeply etched in Messner's soul, these tragic events would redefine his relations with the world and his fellow human beings. The wandering lasted forever, in the intermediate zone between the overwhelming high realm, blue and green with ice, and the golden granite spires towering above, and the upper reaches of plants and small vegetation, where herders and shepherds gather their flock for tender grass and sweet meltwaters.

Then he saw cows grazing in a pasture. Another cruel trick of the mind? "In the state I was now, I would not have been able to cope with yet another disappointment. I think I would have just sat down and died." The cows turned out to be real enough, and so was the man near the little hut, who promptly left after Reinhold called for help. After what seemed an eternity, more people emerged from the woods whence the man had gone; they seemed thoroughly unreal to Reinhold. Communication was very difficult: Reinhold's English was poor, and the men could not fathom that somebody could have come down from the mountain. They wanted to know where he came from and if he was alone. It took him quite a long time just to make it clear that he was starving. They gave him some chapatti, a simple flatbread, his first food in five days. His swollen throat made him choke and feel overwhelmingly nauseous. Somehow, he was able to indicate that he had come over the summit of Nanga Parbat, and lost Günther. The men decided to take him further down into the valley, to a very tiny rural hamlet, called Nagaton; there, children and small goats played while a donkey brayed in the middle of the huts. A soothing feeling of safety finally came over his dilapidated mind.

At the summer settlement he discovered that his feet were by now so terribly swollen and painful, he could not wear shoes anymore, let alone walk. He also needed food, but in liquid form, as his throat caused constant torment. The people gave him lassi, a liquid yogurt with spices and fruit, and chapatti, providing some relief. His situation, though improved, was still dire. He needed to communicate with his saviors, asking them to quickly get him to a hospital for badly needed medical treatment. His feet alone were dangerously close to spreading infection and gangrene, the rest of his body, extremely weary and requiring much rest and recuperation.

At this point, he was still hoping against hope that he would be reunited with the expedition back at base camp, on the Tap alp. Trying to evaluate the distance between Nagaton and base camp, he remembered the Sherpa word for day: *din.* Counting with fingers, the answer came to two; but one of them looked at his feet and shook his head. He was right; he could not even walk at this point. Any such attempt would be suicide. The only way out would be down.

Night brought little sleep; hallucinations and disorientation kept creeping in, half dreams of Günther, nightmares that turned out to be real, an incoherent mind that could no longer process thoughts and ideas in the great whirlwind of the starry skies above. The next day, he enrolled a young lad to help him down to the next hamlet, Ser; payment would come in the form of his headlamp and gloves, precious commodities here. He had no money, but a watch that seemed to delight the local folks could be his best asset for bartering. Walking, even helped with sticks as crutches, became excruciating. His feet were now lumps of throbbing pain, each step an agony. On the small trail, people came and went; at some point, he got some meltwater from a little girl.

They finally reached the outskirts of Ser. There, he saw that his feet were getting worse quickly; blood was now oozing from them, and the swelling was extreme, pressuring his toes, which were becoming dark blue and black. Inquiring for news of the expedition, he realized that Ser had seen no sahibs for a very long time. Two boys took him to a tiny temple, where he could lie down and rest; another boy prepared a grain paste with some water and used the rudimentary unguent on his feet, which were burning with pain. Some local folks visited the prayer hall while he was there; later, two men came in, one of them armed with a gun, causing great fear and alarm to a fragile Reinhold. After a short while, they left.

Hungry, Messner crawled out and bartered for eggs, chapatti, and chai. Some of the children helped him; one brought simple cooking utensils, and another built a fire. They were obviously amazed and entertained by the novelty that he presented. He then tried to enroll their help; in the end two young adults accepted, in exchange for all his remaining gear. Then he realized that his precious boots were missing; this time, he erupted with furious anger. The children, duly afraid, promptly brought back the boots. His only hope now was to make it down to the west, to reach the Indus valley, where the Karakoram Highway would offer the possibility of transportation.

Upon leaving the village, two men accosted him; one of them was the gunman at the temple. They decided to help him—to carry him down, first to Diamirai, the next village along the river. The gun turned out to be unloaded, mostly for show; the two men found his misplaced fear most amusing. The long trek down proceeded. Pain and worry were Reinhold's constant companions, along with the terrible anguish of Günther's disappearance and presumed death. They now had to cross the Diamir's raging waters over a makeshift bridge. Carrying the ailing, disabled climber was not possible, so after much hesitation, Reinhold crawled across, on all fours—another small step toward possible salvation.

Approaching Diamirai, a local farmer helped the disabled Reinhold by massaging his legs and feet, a mixed feeling of ecstasy and agony; meanwhile, help was being organized to carry him farther down. But yet another obstacle awaited him: a terrifically steep gorge, where the raging waters cut their way through vertical cliffs. Treading with utmost precaution, his saviors managed to carry him through these hellish gates. Then the valley became far wider, with fruit trees and orchards, a beautiful vision. Diamirai was a bigger village, with more people willing to help; he was fed and taken in by a farmer for the night. The hallucinations were gone now, and the air was full of oxygen at an altitude of roughly 1,500 meters (5,000 feet); this brought the urgency of his grave foot injuries to the fore: He desperately needed to make it to a big town, the closest being Gilgit. Even local folks were taking pity on him, realizing that he was close to fading away. By then, he was sick with dysentery, and looking skeletal—a shadow of a man, incapable of standing up or walking. The only way he could be taken any farther would be on a stretcher, which he built after unsuccessfully attempting to convey the idea to his minders. A group took him thus, down to the confluence of the Diamir Gah with the mighty Indus, on the Karakoram Highway, within reach of civilization.

At this point, accounts in *Free Spirit* and *The Naked Mountain* differ: In the former, he indicates that the folks helping him dropped him off at the Bunar bridge, were he waited alone for a vehicle going to Gilgit. In the longer version, the porters stayed with him while he drank dirty water in an effort to combat the dangerous dehydration stemming from dysentery. In any event, after some time, a jeep going south, away from Gilgit, passed by, confirming that vehicles did travel the lonely road. A few hours later, the same jeep came back and stopped as Reinhold's porters shouted for help. The military men from the vehicle addressed him in English, enquiring about his identity and whereabouts. A recounting of the salient points of his odyssey left his new minders dubious, but they took him to their barracks, where he ate again and washed.

He then met the Pakistani officer's wife and "two exceptionally beautiful daughters." Afterwards, he told his saga once more, this time with the help of a map. His amazing tale of survival was heard with a combination of respect and doubt. From there, he was transferred and continued on toward Gilgit; the truck driver struck up a brief conversation: "'Well, you say, you are coming from Nanga Parbat?' asked the driver, after a while. 'Yes,' I reply. 'Strange. How can it be possible? Your Base Camp—isn't it on the other side of the mountain?' 'Yes. But I came down the Diamir side.' 'I heard on the radio that two men died there.' 'I am one of them.'"

Some 20 miles from Gilgit, a landslide blocked the road. The driver turned to take Reinhold to a hostel, approximately a mile away, for the night. He was lying on a stretcher, gaunt, sick, looking dreadful; a few people were standing by. The sound of a car broke the calm of the night. Two strangers were coming in: a man and a woman. The man made his way to the stretcher, probably intrigued by the scene; in hesitant shock he recognized the shadow on the litter. Without a word, he gently stroked Reinhold's arm. Herrligkoffer, most implausibly, had reunited with him; this was an astounding turn of events! The woman turned out to be Alex, Alice von Hobe. At Reinhold's request, she carefully removed his boots, revealing the bloody organic mess of his feet. Thus far, he had not talked to anyone about Günther's fate; even as he was about to tell the expedition leader, Herrligkoffer told him that the only thing of importance at this time was his own recovery. While he had been careful with the Pakistani military, the weight of Günther's passing bore heavily on his soul, and he desperately wanted to tell their story; the expedition leadership, however, clearly preferred to focus on the repatriation of the team.

After the main road had been cleared, he was finally taken to Gilgit, where he could be properly cared for. This was where he was reunited with the other expedition members, in a sad and moving moment. The activities at base camp, during his Diamir descent, which thus far had been a mystery, were slowly coming to the fore. Although a completely logical presentation of the multitude of deadly mistakes and fatal errors committed during this first ascent of the Rupal Face of Nanga Parbat is perhaps impossible, one would hope to remove some of the mystery shrouding the enterprise in an effort to understand what really occurred: The Naked Mountain requires nothing less than the naked truth. Before continuing, let us briefly relate the long recovery process that Reinhold had to go through.

The team was flown by the Pakistani military to Rawalpindi in a large Hercules helicopter, giving them a last view of Nanga Parbat, soaring high above all neighboring peaks. Reinhold was infinitely melancholy, deeply saddened by the amazing view. Herrligkoffer sat quietly next to him. They both had lost a brother on that mountain. The impossibility to communicate verbally with Herrligkoffer, however, was becoming increasingly disconcerting, perhaps even alienating to Reinhold: "Were we like two autistics, who had similar experiences, but different recollections?" Reinhold concludes: "We had become complete strangers."

In Rawalpindi, he received a letter addressed to both Günther and him, a sad reminder that loved ones did not yet know the unbearable news. It was later, on July 18, that a memorial mass was held for Günther at St. Peter's Church in Villnöss. Reinhold noted, perhaps bitterly, that neither Herrligkoffer nor Kuen attended. A few weeks after the dramatic reunion in Pakistan, he was admitted to the Innsbruck University clinic, under the care of Professor Flora, a vascular specialist. Amputations had to be performed; he lost toes one to four on his left foot and on his right, the first and second toes were partially removed. Fortunately, his fingers were recovering well, and were spared. After six long weeks, he was discharged: "When I left the clinic I was a cripple." In the end, it took him a year to get to the point where he could run and climb "properly" again.

The Nanga Parbat expedition had profoundly changed Reinhold Messner and his life; he became what he called a "sort of freelance alpinist." He also described his lifestyle by noting that, "Adventurer is not a profession, rather a condition." He went on to become the preeminent mountaineer of his time, becoming the first man to climb all fourteen summits above 8,000 meters without supplemental oxygen, some solo, among many other impressive achievements that give him a singular and distinguished position in the climbing world.

The rather dramatic fate of the other protagonists is encapsulated by Reinhold in the following passage from *The Naked Mountain*:

Peter Scholz, the warm-hearted Munich man, died a short while later on the Peuterey Ridge on Mont Blanc. Felix Kuen went to Mount Everest with Herrligkoffer in 1972. In 1974 he took his own life. No one knows why. Werner Heim also went on to the 1972 Everest expedition. In 1986 he had a bad fall in the Karwendel, broke his back and was paralyzed. Wolfi Bitterling also suffered serious disabilities after an accident. After the arguments surrounding the 1970 Nanga Parbat Expedition, Karl Maria Herrligkoffer emerged victorious and went on to organize several further expeditions: to Mount Everest, Kanch, K2, and again to Nanga Parbat. He died in 1991 in Munich, at the age of 75, without ever having reached any of the highest summits of the Himalaya. In Germany, he came to symbolize Himalayan mountaineering. Michl Anderl, Gerd Mändl, and Hermann Kühn are also dead now. Some of the 1970 team I have lost contact with;

others I meet on a regular basis, amongst them Jürgen Winkler, Gerd Baur, Elmar Raab, and Peter Vogler. Hans Saler is still on his travels, usually somewhere in South America. He has found his peace and his answers in a lifetime of travelling the world.

We now turn our attention to the long-standing controversy that began during the 1970 expedition, and continues in one form or another to this day. It bears noting that the very structure of *The Naked Mountain*, Reinhold's own detailed account of the events on Nanga Parbat in 1970, clearly implies a deep conviction that the expedition leadership is at the very least partially to blame for Günther's death. A substantial initial part of the book is devoted to showing how Herrligkoffer treated Hermann Buhl quite unfairly in 1953; then, as a repetition of those happenings in 1953, Reinhold proceeds to show that the same inept leadership governed the 1970 expedition, this time with tragic consequences. As mentioned earlier, the tragedy on Nanga Parbat resulted from a number of concatenating factors: a series of misunderstandings, misjudgments, and errors—managerial, technical, and strategic. It serves equanimity and verity to accept that these mistakes came from all sides; in order to convey this precept as much as possible, we choose to formulate some critical elements in the form of questions, which are interspersed with quotes from some of the key protagonists.

Important questions center around a series of issues, beginning with the miscommunication between the high camps and base camp. Indeed, the manner of, and personnel involved in, the summit push were clearly predicated on the weather forecast, which was transmitted by the red flare indicating bad weather, putting events in motion. It turned out that the forecast was actually for good weather; a blue rocket should have been fired. Herrligkoffer describes the mistake: "In accordance with the weather report received, Michl Anderl fired off a rocket with a blue seal around it. We were not a little shocked to see a red signal flare rising into the sky." Moreover, it appears that there were no blue flares left, so base camp could not fire blue rockets in an attempt to correct the error.

Reinhold then decided that, according to his agreement with the expedition leadership, he would try the climb to the summit alone. This explains why he did not take a rope; however, it brings up an immediate question: How was he going to descend? The upper part of the Merkl Couloir is very steep, making it difficult to ascend, and nearly impossible to climb down. Was he counting on having fixed ropes set up by Günther and Baur by the time he came down?

Günther committed the next crucial mistake—not because he chose to follow Reinhold, although that was a deviation from the plan, but because of the pace he had to use to do so. By the time he caught up with his brother, he had most likely expended too much energy, so that at the descent, he became far more tired than Reinhold, and highly impaired by altitude. This led directly to his refusal to go down the Rupal Face. Because they both soloed key parts of the Couloir, neither brought a rope; at the same time, no fixed ropes were installed, making the descent extremely dangerous, especially for the exhausted pair after they summited. By contrast, the next day, Kuen and Scholz were able to descend, as a rope, without major difficulties.

Timing was also a key contributor to the debacle: The rule of thumb is that one descends about twice as fast as one climbs, unless the climbing is highly technical. If one leaves high camp at, say, 2:00 a.m., and must be back by sundown, at 8:00 p.m., for example, one would take the total time, eighteen hours in this case, and divide it by three to obtain three six-hour intervals. Then two of these should be devoted to climbing, summiting around 2:00 p.m., and arriving back at high camp six hours later, at the desired 8:00 p.m. The Messner brothers summited very late, which basically condemned them to a very hazardous bivouac. They should have turned around, forgoing the summit. Of course, the enormous investment of time, energy, and commitment to climb a 5-mile-high peak often carries climbers well beyond the "comfort" zone, and some would argue that risks must be taken to break limits.

Finally, as explained earlier, the idea of climbing down the Diamir flank was fraught with the potential for disaster: First, the gentle-looking Diamir slopes on the upper flank quickly give place to precipitous seracs and icefalls and steep rock cliffs; next, navigation in this unknown terrain is extremely hard; third, the brothers did not have any of the appropriate food, liquid, or equipment for a prolonged trek down into terra incognita; and finally, should they have been successful, as Reinhold was, they would have had no way to communicate with base camp, and would have been tens of miles away, surrounded by nearly impassable mountains. Herrligkoffer summarized these facts as follows: "The Messners blatantly broke the number-one rule, never to indulge in extravagances." However, much blame lies on the side of the expedition leadership, and its official summit team. The rocket problem has already been presented; perhaps, during that last radio transmission with Reinhold, Herrligkoffer did not verify what type of flare was available, thus accidentally leading to this important miscommunication.

The episode with Reinhold desperately calling for help while Kuen and Scholz ascended the Merkl Couloir is bizarre and dramatic; many strange occurrences happened in a relatively short time span. The atmospheric conditions and the altitude may explain away some of these, as noted earlier, but others are extremely baroque. The fact that Kuen and Scholz, carried upward by their fever for the summit, seemed to be in complete denial regarding the obvious dire conditions of the Messner brothers after bivouacking at such high altitude is a case in point. The fact that the brothers did not have a rope reinforces that point; nevertheless, the summit team continued, unfazed.

It is true that climbers are often so incapacitated at extreme altitude that rescues are extremely difficult, but every effort should have been made to have an actual meeting between Kuen, Scholz, and Reinhold, perhaps at the top of the Merkl Couloir, so that the situation could have been made clear. Instead, in the *Bunte Illustrierte* magazine, Kuen is quoted thus: "I heard a shout for help in the 500-meter-long Merkl Couloir. When I stood up on top of the ridge at 11 o'clock I could see Reinhold 80 meters above us, and I asked him what had happened. He replied that they had called for help between 6 and 9 o'clock because Günther was suffering badly from altitude sickness, and did not dare to go down the fixed ropes of the Merkl Couloir. Reinhold asked us for a rope. We had already deposited our spare rope at the resting spot above the ridge, however. I suggested that he wait for us to come back."

The discrepancies are discouraging and, perhaps, telling: First, it appears from Kuen's report that the communication was excellent, which is highly unlikely and quite contrary to Reinhold's recollection; next, it is quite improbable that Günther, an experienced climber, would have been worried about the fixed ropes, where one can tie in with a carabiner. He was probably afraid of descending the Couloir unroped; in fact, they would not have needed to rope up if fixed ropes were set up, and that goes for Kuen and Scholz as well. Then there is the infamous "okay": Why did Reinhold use that word, in a context where Günther was dangerously sick and feeble? He meant, as he has explained, that everything else was okay, perhaps as a way to closely define their predicament. In any event, with only partial sentences going back and forth, and even less understood, this word reassured Kuen and Scholz, and further cemented their will to summit and let the Messner brothers, who were okay, figure out their way down.

Once the bothers were committed to descending the Diamir flank, there was no way they could have crossed back to the Rupal Face; they simply had used too much energy to summit, then bivouac. Going down, especially in view of Günther's acute altitude sickness, was the right thing to do at that point. Reinhold noted that, "Karl makes sure the slopes to the left of the Rupal Face are searched, and justifies his stance by reiterating that Günther was not fit to summit: 'I had my reasons for not lining Günther up for the summit.'" This is a justification a posteriori; therefore, it does not bring much new information, simply the fact that Herrligkoffer was attempting to protect his reputation at the expense of Günther, who had died.

Virulent comments arose after the brothers' odyssey, culminating with the mystery of Günther's death, and have continued ever since. While the sum total of these would fill many volumes, it is interesting to present the main lines of argumentation, and to see how they hold, some forty-five years later. One of the most bizarre notions put forth was the idea that the brothers had planned a traverse of Nanga Parbat all along. Why would they be so poorly prepared and equipped? How did they plan to reunite with the expedition, many tens of miles away? Would they actually risk being stranded, just for the sake of secrecy? Finally, if the expedition members were convinced that this was, in fact, what had happened, why would they not alert the Pakistani army?

A number of documents exist that underscore the type of inflaming arguments feeding the controversy, some of them quite valid, while others are simply beyond the pale. For our illustrative purposes, it will suffice to reproduce a slightly edited version of Tom Dauer's "One Truth and Another," and to introduce comments where appropriate:

> *In 1970 Reinhold and Günther Messner stood on the summit of Nanga Parbat. Only Reinhold returned from the mountain. What happened back then? Only Reinhold knows. Why do people keep asking him about it? That is something he does not want to understand. Climbing high mountains broadens horizons, or so climbers say. When you return to the valleys, they say, you become more relaxed, perhaps even chastened. Reinhold Messner does not say it. No wonder, because when he is not on a mountain, he regularly quarrels; especially with people with whom he has just shared success or failure, happiness or sorrow. And he preferably does so in public.*

Here, after a few general comments, the author makes the assertion that Reinhold is not a team player; although that may well be true, it does not serve any other purpose than to cast him in a negative light at the very onset of the piece. As mentioned earlier, we prefer to remain as neutral as possible, so that the truth may be distinguished from the obvious sociopolitical intrigue surrounding the whole Rupal Face first ascent. Dauer continues:

> *This summer [in 2003], a public debate raged . . . about what happened during the Nanga Parbat expedition of 1970. It was a debate that had smoldered unnoticed, occasionally thrown sparks, and then died down again. Until Reinhold Messner himself poured a huge pan of oil into the fire; during a presentation of a new biography of Karl Maria Herrligkoffer, leader of the 1970 Nanga Parbat expedition, he said: "And I am saying today that it wasn't a mistake by Herrligkoffer, it was a mistake by the expedition members, not to go to the Diamir*

valley. Some of them, older than me, wouldn't have minded if the two Messners hadn't returned, and that is the tragedy." Naturally, Messner's former expedition colleagues felt attacked, insulted, hurt. Since then, they defended themselves against the accusation that they had refused to help the Messner brothers after their summit bid.

Most of the contents of this passage appear to indicate that, although the Nanga Parbat controversy had never really gone away, it was Reinhold who reignited it, thus providing license for those on the other side of the debate to deploy the potent counterattacks that follow.

In fact, none of them knew where Reinhold and Günther Messner had gone after June 27th, 1970, the day of their successful ascent of the 15,000-foot Rupal Face, Nanga Parbat's southern flank. Between June 28th, when Reinhold was last seen, and July 3rd, when Reinhold met again with the expedition down in the valley (on the other side of the mountain), they had no way of knowing. Though they suspected that the Messner brothers had descended the Diamir Face, the other side of the mountain, they would not have got there in time anyway— they were still on the Rupal Face when, as it became known afterwards, Reinhold fought his way down the Diamir Valley towards civilization. For the others, there remained only anxiety and fear.

Although factually true, this line of reasoning is not sensible. The brothers were missing at extreme altitude, pure and simple; their lives were clearly in grave danger. At a minimum, while searching the Rupal Face, which the expedition did, they could have alerted the Pakistani authorities of the possibility that the brothers were lost on the Diamir flank; a simple helicopter search might have located them quickly, and even dropped food and supplies for the stranded climbers, either at their location, or below, if their altitude was still too high.

Reinhold acknowledges this sort of concern, albeit with a shrug. "Pathetic kitsch," he says, is this talk of mountain camaraderie (Berg-kameradschaft); "hypocritical mountain-romantics." It possesses no virtue to him, so that is why he cannot understand how deeply he hurt his former comrades with the aforementioned quote. How much salt did he rub into open wounds when he claimed in the Schweizer Tages-Anzeiger/Magazin, *on October 10th, 2002: "All my colleagues from the expedition wish I was dead"?*

The disappearance certainly caused great pressure and distress to the other expedition members; there is no doubt about that fact. Therefore, it is entirely possible that the folks at base camp and higher on the mountain resented being put in such a situation by a couple of "inexperienced" climbers. Here, "inexperienced" describes the Messner brothers' Himalayan skills. The reaction of those climbers and leaders to this pressure, however, appears to have been entirely inappropriate in view of the severity of the actual situation. It seems that, implicitly or tacitly, the brothers were being punished for deviating from the normal course of operation by simply ignoring their predicament, which is tantamount to criminal negligence. Another possibility is that they may have thought both had died almost right away; but, crucially, they did not know this for certain, thus, negligence withstands. A third explanation would have the expedition members completely convinced that the brothers had died while descending the Rupal Face by an alternative route, diligently searching that face while dismantling the camps along their route, and simply not finding them. If such a narrative dominated, the actions of the team would have been fairly appropriate. We know, however, that Kuen and Scholz observed Reinhold atop the ridge delineating the boundary between the Rupal and Diamir flanks, and that they reckoned that Günther would not dare to descend the Merkl Couloir on the Rupal Face. It was therefore clear that both descent routes were possible. Although it is understandable that the expedition did not possess the wherewithal to conduct a search-and-rescue operation on the Diamir flank, a simple radio call from base camp would have alerted local authorities, with potential lifesaving results.

Half a year later, Reinhold Messner is trying to put this quotation into perspective. He had "said it that way, but did not think it that way." In other words, he was completely misunderstood again. He who reads Reinhold Messner should read his writings the way Reinhold Messner meant them—or could have meant them—because his writings have a novel-like quality, even if they are presented as documentaries. Reinhold Messner sells this as "hidden meaning." In reality, he launches oral bombshells and then shuts his eyes and ears off to the effects of the explosions.

Postulating Reinhold as a self-proclaimed victim and quasi-novelist, and using that tenet as proof that his writing style takes so much license as to fully deviate from the truth, for the sake of narrative coherence, is a convenient device to simply dismiss his viewpoint. Here, we choose to consider that arguments made by both sides are primarily true, although, as with all things human, they can be significantly warped through the lens of internal feelings and conflicted emotions.

Messner claims he had "always tried to tell my stories straight." In reality, he is a master of suggestion and in using the ambiguity of words. In his book, The Naked Mountain, *he writes about his thoughts during the descent of the Diamir Face: "Campfires at Base Camp. It is nighttime. Like shadows people stand around the fire. Mood is subdued. No, we don't try to imagine what the others do." An expert knows: The other climbers aren't in Base Camp, but at altitudes between 16,500 and 23,000 feet on the Rupal Face. They know nothing about the Messners' predicament; they are unable to help. Yet an uninformed reader will ask: Why does the rest of the team not help the Messners?*

The exact quote is: "Down at Base Camp they would be standing around the campfire, shadowy figures in the night. The mood would be subdued, I imagined. We did not waste much time trying to imagine what the others would be doing, however." Although this paragraph does show Reinhold's style, is it truly perniciously suggestive, as argued? Factually, of course, some expedition members were at base camp; he also indicates that he imagines a subdued, restrained, or downcast mood, thus clearly indicating the subjunctive aspect of his narrative at that point. In fact, just a few pages later, he recounts that, "Meanwhile, over at Base Camp they were getting very concerned." This directly reflects the facts, as agreed-upon by all involved, and would be contradictory, with a subtle undercurrent of suggested apathy from the expedition members with respect to the dire situation.

Members of the 1970 expedition, like Gerhard Baur, who first saw Reinhold and then Günther setting off from Camp V for the summit, see their reputation at stake due to such (mis-) representations and the media presence of Reinhold Messner. They know that he plays the media game like no other—and that he constantly appears in magazines and talk shows. After the presentation of the Herrligkoffer biography, Baur started critically reviewing Reinhold Messner's accounts of the 1970 Nanga Parbat expedition. "I felt that a story was being fabricated," says Baur. The accusation of negligence, of refusing help—the worst that can be said about a mountaineer—is something he is unwilling to accept. Especially as he has reason to believe that Messner has hidden part of the truth from the public for 33 years.

Naturally, most climbers would be offended if accused of criminal negligence; there is no question that, especially from a public perspective, no one wants to be portrayed as deserting stranded fellow climbers, neglecting to help where they could. Returning to the notion that the Pakistani authorities could have been contacted about the possible whereabouts of the Messner brothers on the Diamir flank, that responsibility would have squarely fallen on the expedition leadership. Therefore, the other climbers may well feel that they did what they could on the Rupal Face, and did not abandon their fellow climbers. Reinhold's accusation was therefore misplaced; he might simply have been quite gauche in trying to deflect blame from Herrligkoffer at an event designed to celebrate the Munich doctor. He certainly should not have added, in jest or otherwise, that the other expedition members wished him rhetorically "dead." The last sentence, on the other hand, is loaded with implications.

Baur sifts the evidence. He is not alone: Jürgen Winkler, photographer and climber during the 1970 expedition, uncovers inconsistencies in

Reinhold Messner's accounts. Hans Saler, an experienced climber now living in Chile, and Max von Kienlin, at the time a close acquaintance of Reinhold Messner, go a step further: They present their views in their own books—and publicly doubt that Günther Messner was killed in an ice avalanche at the foot of the Diamir Face. According to their hypothesis, Reinhold and Günther had separated near the summit; Günther descended the Rupal Face alone and presumably fell to his death.

On the one hand, as will become clearer in the following paragraphs, the abrupt falling-out between von Kienlin and Reinhold shortly after the 1970 events may have tainted the views expressed by the baron. Hans Saler, on the other hand, does not appear to have had specific reasons to dislike Reinhold. It is worthwhile, therefore, to examine the possibility put forth by those two members of the 1970 expedition. The first question would be the motivation for the two to separate: If Günther had decided to go down the Rupal Face, why would Reinhold want to descend, alone, on the Diamir flank? The notion of a preplanned traverse is hard to imagine for reasons already presented; could it be that Reinhold was afraid of going down unroped? Since we know that Günther climbed faster to catch up with Reinhold, all things being equal, it is more likely that he would be more tired, and one can infer that he would also have been more hesitant to climb down the most difficult terrain of the upper Merkl Couloir. Additionally, we also know that the expedition leadership considered Reinhold a superior climber to Günther, since Herrligkoffer had initially chosen Reinhold and Kuen for the summit-assault rope.

The next question is, Why would Reinhold hide that fact? And why would he go back to the Diamir flank to find Günther's body? Of course, it is now known that parts of the presumed body of Günther have been found on the Diamir glacier, in 2004, as reported in *National Geographic*: "From his castle redoubt in Italy's South Tyrol, Messner has now launched a fierce counterattack against his accusers, brandishing as evidence a leg bone he believes to be his brother's, and the DNA tests he says confirm that claim" (Roberts).

In this instance, it appears that logic and facts may well agree; however, the question is still worth asking: If Günther died on the Rupal Face, why would Reinhold Messner insist on locating his brother's icy tomb on the Diamir flank? Well, while a separation of the brothers near the summit would have been a substantial mistake, from a mountaineering logistical viewpoint, it also opens up the question of one climber abandoning a weaker one, with the caveat that, on the face of it, the stronger climber would presumably attempt to descend the harder Rupal Face. Given the pain and suffering endured by the brothers in Reinhold's account, the ethical benefits of having them together on the Diamir flank, versus separated, are somewhat meager, and would probably not justify an error or lie of such glaring proportions.

Of course, Messner fights against the fact that now another version of the events has appeared beside his own. "The truth is a suspicion that endures" wrote Spanish poet Rámon de Campoamor in the mid-1800s. A suspicion has been raised. Time will tell if it endures. In this case, the suspicion may have been thwarted by facts. Reinhold Messner accuses his former colleagues of organizing a "concerted action" against him, to make money at his expense. He fears for his reputation and integrity. For this reason, his lawyers sent the publishers of Saler and von Kienlin's books a letter (dated May 6, 2003—before the publication date), stating that "our client will not accept untruthful reporting and advised us, after review of the manuscript, to take legal action if necessary. . . ." At the time of this writing, the latter has already been attempted: By interim order, the district council of Hamburg prohibited von Kienlin to quote from his diary notes of a conversation with Reinhold Messner (after his descent to the Diamir Valley). Hans Saler is no longer allowed to claim that Messner's own ambition was in part responsible for the death of his brother. The order, however, does not concern copies of the books already sold or in stores. Both publishers lodged an appeal against the interim order.

For Reinhold Messner's former friends this development proves the futility of rational arguments in this case. Months earlier Hans Saler wrote in an open letter to Reinhold: "Your words are armors of self-glorification. You use them uncontrollably, launch attacks blindly. If one of the attacked defends himself, you laconically suspect—preferably in front of TV cameras—everybody were [sic] envious of your success. But you measure success by the standards of a noisy bazaar on which you proclaim wisdom that is miles away from your own behavior."

This type of legal maneuvering tends to raise public awareness, acting as a form of advertising, and may work to the financial benefits of all the authors; otherwise, it simply exemplifies the underlying bitterness surrounding the aftermath of the 1970 occurrence.

The debate about the events, agreements and decisions during the Nanga Parbat expedition has long since escalated to a nasty quarrel, in which factual and personal levels are no longer divided. But it is important to distinguish cause and effect. If this were a quarrel among children, one would point to Reinhold Messner and say, "He started it!" His former comrades could only react. They didn't do it to destroy the "Messner myth." This wouldn't be necessary anyway, because Reinhold Messner is doing it himself—by running amok verbally when he should have been unflappable; by regarding anything and anyone as enemy, because he can't accept criticism; by banning a team from "Bergauf-bergab" [regular TV production on climbing in Germany] from a press conference.

This is an interesting piece of rhetoric, in which the author begins the passage with equanimity, but launches a bitter verbal attack regarding the pitiful "Messner myth." Of course, this does not advance the quest for truth at all; it only operates as catharsis for the benefit of Reinhold's detractors.

In any case, the accusation [that] Messner had left his brother behind on the mountain isn't new. Already in December 1970, a few months after the expedition, leader Herrligkoffer suspected Reinhold could have "sacrificed his brother to his personal ambition."

This pronouncement by Herrligkoffer—a senior Himalayan expedition leader, certainly respected in some circles—about a young, up-and-coming mountaineer may well have been the crux of humiliation for Reinhold: After losing his brother and suffering a great deal, this short and eloquent comment might have reopened all the wounds left to fester after the expedition. Since the statement is vague, encompassing, and accusatory all at the same time, it is virtually impossible to disprove: Does it mean that Reinhold was prepared to kill his brother to summit? Does it mean that his ambition may have played a completely minimal role in the events? Asymptotically, we understand that all Himalayan climbers have some level of ambition; would we then explain any tragedy up in the thin air as the result of this equation involving ambition and sacrifice? It seems that the only way to disqualify the comment would be for Reinhold to have no ambition, to quit Himalayan climbing altogether.

Subsequently, Reinhold charged Herrligkoffer for involuntary manslaughter of Günther and negligence. The district council of Munich dropped the charge on March 14, 1972. At the time, his comrades Saler and von Kienlin supported Reinhold. The team stood unified against its leader. Today, Reinhold Messner has isolated himself with his accusations. He claims that Herrligkoffer's mistakes had been mistakes by the team. . . .

Against this stands the firm belief of his former comrades that Reinhold Messner had planned the traverse of Nanga Parbat all along. Gerhard Baur is convinced beyond doubt that this plan wasn't just a dream or half-baked idea. Messner had thought of the possibilities of a traverse already back home, and at Base Camp talked repeatedly of his idea. He had brought along a black-and-white picture of the Diamir Face and studied it carefully. Besides this, traverses of 8,000-meter peaks had been en vogue at the time.

If he had indeed dreamed of a traverse, his climbing down the Diamir flank would have been uncharacteristically ill-prepared. Before and after the Nanga Parbat Rupal Face expedition, he had been a consistently good planner, logistically and strategically. The last comment, about the fashionable character of traversing high Himalayan peaks in 1970, does not strike one as a strong motivation, especially in view of the cost to the Messners: death and amputation.

Reinhold Messner doesn't want to hear about it. There had been talk about a traverse, but no plan. "Memory deceives us all," is his comment on Baur's belief. It is true that neither the authors von Kienlin and Saler nor the doubters Baur and Winkler had been present when the Messner brothers were fighting for their lives. But their doubts about Reinhold Messner's version of the events are based on rational arguments. Reinhold Messner just brushes them away—without being able to disprove them completely.

This becomes evident in the debate about a diary entry by von Kienlin, allegedly based on conversations between him and Reinhold Messner after July 3, 1970. Von Kienlin writes, in essence, [that] Reinhold Messner had said to him that he doesn't know where his brother was. Messner regards this diary entry as "a blatant hoax, because I never told all of this to Herr von Kienlin." Von Kienlin's alleged reason: late revenge for the love affair Reinhold Messner had with von Kienlin's wife after Nanga Parbat. But why didn't von Kienlin take revenge 33 years earlier? And everyone noticed Reinhold Messner's reaction upon meeting with his expedition after the odyssey. His cries, "Where is Günther?" were heard by several members. Yet only he could have known where his brother was. Today, Reinhold Messner interprets his cries as expression of his continuing search for his brother. During the descent he had gone into a state of schizophrenia. Until today he kept asking himself, "Where did the hallucinations start, where could Günther have gone?"

A number of points can be made about this passage: First, disproving hypotheticals can be quite difficult, especially since Reinhold is the sole witness to the events under discussion. Cross-checking the consistency of his account is probably more worthwhile than attempting to disprove any and all alternative versions; von Kienlin's diary entry may simply reflect the fact that Messner never precisely located Günther's body (it may mean more, but we are back to Reinhold's testimony). Finally, the fact that a distraught Reinhold would lament about his brother's whereabouts and death questioningly is not particularly telling in terms of the circumstances of Günther's passing; rather, it underlines the ragged state of Reinhold's mind.

If true, Reinhold is the only, but also a bad, witness of himself. In fact, to this day he formulates differing accounts of the ice avalanche that allegedly killed his brother at the foot of the Diamir Face. In his latest book, he claims, "I have always regarded the avalanche death of my brother as a possibility, not as proven fact. I wasn't there when he died. . . . Yes, the avalanche was the most likely cause of death. To this day, there is no other answer." In contrast, he describes the event in his book Alle meine Gipfel *[1982, revised edition 2001—note the latter date], "I stumbled ahead to find a way through the dangerous séracs, when an avalanche crashed down behind me. Günther had disappeared, buried under tons of ice."*

Despite his own lapses of memory, Reinhold Messner regards the difference between his version and the hypothesis of his former friends as that between experience and fiction. But is "experience" more to be believed if one can't tell the circumstances of that experience? And where does the provability and consistency of an experience remain if his version changes from account to account? Dramatic events, especially when witnessed under extreme distress, may possess both the quality of a deeply imprinted memory, and a fleeting, evolving character; people are, in fact, notoriously unreliable witnesses, in at least two fundamental ways: First, the accounts of different witnesses of the same event often display a range of discrepancies, from simple details to important, salient facts; second, a given witness's recalling may evolve over time, sometimes quite significantly. No sinister motive is at play here, simply basic human psychology. Closely related is the phenomenon of false or implanted memories, where persons susceptible to being influenced under the guidance of an authority, generally a psychiatrist, are known to develop strong recollections of events that never took place, ultimately acquiring false memories.

Finally, "cryptomnesia occurs when a forgotten memory returns without it being recognized as such by the subject, who believes it is something new and original. It is a memory bias whereby a person may falsely recall generating a thought, an idea, a song, or a joke, not deliberately engaging in plagiarism but rather experiencing a memory as if it were a new inspiration." Furthermore, "The idea that is reproduced could be another's idea, or one's own from a previous time. B. F. Skinner describes his own experience of self-plagiarism: 'One of the most disheartening experiences of old age is discovering that a point you just made—so significant, so beautifully expressed—was made by you in something you published long ago'" ("Cryptomnesia").

Jürgen Winkler, who still sought eye-to-eye conversation with Reinhold Messner at the beginning of the debate, researched various contradictions in Messner's public statements. Yet his conclusions don't make him participating in speculations about what really happened up there on Nanga Parbat. "I don't propose any hypotheses." It is sufficient to let the facts speak for themselves. Facts that prompt Winkler to conclude, "I don't want to have anything to do with Reinhold Messner anymore. I can't believe this person anything [sic]."

Retaliation between antagonists continued:

In a fax sent to several climbing magazines, Reinhold Messner dubbed the publication of the debate surrounding the Nanga Parbat expedition "psychic torture." Strong words, especially when you consider that Messner is largely unscrupulous himself. During the debate, he became chairman of the Deutsches Institut für Auslandsforschung/Prof. Herrligkoffer-Stiftung. *His secretary and his ex-wife got a seat and vote in the committee of the foundation. The foundation was established in 1953 to raise funds for German mountaineering expeditions to the greater ranges. Its founder was the same Karl Maria Herrligkoffer, who led the 1970 expedition and who was subsequently, even beyond his death in 1991, attacked by Reinhold Messner.*

Returning to the basic aftermath of the 1970 expedition, namely death and amputation for the Messner brothers, and assuming for the time being that the events described in *The Naked Mountain* are reasonably close to the truth, it would actually be very painful for Reinhold to endure a constant barrage of insinuations about the facts surrounding Günther's death. It seems that, absent a clear contradiction in Reinhold's narrative, he should be given the benefit of the doubt. In view of this, the passage above shows how a tragic event evolved into a terribly unfortunate political battle.

The politico-legal minutiae go on:

Prior to the publication of von Kienlin and Saler's book, Professor Ludwig Delp, head of the committee, cited the expedition contract from 1970. According to the contract, "publications regarding the expedition require the consent of the Institute." This was promised under the condition that the respective manuscript "represents a faithful account of the events in the spirit of mountaineering fraternity." This was, of course, unacceptable to von Kienlin and Saler. Saler's publisher answered accordingly, "Keeping in mind the public right for and demand of information, we find it questionable that an institution, headed by Reinhold Messner, asks for 'a faithful account' of events, in the context of which Reinhold Messner publicly voices incredible accusations against other expedition members."

A sideline, maybe. But such tactics show the depth of the wounds Günther's death inflicted in all participants. On one hand, there is Reinhold Messner, who accuses his former partners of "meanness." On the other hand are those climbers who followed Messner's career over decades. They believe that there is more than just one truth to the climb and tragedy of fate that sowed the seed for Messner's popularity back in 1970.

Perhaps an underlying taint of envy may be detected in the motivation of Reinhold's detractors, who describe his privileged relationship with the media and his political positioning within the German-speaking mountaineering community, a continuation of his ambition, as it were, as negatives. It seems that if he has sacrificed to his ambition, it is diplomacy and friendship that have gone by the wayside, rather than family. In some sense, Reinhold has "bulldozed" his way to the top politically, much as he has blazed impressive trails to the summits of the 8,000-meter peaks. As a result, a tragic opening on Nanga Parbat to climbing 5 vertical miles above sea level, has become a Sisyphean torture: Every time a modicum of closure appears to be reached, a new wound opens up, followed by the aforementioned tortuous politico-legal processes in the court of public opinion.

The discussion by Tom Dauer then waxes philosophical:

> *Truth has become questionable since post-modern reflection of the "conditions of perception and knowledge" has even affected the moun-taineering world. Before that, word of the participant was trusted without exception. Perhaps there will never be a conclusive answer, any kind of proof for one truth or another. Awkwardness will remain. Because Reinhold Messner's banal statement that there are "as many truths to the Nanga Parbat expedition as there are members" can't bring any consolation in the face of death; neither to him, nor to every other member.*

After this lengthy initial commentary, focused mostly on the various public actions taken by Nanga Parbat 1970 protagonists, Dauer provides a comparison of the different versions of events. He begins with a summary of Reinhold's numerous public pronouncements on the matter, including sources where available:

> *"Only I know what happened at the summit, I remain the sole wit-ness" (Interview,* Stern, *3/7/2002).*
> *In a summary of Messner's accounts, the following seems to have happened: Around 2 p.m. on June 26, 1970, Reinhold Messner and expedition leader Karl Maria Herrligkoffer agree via radio on a solo bid for the summit by R. M. in case of bad weather the following day. At 8 p.m.—Reinhold and Günther Messner, and Gerhard Baur, are on their way to the single tent of Camp V (7,350 m)—a red rocket is*

fired from Base Camp, the agreed sign for bad weather. But the red rocket was a mistake—it was fired despite a good forecast.

At 2 a.m. on June 27, Reinhold prepares for the summit attempt. He leaves Günther and Gerhard Baur while it is still dark. Reinhold climbs the Merkl Gully. At its end (where it becomes vertical), he leaves it over a ramp on the right, leading to easier ground. His brother Günther, who follows him spontaneously a few hours later, catches up to him at about this point. Together they traverse right around the South Shoulder (8,042 m), reach the notch between South Shoulder and summit ridge, and follow the latter to the main summit (8,125 m). They reach it at 5 p.m.

After an hour Reinhold and Günther start their descent. Günther is weakened, lags behind. He voices his fear of descending the Rupal Face (way of ascent). Reinhold agrees with reluctance to descend from the notch between South Shoulder and summit to the Merkl Notch (at the exit from the vertical top of the Merkl Gully), where they bivouac. The following morning there is a shouting exchange between Reinhold and Felix Kuen (who, with Peter Scholz, is about to make the second ascent). Kuen doesn't seem to recognize the Messners' predicament and continues towards the summit.

The brothers are now forced to descend the Diamir Face. After a second bivouac they reach the base of the wall. To reconnoiter the way, Reinhold is one to two hours ahead of Günther—sometimes losing sight of him. After waiting for some time below the glacier, Reinhold returns to search for his brother. He can't find him. Reinhold reports later that Günther was probably buried in an ice avalanche.

This is in line with Messner's *Naked Mountain*; the only new point is that the time between the brothers, when they are separated at the bottom of the Mummery Spur, is now quantified: one to two hours.

The next section is devoted to the unfolding of events, according to Saler and von Kienlin:

"When I piece together all the facts chronologically, they fit the following version best" (Saler, 148). "What decision was really made [at the

summit]? There is only one logical, plausible, very probable solution"
(von Kienlin, 202). Leaving aside some differences in detail, Max
von Kienlin and Hans Saler present the following version: When
Reinhold and Günther start their descent from the summit, Gün-
ther—exhausted, but not suffering from altitude sickness—decides to
go down the known way via the Rupal Face. He counts on other expe-
dition members having fixed the Merkl Gully, thus facilitating the
descent. The brothers separate. Reinhold descends to the Merkl Notch.
After his bivvy, on the morning of June 28, he looks down the Rupal
Face with the hope of seeing Günther, or traces of him. Without success.
At 6 a.m. he starts shouting for Günther. 8 a.m., 9 a.m. passes [sic].
No trace of Günther, who should long since have been on the way
down. Instead, he sees Felix Kuen and Peter Scholz ascending from
Camp V, separated by c. 100 feet of rope.

Around 10 a.m. Reinhold has his exchange with Kuen. Now he
knows that they hadn't met Günther. According to Kuen, Reinhold
advises him and Scholz to circumvent the South Shoulder on the left,
this being the easier option. Perhaps Reinhold hopes they may find
Günther there. He tells Kuen of his intention to descend the Diamir
Face: he can't help his brother no more [sic]. Then he starts down. Five
days later, on July 3, he meets the expedition team. Where Günther
died remains unknown.

In order to analyze the merits of the alternative version summarized
above, additional information is needed—namely, the various hints and
clues that logically guided both Saler and von Kienlin toward this conclusion. Tom Dauer's comments on these "key pitches" at the exit of the
"Merkl Gully" are particularly important in this respect:

Did Reinhold Messner know that the terrain between the Merkl
Notch and the point where he, Günther, and later, Kuen and Scholz,
traversed out of the Merkl Gully was unclimbable? Could he have seen
this on the way up? If the answer is "yes," his reasoning that he and
Günther had descended to the Merkl Notch in order to traverse back
into the Merkl Gully is questionable. Equally questionable would be

*his hope of Kuen and Scholz coming to their aid. "I will give up . . .
but there is just one other possibility, a last way out; a down sloping
ramp, slanting up to the right. . . . I must be close to 7,800 m. To the
left, above me, I can see a notch. The end of the Merkl Gully? So I am
on top soon, on top of the gully"* (Naked Mountain, *191f.*). *"In the
upper part of the Merkl Gully I traverse via a ramp to the right, onto
the ice fields. Below the South Shoulder. The upper part of the gully is
above me to the left. But that terrain is of no interest to me. My way
is to the right"* (Weisse Einsamkeit, *35).*

The precise quote in *The Naked Mountain,* as listed in the reference section, reads, in its entirety: "I was about to give up and go back down to
Camp 5 when another possibility presented itself, a last chance, in the shape
of a sloping ramp leading up and right. It seemed to offer the only possibility, my last chance, if you like. The climbing was easier than I had thought—
Grade III perhaps—and the rock was only partly verglassed. Only the flatter
holds were full of snow and the ramp was long enough at two pitches not to
be missed on the way back down. This was it: the key to avoid the difficult
steep section in the Merkl Couloir. Suddenly I felt safe again and every bit
as sure as I would have felt on a route in the Alps. I must now be at about
7,800 m, I thought. To the left, high above me, I could just make out a notch
on the skyline—the end of the Merkl Couloir? I would soon be out of the
gully then. There was just one last steep section to do before I reached the
ramp that led across below the South Shoulder to the South-East Ridge."

Dauer continues: "Reinhold Messner's former comrades doubt that
an experienced mountaineer, climbing in unknown terrain, wouldn't scru-
tinize closely any possible way of ascent." In view of this, it is interesting
to quote Messner regarding his decision to climb down from his upper
point in the Merkl Couloir only to discover the slanting ramp discussed
previously: "At this altitude and with the clumsy, heavy boots I was wearing, such a steep pitch was clearly too dangerous, maybe even impossible.
At any rate, I would not be able to down-climb it. I had gone too high."
This clearly shows that the severity of the descent was on Messner's mind;
he also made mental notes, and remarked that the slanting traverse was
long enough not to be missed on the way down.

The subject of descending on the Rupal Face becomes the focus of Dauer's running comments:

How did Reinhold Messner judge the difficulties of the descent from the notch between South Shoulder and summit to the Merkl Notch? The decision to descend to the W to the Merkl Notch does only make sense if this possible way of descent was visible, as well as considerably easier than the known way of ascent from the end of the Merkl Gully. Notably, the latter was so easy that Kuen and Scholz cached their rope at the end of the Merkl Gully. Once at the Merkl Notch, the Messner brothers were only at the beginning of the difficulties of the descent. If they had gone down the Diamir side towards the Merkl Notch, despite the terrain being more difficult than the way of ascent, or invisible, this would speak for a planned traverse. "Günther . . . points with his ice axe to the right. Will he descend to the west? At first I don't understand his idea. To go down the Diamir side? . . . 'Here, to the west, it isn't easy either,' I say" (Naked Mountain, *201f.*).

The exact quote from *The Naked Mountain* reads as follows: "I stopped and waited at the col between the South Shoulder and the ridge. Günther arrived and pointed with his axe to the right. It looked like he wanted to descend to the west. At first, I did not understand what he was suggesting. Down the Diamir Face? I waved back, dismissing the idea out of hand. 'No, we can't do that,' I said. 'It's easier,' he countered. 'We have to go down the way we came,' I said, trying hard to hide my concerns. 'Too difficult,' said Günther. 'But we came up the Merkl Couloir.' 'I'm so tired.' 'We'll be even more tired tomorrow. We have to lose some height before it gets dark.' 'But not the way we came up. We have to find an easier route.' I did not insist. Perhaps I should have done."

Here, the discrepancies between the actual narrative from Reinhold and the transcript used by Tom Dauer are important, especially the fact that Reinhold does not dismiss a descent on the Diamir flank because of technical difficulties, but because they have no supplies nor equipment to traverse the mountain to that side. In fact, a cursory look at maps or satellite photos clearly shows that the Diamir flank *does* look considerably easier than the Rupal Face; as explained earlier, this is somewhat decep-tive, because the relatively gentle upper slopes are barred by seracs and ice cliffs further down to the west, and the connection to the upper Mum-mery Spur is difficult, especially in terms of route-finding.

Dauer continues:

"At the South Shoulder I look to the west. The way to the Merkl Notch is easy. The photo of the Rupal Face we took along suggests the pos-sibility of traversing back to the gully from there. . . . No details are discernible" (Weisse Einsamkeit, 36). *"No, from the South Shoul-der no one can see the Merkl Notch"* (Weisse Einsamkeit, 41). *In 1976, four Austrian mountaineers climbed on the Diamir side from a point a little below the Merkl Notch to the South Shoulder and sum-mit. Robert Schauer belayed his partner Hanns Schell over passages of up to Grade III of difficulty. According to Schauer, the descent to the Merkl Notch is not visible from the South Shoulder. "It goes down really steeply from there."*

At the risk of reiterating previous comments, the general logic for the Messner brothers' decision to separate and climb down via different routes should be reexamined. Essentially, all versions of events agree all the way to the summit, except for hidden intentions that are not within the pur-view of logical examination. The difference of physical states between the brothers on the summit clearly favors Reinhold: He was not catching up and climbed at his own pace; he was recognized as the stronger of the two, including by Herrligkoffer, who teamed Reinhold up with Kuen in his initial plans for the summit, and expressed doubts about Günther's abilities. Following the summit push from Camp 5, via the highly techni-cally demanding Merkl Couloir, would have taken a considerable amount of energy from the brothers; as a result, the climb down would present a very serious problem, especially on the steepest, unequipped parts of the Couloir, and without a rope to provide a measure of safety.

At that point, separation would provide no advantages whatsoever; in fact, even unroped, a team is stronger than individuals, and offers the pos-sibility that one climber could report on the other in case of an emergency.

The Messner brothers simply did not have the luxury of separating, much less for the sake of performing a traverse of the mountain under suicidal conditions. It is entirely possible that the much easier upper snow slopes of the Diamir flank would have appeared to offer a tempting alternative, especially after the bivouac under the ridge, and given the daunting terrain connecting the Merkl Notch to the upper parts of the Couloir.

The brothers felt trapped near the summit, high in the lethal zone, and tried to climb down as quickly as possible, on the easiest-looking terrain, reaching the Merkl Notch and realizing that they had missed the proper entrance point to descend the Rupal Face. Such seemingly small errors are considerably amplified by altitude and exhaustion. At that point they did not have enough energy to climb back up to the col below the South Shoulder and reconnect with the established route. They were also fearful of the extreme steepness of the terrain above Camp 5, especially without fixed ropes in the upper sections. The combination of these elements, along with Günther's overnight deterioration due to acute altitude sickness, pushed the brothers to the brink of their fateful decision to go down on the Diamir flank. The last precipitating factor was the deaf-and-dumb exchange between Reinhold and Kuen, which catalyzed the final verdict to head down to the west, where Günther would perish. Notions about better weather and other climbers equipping the route with fixed ropes were no longer relevant; they knew they would not survive a second bivouac at circa 7,900 meters. Going down on easy terrain solved many immediate problems, including altitude sickness, the absence of a rope, and a second bivouac in the death zone.

In fact, the somewhat moot question of additional team members equipping the route is discussed by Dauer as well:

*Did Reinhold and Günther Messner know that other expedition members would try a summit bid after them? If so, a descent to the Diamir side in spite of Gunther's weakness is hard to explain, as they could have counted on the help of their comrades in the Merkl Gully at the latest. "Where could we bivvy, I ask myself, and where can we be seen from the Merkl Gully?" (*Naked Mountain, *202).*
"Perhaps we could traverse back into the gully lower down, at the

Merkl Notch. Otherwise we'd have to ask for a rope. The others will fix the gully" (Naked Mountain, *202, quote attributed to Günther).* "But on this morning Felix Kuen and Peter Scholz climb the Merkl Gully. They should go for the summit, too. Behind them Werner Haim, Hans Saler, and Gerd Mändl, who equip the Merkl Gully with fixed ropes in order to facilitate the descent of exhausted parties coming down, including us. Günther and I couldn't know any of this" (*Weisse Einsamkeit, 37).*

Reinhold Messner claims that because of the mistakenly fired red rocket he assumed the weather to be turning bad soon and [that] nobody else would ascend. Von Kienlin and Saler disagree, saying it had been apparent that the weather would stay reasonable. An expedition climber would always trust his own observations more than a weather forecast (i.e., the red rocket). Saler: "Gerhard Baur later said that the Messners and he were very skeptical about the rocket, especially as the special weather forecast by Radio Peshawar had often been a lottery game" (Saler, 113). Even if Reinhold Messner hadn't known about the others' plan, it should have been logical to him that others would be in the Merkl Gully. Baur swears he'd been talking to Günther before the latter's solo bid about others coming up—so Günther had known. Saler: "Where else should the other climbers have been during good weather? At Camp IV, playing cards?" (Saler, 128).

The discussion regarding technical difficulties on the western descent and the possibility of having other team members setting up fixed ropes is described quite briefly in *The Naked Mountain*: "It was then that I remembered the red rocket. The bad weather would be coming in soon. We needed to get out of there, fast. I knew only that we had to get down, somewhere. Where could we bivouac, I asked myself, and where could we be seen from the Merkl Couloir? Günther still wanted to drop down to the right of the ridge. 'It is not easy down to the west either,' I said. 'But easier.' 'And tomorrow?' 'Maybe we could traverse back into the Couloir lower down, at the Merkl Gap. Otherwise we'll have to shout for a rope. The others will fix the Couloir.' We did not have a rope, since we both had set off soloing from Camp 5. It was looking bad."

The much-maligned episode where Reinhold and Kuen attempted to exchange information was reported by Dauer thus:

> *On the morning of June 28, 1970, Reinhold Messner gets in touch with Felix Kuen, who is climbing towards the summit with Peter Scholz. Between them and Messner, the terrain is vertical, unclimbable at this altitude. Conversation over the distance of 250 feet is difficult. "Did you get to the top?" asks Kuen. "Yes!" Indiscernible words follow, then Kuen's question, "Is everything alright with you?" "Yes, everything alright [sic]," answers Messner. Then he signals to Kuen that he will descend the other side of the mountain, and disappears behind the ridgeline. The question remains: why didn't he vehemently plead the others to come to his and his sick brother's help?*

Of course, Reinhold's version contradicts this notion that he was not desperate for help. To buttress his assertion, Dauer discusses the admittedly bizarre use of the word *okay* by Reinhold in an equally bizarre paragraph:

> *"His question, interpreted as 'Are you O.K.?' can I confirm. 'Yes, everything alright, Felix' I call back. As mutual reassurance. A question about our health can only be followed by a calming answer. Health in the death zone is a relative thing"* (Naked Mountain, 212). *"I signal 'everything O.K.' and descend on the opposite side. Why? Because I didn't want to force Kuen and Scholz into a life-threatening action"* (Weisse Einsamkeit, 23). *"I feel it. I mustn't force Felix into a deadly risk. A fall had meant a shock and the death of all four of us. That was the reason for my 'Yes, everything alright' in response to Felix's question, 'Is everything alright.' I couldn't have done anything else"* (Weisse Einsamkeit, 38).

Here, Reinhold puts forth a new reason for the use of the word *okay*; unfortunately, it does not clarify things very much. Further elaborating on the willingness by Kuen and Scholz to help, Dauer writes:

According to several witnesses there is no doubt that Kuen and Scholz would have helped the Messner brothers in case of an emergency, if this had been made clear to them. Saler quotes Kuen: "There was no word about help, no word about a rope, no word that Günther was ill. . . . We had helped, had climbed left around the South Shoulder and gone down to Reinhold and Günther from there. To imagine Peter and I wouldn't have done so is incredible. . . . Not only could we have helped—we would have helped!" (Saler, 140f.).

This definitely contradicted Reinhold's account, and the quote attributed to Kuen by Saler makes it appear as if Kuen and Scholz had deviated from their route. In fact, if one uses the subjunctive, the quote makes better sense: "We would have helped, would have climbed left around the South Shoulder and gone down to Reinhold and Günther from there."
Dauer goes on:

Both accounts agree that the conversation between Kuen and Messner took place around 10 a.m. Afterwards, Kuen and Scholz rested for an hour. Reinhold Messner didn't reappear. He writes, "Around 11 a.m. we began the descent of the Diamir Face . . . Reinhold once more looks back at the summit, then down the Merkl Gully. No one" (Red Rocket, 141f.). Why did he wait for an hour before looking down the Merkl Gully again? Didn't he and Günther need to go down as quickly as possible? Günther: "We got to hurry, we can't wait forever. (After a pause.) I won't survive a second bivvy." Reinhold: "Yes, we must get out of here" (Red Rocket, 139f.).

Finally, Dauer describes the reunion of Reinhold with the rest of the expedition:

When Reinhold Messner met the expedition members after the odyssey on July 3, 1970, alone and more dead than alive, he embraces von Kienlin. In his diary, von Kienlin wrote: "He [Reinhold] stares at me with wide eyes, sobs and cries out, 'Where is Günther?' I am shocked, hold him tight, how? Günther isn't there? I am unable to ask.

*Reinhold cries out again, 'Where is Günther?'" (von Kienlin, 137).
Only Reinhold himself should know the answer.*

*During the journey home, Reinhold is in apathy, depressive. Von
Kienlin is concerned about the "psychic and social survival" of his
friend. He advises him to think about what he is going to tell the public back home, the parents. This way, the ice avalanche became a fact,
and today, it is still regarded as a possible cause of Günther's death.*

What are we to conclude? Is the alternative version of the facts stronger, more persuasive, more logical than Reinhold's own narrative? The
reader can judge on the basis of the numerous documents that are available. The key question may well be, Why? Why would Reinhold recount a
false story and doggedly insist on it being the truth; what purpose does it
serve? In other words, what would motivate him to do so? Both stories are
glorious, inglorious, and tragic; neither makes Reinhold Messner more
or less responsible for his brother's death, notwithstanding the exchange
between Reinhold and Kuen, which came to naught. Neither absolves the
expedition leadership of all responsibility for Günther's passing. Whether
killed by an avalanche or a fall, Günther's early death is tragic. Reinhold's
physical suffering during this ordeal is obvious; in fact, he barely survived.
Was it foolishly self-imposed with dreams of a traverse, or dictated by dire
circumstances with Günther in grave danger? Whatever the case may be,
Reinhold had to go through amputation, rehabilitation, and grieving the
loss of his brother.

All in all, the surfacing of an alternative narrative, over the course of
many years of bitter dispute between Reinhold and the other expedition
members, seems to function more as a potent way to indicate that he may
not be trustworthy, rather than as an attempt to set the story straight. It
is not a cause of the quarrel, but an effect, a symptom. The truth can be
messy, and it would be very Manichean and quite naive to attempt to
lay blame on one party or another. With this caveat, we choose Messner's narrative. For a mountaineer, even though the logical flow of the
story is interrupted by bad decisions, the glorious ascent to the summit,
a remarkable climb by any standard, followed by the agonizing misery of
the descent into the west, the terrible physical and mental deterioration

due to the concatenating effects of extreme altitude, debilitating thirst, ravaging hunger, and deep exhaustion—all are the signature of the profound, potent combination of life at the edge of death, exhilaration, and despair that define extreme mountaineering.

Incredibly, Reinhold was to return to Nanga Parbat no less than three times. Interestingly, he always came back to the Diamir flank: first in 1971, with Uschi von Kienlin, Max von Kienlin's wife, with whom he had fallen in love while she was helping him recover from his amputations; next in 1978, when he performed the first solo ascent of an 8,000-meter peak; and finally, in 2000, with his brother Hubert and two South Tyrolean climbers, Hans Peter Eisendle and Wolfgang Thomaseth, when they opened a new route on the Mazeno face, and were turned away from the summit by bad weather and fresh snow.

The goal of his first return to the Naked Mountain was to meet again with the folks who had saved his life, to whom he owed a debt of gratitude. This voyage back into the Diamir and in time must have been cathartic on many different levels. In 1978, Reinhold was back at Nanga Parbat with the intent of performing the first solo climb of an 8,000-meter peak. Why Nanga Parbat? Was it the fact that he knew the terrain? He certainly had spent a great deal of lonely, miserable time on the Diamir flank of the mountain, searching for Günther in vain. Did he want to meet once again with the simple people who had saved his life? A brief account of this climb is given in his *Free Spirit*, where most of the action described takes place at altitude. In this short piece, he contrasts the feelings of reaching the summit of his first 8,000-meter peak, with Günther in 1970, with the lonely, sobering experience of 1978. The brief mention of this first successful solo ascent of an eight-thousander, in *The Naked Mountain*, is an apt antonymic epigraph: "It was and remains the boldest climb of my life."[3]

NOTES

1 A methamphetamine stimulant used by soldiers during World War II.

2 An enzyme preparation for kallidinogenase, made from urinary, plasma, or renal tissue kallikrein, with accompanying substances from porcine pancreas. Kallikrein is a subgroup of serine proteases, enzymes capable of cleaving peptide bonds in proteins.

3 After the 1970 tragedy, Nanga Parbat received continued attention from the mountaineering community. The English version of Wikipedia provides extensive climbing annals for Nanga Parbat under its namesake entry (Nanga Parbat).

SOURCES
The preceding account is based on the two Messner books. Other material is documented textually.

"Cryptomnesia," Wikipedia, en.wikipedia.org/wiki/Cryptomnesia.

Dauer, Tom. "One Truth and Another," Affimer. May 2003. www.affimer.org/np -tom-dauer.html.

Eddison, E. R. "Mistress of Mistresses," Wikipedia. en.wikipedia.org/wiki/ Mistress_of_Mistresses.

Messner, Reinhold. *Free Spirit*. Seattle: Mountaineers Books, 1989.

Messner, Reinhold. *The Naked Mountain*. Seattle: Mountaineers Books, 2002.

"Nanga Parbat," Wikipedia. en.wikipedia.org/wiki/Nanga_Parbat.

Roberts, David. "Messner's Burden," *National Geographic Adventure*. May 2004. Reprint. www.nationalgeographic.com/adventure/0510/0509/whats_new/ reinhold_messner.html.

PART TWO:
BRIEFER OVERVIEWS

DURING THE COURSE OF ANY GIVEN YEAR, MANY ACCIDENTS AND TRAG-
edies occur in the mountains. The extent of this can readily be seen in the
American Alpine Club's annual *Accidents in North American Mountaineering*, the 2013 issue of which offers 126 pages of devastation. In broad
summary, in the United States and Canada from 1951 through 2012, a
total of 8,026 accidents were reported, involving 15,131 people, resulting, horribly, in 1,838 deaths (*Accidents*, 118–19). Worse, because many
fewer people participated from the beginning of Himalayan climbing
until 1999, there were a total of 591 deaths on the fourteen 8,000-meter
peaks; the mortality rate per peak ranges from 2.1 percent to a high of
50.5 percent (Hartemann, 2). Specific debacles occur so often that readers
and viewers quickly forget even the most horrifying of incidents.

In July of 2012, for example, an avalanche killed nine climbers and
harmed eleven others on Mont Maudit in the French Alps (Bilefsky).
Then, in late September of the same year, a devastating avalanche on
Manaslu in Nepal killed nine primarily German and French climbers,
with six missing and others hurt ("Avalanche"). Most people did not even
notice these tragedies. In mid-October 2014, in Nepal's Annapurna massif, hundreds of trekkers were caught in a freak blizzard or inundated by
an avalanche, and at least twenty were killed (Sharma). It later turned
out that as many as forty people lost their lives. In light of the disasters
included in this book, the people's extreme suffering, and their extraordinary fights to survive, it is both shocking and extremely sad that large
groups of fit adventurers are wiped out in a brief moment.

Here follow some concise overviews of controversies, hoaxes, and
disasters that have plagued those who venture into the mountain environment. These problems arise because adventurers are dishonest, greedy,
foolhardy, overconfident, ill-prepared, choose to avoid warnings and

weather auguries, and make bad (often very bad) choices and decisions. Most notable is the fact that even sophisticated and knowledgeable people do not give smaller mountains the respect they deserve. That is why New Hampshire's comparatively diminutive Mount Washington, at 6,288 feet, has more deaths than any other American peak. People wander up on a lovely, warm July afternoon in shorts and T-shirts only to find themselves in a devastating blizzard; hypothermia follows, and they sometimes succumb. The junior author of this compilation recalls seeing a man and teenage boy both clad only in wet cotton sweatshirts wandering around on the summit of Maine's Mount Katahdin on a cold, rainy day. They were lost and did not know precisely which trail to take to get back to their campsite. They could easily have died. Friends who have worked on and off as fire lookouts and caretakers for almost half a century on a mountaintop, across which the Appalachian Trail rolls, report that at least two or three times a season some people (even through-hikers traveling from Georgia to Maine, who must know better) are ill-prepared for the cold and rainy storms that one encounters in all seasons in the mountains. They must be rescued, brought into their home (a diminutive 10-by-12-foot cabin), warmed at the woodstove, and plied with hot tea to avoid a hypothermic tragedy. In the spring of 2014, a hiker died from hypothermia on Camel's Hump, a diminutive Vermont mountain. Adventurers must be more cautious in order to prevent tragedies.

SOURCES

Accidents in North American Mountaineering (10.3, issue 66). Golden, CO: American Alpine Club, 2013.

"Avalanche Kills 9 Climbers in Nepal," *New York Times*. September 24, 2012: A6.

Bilefsky, Dan. "Avalanche Kills at Least 9 Climbers in France's Mont Blanc Mountain Range," *New York Times*. July 13, 2012: A4.

Hartemann, Frederic V., and Robert Hauptman. *The Mountain Encyclopedia*. Lanham, MD: Taylor Trade, 2005.

Sharma, Bhadra, and Nida Najar. "Blizzard and Avalanche Kill at Least 20 Trekkers in Himalayas," *New York Times*. October 16, 2014: A5.

McKinley, 1906:
Dr. Cook's Deception

DR. FREDERICK A. COOK WAS AN HONORED GENTLEMAN, A DOCTOR, AN explorer who had sailed with Peary and Amundsen, a respected ethnographer, a popular lecturer, and a founder of both the American Alpine and Explorers Clubs. He had worked hard delivering milk at night and simultaneously studying to become a physician. He suffered greatly when his new daughter and wife both died. He ministered to Peary when he broke his ankle and Amundsen lavished high praise on him. As he accompanied others on various expeditions, he began to relish the possibility of being the first person to reach the North Pole. But this took money, and he decided that he would have to do something really outstanding (spectacular, as Bradford Washburn puts it) to gain the respect necessary to raise funds and lead a major expedition. This is where McKinley came in.

In the spring of 1903, he mounted an expedition, the goal of which was to be the first person to summit North America's highest peak. In Alaska, he split the members up, but they later met again closer to the mountain. Cook was essentially a good man, but apparently an incompetent leader, one who knew little about the scientific instruments he carried, and who had no Alpine climbing experience. It took a long time, but by August 16, they arrived at the northern side and soon began to climb. They were ill-equipped for glacier travel, having only "a few ropes, sun goggles, and three ice axes." Two men had only tent poles! Amazingly, they managed to reach 10,800 feet without any mishaps. They then descended and continued, circumnavigating the mountain, "a remarkable feat that would not be repeated for a half century." Upon his return to New York, Cook offered lectures, but negative pieces written by a reporter who had accompanied him caused some harm. Instead of manifesting outrage, Cook defended the man, thereby enhancing his own reputation.

In 1906, he raised financial support in various ways, tried again, but failed—at least, at first. Among the many expedition members was the artist Belmore Browne. Once again, the group split up, some traveling by boat, others by pack horses. They reunited, and by July 19, they still had not reached the mountain. This left little time for the climb. They gave up, and some of the members left to do other things. Eventually, Cook and just two men headed in on the southeastern side. "Less than three weeks later, on September 22," Washburn reported they were off the mountain, claiming that Cook and a companion had summited by a northern route, which obviously conflicted with his earlier indication that he was in the south. Browne did not believe that the ascent was possible. Cook had apparently reached a point 4 miles below 10,600 feet. But then, his account offers only vague generalizations and makes little sense. Nevertheless, his claim was accepted and he thereby accomplished his goal: He had certainly done something spectacular.

He was now a real hero, even though he failed to pay his debts. In November, five hundred people in Seattle showed up to hear his first talk, at which time he discussed the climb and his equipment. He claimed that he and his partner moved very quickly, carrying "light" (50-pound) backpacks with rope, tent, stove, camera, pemmican, etc., and wearing some inadequate clothing. Then he was off to New York and Washington, where he addressed august groups of well-known men, including Peary and Theodore Roosevelt. He next received backing and headed for Greenland; his ultimate goal was still the North Pole.

None of the explorers and adventures who heard him speak nor the general public doubted the veracity of his claims. But some Alaskans, especially Reverend Hudson Stuck, who were more familiar with McKinley and its rigors, did not believe that it was possible to ascend in just eight days and descend in four. And two collaborators, Browne and Herschel Parker, who earlier had been with Cook, also were skeptical. After seeing some inadequate photographic evidence, they mentioned this to people at the American Alpine Club, which resulted in mumblings that Cook had fabricated his accomplishment. Cook threatened to sue, and so the two men held back, awaiting more narrative and photographic evidence.

This appeared in the May 1907 issue of *Harper's Monthly Magazine.* The summit image of Cook's partner depicted him standing in soft fluffy snow, which would have been blown away on the wind-lashed 20,000-foot summit. None of the other images offered down-sweeping views of "recognizable landmarks," according to Washburn's account. Browne and Parker kept silent because Cook had already left on his northern voyage. Later, they discovered many differences between the article and Cook's monograph, *To the Top of the Continent.* Captions were altered, and the summit photo now showed a higher peak in the distance, which apparently had been cropped in the article but not in the book. They awaited Cook's return.

Next came Cook's claim that he had reached the North Pole on April 21, 1908, although news of this did not reach the world until September 1, 1909. Now that he was once again a major hero, the Explorers Club people did not feel comfortable accusing Cook of dishonesty. On September 6, Peary announced that he had reached the Pole on April 6, a year after Cook. Peary indicated that the two natives who had been with Cook insisted that he had not gone north at all. Suspicion increased, and the *New York Sun* published an article questioning Cook's purported triumphs. Interviewees had bad things to say.

Something that strikes an objective person negatively, and that at first was not widely recognized, was the fact that Cook failed to pay the various men who accompanied him, or who had rented him horses in Alaska. That a benefactor did not follow through with a gift was irrelevant. The hero did not live up to his commitments, and he lied about it. Edward Barrell, the man who had purportedly accompanied Cook to McKinley's summit, shared his diary for a payment of $5,000, and then signed an affidavit to the effect that they had not even gotten close to the summit. Browne and another witness spoke up at the Explorers Club. And two men came forth and swore that Cook had had them create false latitude and longitude coordinates to prove that he had reached the Pole. Both the Explorers and the American Alpine Clubs dismissed him. The

Explorers Club and Browne mounted an expedition (as did other parties, one of which falsely claimed a summit as well). Browne located the spot from which the "summit" photo was shot; it stood at just over 5,000 feet! Another investigating party reached a similar conclusion, viz., that Cook had lied. Despite the overwhelming evidence that Cook was a fraud, his supporters refused to capitulate; indeed, they accused the detractors of dishonesty. Even today, the Dr. Frederick A. Cook Society (founded by his family) continues to advocate for his accomplishments.

In Cook's book, the early part of the climb is detailed, but as he ascends (at least imaginatively), his descriptions lack precision. It is impossible from his metaphoric remarks to pinpoint any precise geographic locations. He also indicated some things that are impossible, such as seeing the Yukon River or building an igloo (although he had no tools with him). He refused to share a putative field diary, because none existed. Fifty years later, one was discovered, but it was written in pencil, and might have been composed at any time after the climb. Eventually, matters degenerated to such a point that Cook ran a Ponzi scheme, was found guilty, and actually spent some years in prison. A number of more-recent attempts to duplicate Cook's route failed, even though one group included Vern Tejas and Scott Fischer, two extraordinary climbers.

The photographic evidence, including images re-created at the precise locations from which Cook's photos were made, offer conclusive proof that he did not get higher than 5,400 feet. In 1995, an examination of all of the evidence showed that his summiting "was the clever hoax of a brilliant charlatan."

Washburn has done an excellent job of combing the historical record, gathering the evidence, fairly assessing it, and concluding that Cook was a consistent fraud, one who apparently was never embarrassed by his deceptions. Washburn's successful search for the precise locations from which he was able to duplicate Cook's images in a series of exquisite photos is an extraordinary feat of commitment, determination, and skill. They prove conclusively that Cook was not the first ascender of McKinley. And he probably did not get anywhere near the North Pole. This is a depressing tale of a convincing con man who did some good, but also caused a great deal of harm.

Thirteen years after Washburn published his exposé, Jennifer Bleyer offered a brief historical overview and an attempt to rehabilitate Cook's reputation. She cited two supporters who claimed that Cook succeeded on both McKinley and in his North Pole quest. That a guide may have been corrupted by a payment to deny the McKinley conquest, and that Peary, too, may have been a liar, hardly redeems Cook and his reputation. In fact, Bleyer does not mention Washburn and his convincing study at all.

Sources

The Washburn work (which is the basis for this chapter) contains an extensive bibliography. Readers interested in additional details, perhaps not covered by Washburn, can contact the Belmore Browne collection via e-mail (brownecollection@gmail.com) and also see ead.dartmouth .edu/html/stem190_fullguide.html, the finding aid to Browne's papers at Dartmouth College.

Bleyer, Jennifer. "90° N, 0° W," *NYU Alumni Magazine* 22 (Spring 2014): 41–47 [images at www.nyu.edu/alumni.magazine/issue22/pdf/NYU22_FEA_COOK.pdf].
Washburn, Bradford, and Peter Cherici. *The Dishonorable Dr. Cook: Debunking the Notorious Mount McKinley Hoax.* Seattle: The Mountaineers, 2001.

Annapurna, 1950, Revisited:
David Roberts vs. Maurice Herzog

MAURICE HERZOG WAS AN INTERNATIONAL HERO; THE LEADER OF THE expedition that first conquered an 8,000-meter peak; the author of *Annapurna: Premier 8000* (with *at least* eleven million copies published, the best-selling mountaineering book of all time); the mayor of Chamonix; and the Minister of Youth and Sport under Charles de Gaulle.[1] In *Annapurna*, he depicted a pleasant, cooperative group of men who climbed a mountain optimistically and harmoniously. It is "a stirring saga of teamwork and self-sacrifice," and the men manifested "loyalty, teamwork, courage, and perseverance."[2] David Roberts expends more than two hundred pages showing that this is a false picture; the truth turns out to be extremely unpleasant: "*Annapurna* [is] a dishonest, semi-fictionalized account" is how Roberts puts it ("Best Mountain Book"), replete with "concocted dialogue."

The group consisted of nine men, including Herzog (the leader), Lionel Terray, Gaston Rébuffat, Louis Lachenal (three extraordinary guides from Chamonix), Marcel Ichac, Jean Couzy, and Marcel Schatz. Before the trip began, Herzog surprised them by insisting that they sign an oath of allegiance, demanding that they obey Herzog unconditionally. This seems to be unprecedented; imagine if a friend or skiing or climbing partner asked you to sign such a document before leaving on an adventure. Then just before getting on the plane to India, the men were forced to sign a contract prohibiting them from publishing or publicly indicating anything for five years, leaving the field open only to Herzog. Most people, especially such strong, intrepid, and autonomous climbers, would have refused. But these men really wanted to go, so they acquiesced.

These nonnegotiable demands embittered at least some of the men. (Incredibly, on the return, once they reached India, Herzog confiscated the men's passports so that no one would arrive home before he did.) But even after the moratorium passed, no one told the true story. This is surprising, but Roberts provides a reason. In 1956, Lachenal posthumously published *Carnets du Vertige*. Roberts had read it and discovered that it jibed with Herzog's version of the events. Only later, in conversation with Michel Guérin, did he discover that Lachenal had died before publication and Herzog, his brother, and Lucien Davies usurped the manuscript and expurgated Lachenal's sardonic criticisms. In 1996, there appeared both the uncensored version of Lachenal's book as well as a biography of Rébuffat, based in part on his caustic letters. The real story was very different: Because of the coerced legal requirements, the men were "torn by conflict and resentment" even before they boarded the plane, and the final assessment was that "the team had been frequently and rancorously divided; Herzog's leadership had been capricious and at times inept," and the expedition's culmination and peroration were mysteriously unclear.

In his narrative, Herzog suppressed the bickering and conflicts that occurred; when he did indicate a problem, he was always the one to wisely resolve it, but at the same time he *did* give credit to the skills of his colleagues inspired by their ultimate goal, the conquest of the mountain. As Roberts observes, Rébuffat, in a letter, declared that his teammates were egotists lacking in team spirit. (The truth probably lies somewhere between these two extremes.) Another important lacuna in the expurgated version of Lachenal's memoir (and, of course, in *Annapurna*) is the absence of all maladies, illnesses, and other human debilities from which many of the men suffered. This was extremely misleading, because although it is now common knowledge that almost all Westerners get ill on Himalayan expeditions, in the early 1950s readers may have thought that one could spend three months in this alien environment, eating and drinking contaminated products, yet somehow avoiding stomach upsets and diarrhea, as well as the bronchial attacks with coughing so severe that it can result in broken ribs. Also missing were reports of the unseemly in local populations, e.g., barbaric funeral practices or the proffering of children for sex. Herzog did not seem to be bothered by his censorious actions; he retorted that the passages were deleted "because they didn't interest the editors."

Herzog apparently was a controlling and domineering person. He became the leader of this important, nationally sponsored expedition through political manipulation; he was friendly with the empowered. Additionally, he was a competent amateur, worldly and cosmopolitan, and a corporate executive, whereas the professional Chamonix guides were considered unsophisticated bumpkins who lacked the requisite skills to lead a prestigious expedition, although their superb mountaineering capabilities were never questioned.

After spending seven weeks failing to find a viable route on Dhaulagiri, they encountered a second major problem: They could not locate Annapurna, and "wandered aimlessly," searching for it. Their chronology, however, is truly amazing: They left France on March 28; their peregrinations brought them to Annapurna base camp on May 18; they wasted five days on an impossible route; they summited on June 3. Normally it takes many months and the help of innumerable high-altitude porters to set up and stock as many as nine camps. (This was in the past; these days, four or five are more typical. The Herzogians had seven.) Somehow they managed this entire feat in just seventeen days, and unlike many expeditions, they did not lose anyone, although some of the men suffered extreme harm, from frostbite, for example.

Another controversial personal dispute involved Rébuffat, who, while others were scurrying around in the wrong area, discovered the perfect route. He was proud of this but very embittered that Herzog not only did not acknowledge his role, but instead appropriated the credit: "I felt in my bones if there were a way up Annapurna, this was where it lay." And, naturally, the men had various disagreements with each other, but only infrequently are these indicated in *Annapurna*. After summiting, Herzog and Lachenal descended to Camp Five, where they encountered Terray and Rébuffat, who had come up to try for their own summit. But a bad storm was raging and the two triumphant climbers were badly frostbitten. They needed help to descend. And so Rébuffat was further upset because Herzog neither indicated that the rescuers abjured their own attempt nor acknowledged their help in saving the summiters' lives. In his letters, jottings, and then in Yves Ballu's biography, Rébuffat indicated frustration and a strong dislike for what had occurred, and how Herzog had distorted matters and overdramatized his own role as a hero. And sometimes, the other expedition members were expunged from various proceedings. As they went down, they passed through thigh- and waist-deep snow. With the two summiters frostbitten and the two rescuers snow-blind, it was not surprising that just a short distance from Camp Four A, they managed to get lost. They spent the night in a crevasse, where their boots were buried in a small avalanche.

In commenting on discrepancies between Herzog's account and a much later memoir, Roberts remarks that Terray's *Conquistadors of the Useless* (one of the finest of all mountaineering books) "is equally a partial fiction—as, some would argue, are inevitably all memoir and biography." This is too easy, too simplistic: all (auto)biography is not necessarily fictionalized. Some authors distort reality inadvertently or purposely, but others attempt to reproduce it to the best of their ability, respecting the truth despite the harm its articulations may engender.[3]

Next comes a difference in Herzog's two books in describing a scene at the crevasse. Herzog admonishes Terray to leave him; Terray refuses. In his later memoir this is much expanded into a dramatic dialogue through which Terray indicates his loyalty to Herzog. Roberts is skeptical. Other petty discrepancies exist. On the long march out (it lasted more than a month), "the expedition began at this point to unravel." There is no unraveling in the sanitized *Annapurna*. A sympathetic reader can well imagine how and why these men were at such odds with themselves and each other. They were exhausted, ill, or injured, some so badly that they had to be carried. They suffered excruciating pain from their frostbitten fingers and toes, but also from the horrible but ineffective "cures," such as flagellation or stomach injections. And their mental anguish, knowing that soon they would lose fingers and toes (some of which were amputated as they rode through India on a train), must have been unbearable. Neither *Annapurna* nor Lachenal's expurgated *Carnets* contains much mention of "conflict, disgust, despair," or even morphine.

Early on, Roberts claims that what occurred on summit day presents a mystery. He never reverts to this but perhaps he is referring to the culminating ironic controversy that has raged, albeit rather quietly: The summit photo of a triumphant Herzog shows a slope rising above him, leading some skeptics to believe that he and Lachenal never reached the summit. Lachenal was a man of integrity and presumably would not lie about, and thus detract from, his life's work as an honored Chamonix guide. If the two men were truly trying to deceive, it would have been quite easy to dissemble by shooting the image from a different angle, or at a less-steep location. Roberts concludes that they did summit.

In 1999, Roberts interviewed Herzog in Paris. He wondered whether the recently published unexpurgated Lachenal diary and the Rébuffat biography, with all of their unseemly revelations, had upset Herzog. Apparently not: "I have a clear conscience and the experience of the truth. No one has doubted what I wrote." He often repeated this like a mantra, but it is simply not so. Indeed, the journalist Benoît Heimermann noted that Herzog was distraught.

And then Herzog insisted that losing his gloves did not result in his devastating frostbite, a statement at odds with his account in *Annapurna*. Herzog was repeating this new version of events, first mentioned in the 1998 memoir, *L'Autre Annapurna*. Additionally, there exist other discrepancies between Herzog and the articulations of members of the expedition, as well as between Herzog's two books. When questioned, he replied: "Why did it sell fifteen million copies? *Annapurna* is a sort of novel. It's a novel, but a true novel." He also admitted that he paraphrased dialogue and even constructed it, ab ovo. Roberts comes up with three possible excusing explanations, but we are skeptical.[4] The real explanation seems to be that Herzog simply created a truth that he preferred; it just did not happen to jibe with reality.[5]

NOTES

1 Herzog was also very kind to the authors of this book.
2 These are the very terms that might be used to describe the 1953 Houston expedition to K2 (see above), but in that case, the men really were caring brothers of the rope.
3 The literary conceit, affirmed by pop psychology, that individuals each perceive a precise tableau from different perspectives and therefore must of necessity see it differently and thus draw differing conclusions is nonsense, despite the persuasive depictions in Faulkner's *The Sound and the Fury* and Kurosawa's *Rashomon*. A group of people admiring a circling eagle see a soaring bird, not a loping gazelle. All judicial systems are based,

in part, on the testimony of witnesses whose *perceptions* are never questioned, except by badgering prosecutors. People may see what they want to see, but this does not mean that every work of nonfiction is a series of distortions.

4 Roberts is perhaps unwilling to seriously criticize or denigrate a mountaineering icon, and this is understandable; nevertheless, the existence of *True Summit* and its revelations speak for themselves, and readers have no choice but to draw the disheartening conclusion that Herzog was purposely deceptive (in order to serve some higher purpose, which is always the excuse offered, as with Rigoberta Menchú, for example).

5 In a *New York Times* obituary, the author quotes Herzog's daughter, who claims that her father was a megalomaniac: He "rewrote history, betrayed and neglected his entourage without ever having the sense of hurting anyone because society judged him to be so good" (Weber).

SOURCES

This chapter is based on David Roberts's revelatory monographic study, which contains a useful bibliography. Other sources are cited in the text.

Herzog, Maurice. *Annapurna*. New York: Lyons Press, 1997.

Roberts, David. "The Best Mountain Book Ever Written." *The Active Times*. November 15, 2012. www.theactivetimes.com/best-mountain-book-ever-written-banff-2012 -part-iii.

Roberts, David. *True Summit: What Really Happened on the Legendary Ascent of Annapurna*. New York: Simon & Schuster, 2000.

Weber, Bruce. "Maurice Herzog, 93, Dies; Led Historic Himalaya Climb," *New York Times*. December 15, 2012: [A]8.

The Pamirs, 1974: Fifteen Climbers Die

In the early 1970s, as the Cold War receded, mountaineers from countless countries began to descend on the Soviet Union in order to climb in its many ranges, including the Caucasus, the Urals, the Tien Shan, and the Pamirs. The American Pamir/USSR Expedition arrived in July of 1974, along with groups from eleven other countries. Scotland, England, France, Germany, and Japan, as well as Austria, with its 62 climbers. There were 160 foreigners at base camps and many Soviet and Communist climbers, including an 8-member Soviet women's team. The American leaders had culled 19 men and women from a group of more than 200 people who wanted to take advantage of this unique opportunity. They acquired and organized equipment (subsidized by Eddie Bauer). They also raised funds, one of the more irritating chores necessary when organizing an expedition; this is especially onerous for Americans because, unlike some countries, the US government does not underwrite mountaineering ventures.

The nineteen climbers included Robert W. Craig, author of *Storm and Sorrow*, the expedition account, and a member of Charlie Houston's famous 1953 K2 climb (see chapter 4); Marty Hoey, who soon thereafter got very ill on Nanda Devi; Jeff Lowe; John Roskelley, who was also on the tragic Nanda Devi climb; Peter Schoening, who famously held five men on The Belay on the Houston climb; Gary Ullin; and Christopher Wren, who worked in Moscow for the *New York Times*, and whose many articles JA has read over the years. They seemed to be a compatible group, and no one, not even the organizers or leaders, were autocratic demagogues.[1]

The logistical arrangements at the base camps and the subsequent climbs are perhaps the most peculiar ever recounted in the mountaineering literature. The Soviets played host to a lot of diverse people ("the greatest gathering of international mountaineering teams in climbing history," more than 150 people from at least twelve countries) out in the middle of a glacial wasteland. Some local people and their herds were nearby, since arable land ran right up to the ice, but otherwise they were far from civilization. The hosts set up a regimented enclave, a small city of tents (sleeping, mess, and theater) and tables, communication devices, and rules, and supplied the climbers with food and drinks. When the foreigners visited with the local population and ate their food and drank their unpasteurized *kumiss* (which is fermented milk from mares or camels and sometimes cows) and vast quantities of alcohol, they often got violently ill,[2] or drunk.

From the base camps, the various national groups sallied forth to their appointed climbs. No one appeared to break the rules and climb an undesignated peak. The Americans divided into four separate groups with four different distant objectives. This too is most unusual, though it has occurred (for example, in 1962 on Everest, when Willi Unsoeld and Tom Hornbein did the West Ridge, traversed, and met those who had come up the normal South Col route).

Before leaving for Moscow, the group had procured, with much trouble, seven radios. Once airborne, they discovered that they had left them at the airport. This was both a terrible loss and a bad augury. Even if they had had the radios, Customs might have confiscated them, but once they were retrieved and sent to the USSR, they were not allowed to rejoin the men. Craig hypothesizes that had they had some (better) means of communication, the horrible tragedy that ensued might have been averted.

The Americans' chosen and assigned mountains were four in number: Lenin Peak; Peak 19 (Peak of the 19th Party Congress, 19,423 feet); 6,852 (meters); and the Dzerschinsky area, which was not well-explored, and had many unclimbed peaks. Indeed, except for a single image, no photographs or information on the glacial terrain existed, so it was much coveted. Everyone wants to be a discoverer and hold first ascents. Nine Americans in two groups were up high near Krylenko Pass, when one man fell into a crevasse (a second augury); fortunately, he managed to extract himself. It was snowing but warm, and Peter Lev, one of six Americans at this point, felt very uneasy about the state of the snow. The others were also nervous because of the potential avalanche danger. On July 23, four men descended. The second group was also nearby. Suddenly an earthquake[3] triggered an avalanche (a third augury), which inundated the remaining climbers; it is truly miraculous that all of them survived, some by jumping into a nearby crevasse over which the snow rolled. The men who had left earlier also were caught. A few were buried and one had to be laboriously dug out. The second group then descended 4,000 feet to a lower camp; the trip down was terrifying. Some men were hurt, but none badly, and they all survived.

By July 17, another group of men, Ullin, Roskelley, Craig, and John Marts, were working their way up Peak 19, as were other national groups. The Americans were operating on a new, difficult route on the north face. The others were following a traditional path. They hauled loads, sometimes as heavy as 80 pounds, up steep and avalanche-prone ice slopes, set up camps, and retreated. Camp 3 was at 15,400 feet. The summit was about 5,000 feet above. Two unusual features nearby derive from the proximity of the arable land mentioned above: a profusion of flowers and wild yaks.

The weather was uncooperative, and four days of rain were followed by a blizzard. As usual, as reported consistently in the literature, Roskelley was exceptionally strong, as was Ullin, both of whom did potent leads. Here the problem was not deep snow but rather steep ice (70 degrees or more), on which ice-screw belays were sometimes required. Worse, on a descent, their crampons balled up, "directly over the almost vertical section of the north face ice wall." Then Craig slipped on some snow over ice and pulled Roskelley off; luckily, they were both able to self-arrest. On July 23, they went up and set up Camp Four at approximately 17,000 feet. Waist-deep snow and very hot weather drained them and caused a feeling of extreme lassitude. As they rested, part of the glacier (snow, ice, seracs) broke off and headed toward them in the form of an enormous avalanche, which luckily veered off. They were upset. Shortly thereafter, Craig kicked the tent to remove the snow and suddenly the entire mountain began to shake in the roughly five-second earthquake, noted above.

They were terrified. By the morning of July 24, an additional 18 inches of new snow had fallen, and by 1:00 a.m. on July 25, 6 to 8 more inches had accumulated. Things were not going well.

At about 3:00 a.m. on July 25, a hissing sound preceded the collapse of the tent that held Craig and Ullin; it was covered by another avalanche. Craig had slept with his arm outside his bag and this created an air pocket in the solidified snow. He called out to Ullin who had been at his side, but there was neither answer nor movement. He hoped that the two other men, who had been in a second tent, might be able to free him. He thought about many things, including his family, but he did not focus on escape—not that there is much one can do when pinioned under solidified snow with very little air to breathe. After perhaps fifteen to twenty minutes, he decided to try to get out. He managed to retrieve his knife, but hesitated to cut because the snow would inundate his airspace.

Just then, a voice called to him; he answered, "I'm okay. Get Gary; I can't hear him! Get Gary; he's on your right!" Roskelley and Marts dug feverishly, removed Ullin, and tried mouth-to-mouth resuscitation, but it was too late: Ullin was dead. As they continued to try to free Craig, another avalanche inundated them, and Craig was reburied in what he termed "the most despairing and hopeless moment of my life." But just a few seconds later, they dug him out. It was dark, snowing hard, and very cold. Much of their clothing and other belongings were buried. Craig rescued some of his stuff and they all moved 300 feet up to a *bergschrund* to avoid the continuing avalanches. There they dug a small cave. They suffered in what Craig described as a more horrific experience than the night he had spent on K2 after Art Gilkey had been killed (see chapter 4). At least there they had their clothing and equipment. An additional burden was that Craig had become very fond of Ullin. They discussed a rescue and whether they could escape from the nightmare that engulfed them.

At 6:00 a.m., it was very cold, and they had become hypothermic; things looked dismal. They began to send out Mayday calls on a Russian radio that Craig had grabbed as he raced to the *bergschrund*. Eventually, they made contact. They requested an air drop that was to include a shovel so they could dig out a storage area they had created earlier. This was where they had stored the climbing equipment they would need in order to descend. As the temperature warmed up, they left their cave, returned to the tent platform, and retrieved what they could. Marts, it turned out, had become snow-blind, but amazingly, they found some eye ointment. Rescuers were moving toward them, and an air drop the following day brought them the shovel and other material they needed. They dug out their equipment and decided that since the weather was good, they would descend. They dreaded crossing the avalanche-prone face (in order to reach the ridge). Just before they left, they buried Ullin and marked the spot for later retrieval of the body.

They started down on July 26, taking a more-difficult ascending route to the ridge in order to avoid the dangerous face. Soon thereafter, they heard voices and were met by the rescuers. The next morning, not far from base camp, they spotted, just 50 yards off, a snow leopard, one of the most elusive animals on Earth (which might have been taken as a positive augury). This had been a very dicey situation, one that could easily have ended with the deaths of all four men. They were very lucky; they would have had better luck had they not set their camp on a slope that was constantly bombarded by heavy avalanches.

Once safe at base camp, they obsessed about reburying Ullin. The Soviets had other problems, since a five-person Estonian group was lost. By the time they were found, three had perished in an earthquake-induced avalanche, and the others died later in a hospital in Osh. But despite the Soviet disinclination to sanction a reburial party (in bad weather after six people had perished), Roskelley, Lowe, and Marts went up, reburied Ullin, and then Roskelley and Lowe headed for the summit, which they reached on August 2. Also on August 2, a four-person American group reached the summit of Lenin Peak (23,406 feet), as did a second group of four. As the storm increased in ferocity, there were more than forty climbers at or above 20,000 feet. The Americans below wanted to mount a rescue despite the Soviets' understandable hesitation. The eight Soviet women, attempting a traverse of Lenin, also made the top, but refused to descend, claiming that they were strong Soviet women. They would camp on the summit despite the horrific storm. Things degenerated. Finally, not wishing to abandon their sick and dying comrades, even those who might have escaped succumbed. Their dramatic ongoing calls to base camp caused sadness and tears. Horribly, all eight died. Another woman passed away, bringing the total to fifteen sacrificed in this most unpleasant climbing season in the Pamirs.

On a now-clear day, yet another small group of Americans stumbled on the bodies of the Soviet women. They were unaware that the tragedy had occurred, and so the discovery was a shocking and traumatic experience. An immediate inquiry cleared the officials in charge of any wrongdoing. The last climbers returned to base and were greeted, early on August 10, by another powerful earthquake. It was followed by others, and massive avalanches across the upper mountains. Before the climbers departed, they held a series of services at a memorial cairn that they had erected.

In 1990, Craig's book was turned into *Storm and Sorrow*, a powerful film with Hollywood actors rather than the actual participants. In order to overdramatize matters (which was entirely unnecessary), the director and scriptwriters included much that is not in the original, emphasizing a single climber (one of only two females in the American contingent) who was portrayed as incompetent. As it happens, she summited whereas many others did not. The scenery is beautiful, and the tragedy heartrending.

The Pamir region has not been kind to visitors. In 1990, forty climbers were killed in a single incident, perhaps the worst accident in the history of mountaineering, a sport that entices many and which, we would presume, harms, maims, and kills at a higher percentage than any other endeavor except war; on some mountains, one-quarter to one-half of all attempts end in death.

NOTES

1 On (very) large mountaineering ventures, the organizer and leader has often been unrelentingly controlling and harmful (see chapter 5 and "Annapurna," above, for examples). Occasionally, members have complained that their leader failed to exercise his position—that is, he did not provide strong leadership—but this has occurred much less frequently. When small groups (two, three, or four people) fly off to New Zealand together to climb, they usually self-direct, with no real "leader" attempting to control the others. When this does occur, some folks leave in disgust.

2 Mountaineers and trekkers, in Nepal, for example, often get ill, because they are not used to the local food and contaminated water. (Bottled water did not exist fifty years ago.) But there is a much more pressing problem involved here: When Westerners venture into distant cultural milieus, they often think that if they refuse to participate in some customary necessity, action, or ritual, they will insult their "hosts." Thus, they force themselves to eat repugnant detritus that cause their bodies to revolt in disgust, or they imbibe contaminated foodstuffs, get ill, and sometimes die. JA, as an ethical vegetarian, has spent sixty years fighting against this insane attitude (in some forty countries). He never capitulates by eating dead animals, and cares very little about his "hosts" (not just in Turkey or China, Fiji or Japan, but also in America or Wales or Germany) and their barbaric customs. It is he who is highly offended. Ironically, when foreigners come to the Western world (England, France, Belgium, or the United States, for example), they bring their beliefs and customs with them and do not go out of their way to accommodate to Western ways. It is an unpleasant situation.

3 One does not normally associate earthquakes with mountaineering tragedies, but on April 25, 2015, a 7.8 earthquake devastated Nepal, reportedly killing more than 1,300 (actually some 8,700) people. On Mount Everest, the temblor precipitated an avalanche that killed at least ten (actually, nineteen) and injured many climbers, all at base camp (Harris).

SOURCES

Craig's book is the primary source for this chapter. Others are cited in the text.

Craig, Robert W. *Storm and Sorrow in the High Pamirs*. New York: Simon and Schuster, 1980.

Harris, Gardiner. "Mount Everest Climbers Killed as Quake Causes Avalanche," *New York Times*. April 26, 2015, 10Y.

Storm and Sorrow. Dir., Richard Colla. Accent Entertainment, et al., 2002 (1990).

Terrorism: The Yellow Wall, 2000: Kidnapping and "Murder" in Kyrgyzstan, and Nanga Parbat, 2013: Eleven Mountaineers Murdered

MOUNTAINEERING IS AN INHERENTLY DANGEROUS PURSUIT WHERE PEO-
ple are harmed and killed with great frequency. It is obvious merely from
general newspaper and other media accounts of storm and avalanche
debacles that catastrophe is an ongoing risk. In addition, we have a host
of articles, books, television specials, documentaries, and popular Hollywood spectacles that keep the public informed concerning the astonishing number of adventurers who head out into the mountains in all
seasons. Rock and ice climbing and mountaineering have grown into
extremely popular sports, and the young and naive have joined a cadre
of experienced amateurs and professionals who inundate mountainous
areas all over the world, creating an enormous guiding industry and turning heretofore pristine unexplored areas into crowded base camps with
accompanying garbage dumps. The authors are not necessarily lament-
ing nor complaining here, since they too enjoy the world's natural areas
(although it would certainly be both responsible and beneficial if a very
popular large Mexican hut had an outhouse, or if a French refuge's toilet
did not empty directly onto the rocks below).

These are the facts, and it is not necessary to climb in Mexico or the
French Alps to confirm them. All one must do is visit an EMS, REI,
or independent sports emporium (anywhere in the world) and observe
the arrays of mountaineering and climbing boots and shoes, suits and

equipment, harnesses, ropes, and crampons, ice axes and racks of carabiners, ice screws, nuts, cams, and pitons (do we still drill holes and pound pitons!) to confirm that climbing generally is now almost as popular as skiing (or bowling).

Because climbing and mountaineering, especially among the high peaks, are such risky sports, real and extremely frightening peripheral dangers are often ignored: Car, bus, and plane accidents, food poisoning, ailments, diseases, animal attacks, and weather problems, such as lightning strikes, are all possible hazards that most adventurers take for granted. On June 22, 2013, a group of men attacked base camp on Nanga Parbat, adding terrorism to the list of potential horrors. They murdered eleven innocent people. But this comes as no real surprise, since there is strong precedent for it. In the summer of 1999, Islamic militants kidnapped and then released nine Uzbek climbers. On August 11, 2000, in the Kara Su valley of Kyrgyzstan, they took German and Ukrainian climbers hostage and then attacked a small campsite, kidnapping four American climbers and killing their accompanying Kyrgyz soldier. As it happens, two of them, Tommy Caldwell and Beth Rodden, were (and are) among the world's finest rock climbers. What follows is the narrative not of an extreme or onerous or triumphant climb or the establishment of a new 5.15 route, but rather, the astonishing tale of how four young people survived for six days as captives of these repugnant terrorists and then managed to escape.

The area in which the Yellow Wall is located in Kyrgyzstan is near Uzbekistan, a hotbed of terrorism, and the perpetrators sometimes crossed borders in order to wreak havoc. The four climbers, Caldwell, Rodden, John Dickey, and Jason Smith, were well aware of the potential danger, and perhaps should have gone elsewhere (although Dickey has returned to Kyrgyzstan in order to climb again, in June 2011, for example ["Memories"]). The Yellow Wall seduced them, however, and up they went in an extended big-wall climb. One morning, partway along, while hanging in their bags on portable platforms, they were peppered with bullets. As recounted in Greg Child's exquisitely detailed and heartrending narrative, they reacted calmly and rationally (instead of having strokes or nervous breakdowns). This is especially astounding because they were mere youngsters, barely out of their teens, and their photographs imply a childish naiveté better suited for college partying than parrying with wanton murderers. But their ages and images belie their courage, inner strength, fortitude, and resourcefulness.

Prior to the attack, while Dickey and Smith took a long (four-day) hike in order to locate a telephone (to trace a lost duffel bag), Caldwell and Rodden remained at camp. Simultaneously, other nearby groups of climbers were hassled by the authorities, informed that they had invalid permits, and turned back at various checkpoints and borders. The Kyrgyz military was acting cautiously and with good reason: Uzbek insurgents were flooding the area, subsequently killing many soldiers.

The kidnappers captured a group of German and Ukrainian climbers, but insisted that they did not want to kill them; they were merely hostages who would be held for a month. Next, they rounded up the four American climbers, along with a Kyrgyz soldier. Two of the Americans considered using sharp tent stakes as weapons, but this was a bad idea, since the captors had assault rifles and were ready to use them. Instead, on August 12, they packed up some of their necessary things (credit cards, money, antibiotics, food) and prepared for a long walk. The insurgents looted the camp of food. Whenever officials appeared nearby (in helicopters), the rebels forced everyone to hide in the bushes. They were heading for Uzbekistan, whose border, like Tajikistan's was nearby. Burdened with heavy baggage, the forced march was unpleasant. When thirty-eight soldiers emerged and began to approach, they had to hide and cower. Then the bullets started flying. This is not what these climbers had come to the Kara Su valley to experience. The rebels murdered the Kyrgyz soldier, who was an unnecessary burden. The Americans, on the other hand, were kidnap victims who might prove very valuable. These insurgent men of God kill and pray. The soldiers' fire homed in on them and the Americans feared that they would either be killed by their putative rescuers or dragged along by the kidnappers to an uncertain fate.

At night, they all ran away from the soldiers. They had nothing to eat or drink and were dehydrated. Obid, one of the many rebels, gave them each a candy and they tried to talk, though neither knew anything of the others' languages. Very early in the morning of August 13, they reached a river. The rebels divided the Americans and forced them to hide in a tiny cave, under an overhang. As they waited for night, water seeped in and they got wet; they were fearful that loose stone would fall on them. And they were hungry, thirsty, tired, stressed-out, and afraid. The same business dragged along: In the early-morning hours of August 14, 15, and 16, the hiding was repeated. They waited until darkness and then traveled again.

Only two rebels remained with the four Americans by this point: Abdul was tough and perhaps cruel; Su was apparently not too bright. The Americans remained sane by talking about their lives and relatives back home. They also discussed escape and how they might kill their well-armed captors, who had automatic weapons, pistols, knives, and hand grenades—they were walking armamentaria. What the kidnappers didn't know was that these little, weak-looking children were among the strongest athletes in the world. They have extraordinary strength in their index fingers, and they are very well-conditioned.

The group reached the roaring Jopaiya, which was a real problem, because the rebels did not know how to swim. The Americans helped their captors get a log across to serve as a bridge, and they continued their trek. At one point, soldiers stood right near the captives, but did nothing. It turned out that they knew the Americans were there, but they had orders not to harm them. The soldiers had killed many of Abdul's comrades, but he may have been unaware of this, although his unresponsive radios indicated something was amiss.

While all of this movement and suffering were taking place, three other things are worth mentioning. First, the group tended to walk in purposeful circles in order to avoid interactions with soldiers, so that even after six days of misery, they were just three miles from the Yellow Wall. Second, these insurgents were slowly being encapsulated and more than half had been killed; soldiers told escapees "that they had been expecting an invasion for months." It is incomprehensible that all of these peoples' governments (Germany and Ukraine, for example) allowed them to travel to this area without dire warnings, that Kyrgyzstan issued visas (that sometimes were not in order), and that the climbers themselves did not have the good sense to stay away, when there exist thousands of safer environments in which to ply their hobbies. Third, the other groups of captives also were pummeled into wandering submission. One day, some awoke and discovered their passports on a rock and their captors gone. They were very lucky that the rebels did not simply murder them.

Things were moving toward a conclusion. Abdul, the leader, left on a mission. The four captives were in the hands of Su, a naive nineteen-year-old. They had to climb a 3,000-foot "hillside" of brush and rubble, but also cliffs. As they ascended, they considered ways of regaining their freedom, all of which entailed killing Su (who had a hard time climbing), and with whom they had become quite friendly. Caldwell and Rodden were squeamish, the others determined, but nothing happened. They were also worried that a bad storm was coming and that it would inundate them, and hypothermia would follow. Suddenly Caldwell grabbed at Su's rifle and yanked him off the wall. He tumbled down and Caldwell was very upset: "Holy shit, I killed a guy!" They ran away quickly and reached the river on August 18, a bit after midnight. They crossed and headed for the shrine of Mazur, where they were greeted by bullets from every direction. But they were safe. Eventually, they were flown to Bishkek on the Kirgiz president's plane.

The aftermath included an onslaught of journalists, meetings, interviews, television appearances, and other annoyances. For some reason, a number of unconnected people disputed the accounts of who had pushed Su, and they wrote articles and letters libelously condemning the climbers' putative distortions, which they claimed the escapees had insinuated in order to make more money from their story. Months later, it turned out that Su was alive, and Dickey and Smith, along with Greg Child, the author of the book on which this account is based, returned to Bishkek to speak with him. Caldwell was happy to learn that he was not a killer. The experience they had gone through created a powerful bond, but it proved elusive. Caldwell and Rodden subsequently married, had a child, and later divorced. Time passed.

Then on January 5, 2015, Caldwell turned up on the front page of the *New York Times* in eight column inches surrounding a large and impressive photo of Caldwell and his partner on the Dawn Wall of El Capitan. The story continued on a full secondary page with five additional exquisite images. The reason for this extraordinary coverage is that the partners were attempting to free-climb this smooth wall (without any aid), something no one had ever done before. In free climbing, ropes are only used for protection against a fall; they and other devices are not employed to help the climbers ascend. It is amazing to note that the men spent five years planning and practicing on El Capitan for this attempt (Branch). The *Times* followed up with additional extensive coverage on six subsequent days. The two men succeeded.

Caldwell and his friends' horrible experience in Kyrgyzstan might have been more than enough to deter most people from visiting there (although JA met a young climber who recently had a wonderful and safe time there), but the vilely wanton murders on Nanga Parbat should give real pause to all adventurers. Potential natural disaster is more than enough to have to cope with. Terrorists intent on murdering people in cold blood are insurmountable. It is certainly ironic that it was possible, even one thousand years ago, to travel in or visit strange and distant lands with impunity (think of the great adventurers—Marco Polo, Vasco da Gama, Giovanni da Verrazzano, Henry Hudson, Ferdinand Magellan, Marc Aurel Stein, David Livingston), be welcomed and honored in many cases, and come home unscathed, whereas in the twenty-first-century global village, we may be unrealistic not to expect to be murdered by evil maniacs.

Nanga Parbat has killed many people. On June 22, 2013, a group of about twelve terrorists murdered eleven innocent mountaineers at Nanga Parbat's base camp. The killers were dressed in paramilitary police uniforms and managed to alienate a host of countries by shooting Chinese, Nepalese, American, Pakistani, Ukrainian, Slovakian, and Lithuanian mountaineers. A single Chinese victim was rescued (Masood). Annabel Symington also includes a Russian as well as a Pakistani cook. She notes that thirty-five terrorists were subsequently arrested. The Taliban claimed that the murders compensated for drone attacks. The political ramifications of this massacre further strained relations between Pakistan and the United States, and altered China's positive attitude toward Pakistan (Masood). Only the truly courageous (or foolhardy) would now attempt mountains in Pakistan.

As it happens, on June 23, 2013, John Quillen and his partners were trekking in to Broad Peak, not far from Nanga Parbat, when they learned of the tragedy and were deeply affected. This was a very bad year in the Karakoram: Twenty-one people died, eleven at Nanga Parbat, seven on Broad Peak, and three on K2 (Quillen, 145, 1). A Sherpa on Broad Peak lost a cousin in the massacre; normally pacific by nature, he nevertheless reacted passionately, and his sentiments probably reflect the general tenor of how people around the world reacted: "I'm never coming back to this f***ing hellhole" (Quillen, 77). Because his partner broke his leg and had to be evacuated, Quillen left sooner than expected. The entire business had a devastating effect on his life.

SOURCES
The Yellow Wall narrative is based on Greg Child's horrifying account; other sources are noted in the text. Nanga Parbat is textually documented.

The Yellow Wall

Branch, John. "'Battling' Up a Sheer Yosemite Face, Seizing a Dream, Not a Rope," *New York Times.* January 5, 2015: A1, D7.

Child, Greg. *Over the Edge: The True Story of Four American Climbers' Kidnap and Escape in the Mountains of Central Asia.* New York: Villard, 2002.

"Memories of Captivity Await Climber in Kyrgyzstan." Npr.org. June 18, 2011. Accessed February 21, 2014. www.npr.org/2011/06/18/137267478/memories-of -captivity-await-climber-in-kyrgyzstan.

Nanga Parbat

Masood, Salman, and Declan Walsh. "Militants Kill 10 Climbers in Himalayas of Pakistan," *New York Times.* June 24, 2013: A4.

Quillen, John. *Tempting the Throne Room: Surviving Pakistan's Deadliest Climbing Season 2013.* San Bernardino, CA: n.p., 2014.

Symington, Annabel. "Pakistani Militants Strike Climbers' Camp, Killing 11." *Wall Street Journal.* June 24, 2013: A9.

Kings Canyon National Park, 2003:
Amy Racina's Angels

IN THE CASE OF SEVERE DISASTER, THERE EXIST THREE PATHS TO SALVA-
tion. One may draw upon an indomitable inner spirit, will, strength, and
exemplary courage, as was the case with Joe Simpson (see above), one
may be helped or rescued at the outset, as was Marty Hoey when she
succumbed to AMS on Nanda Devi; or one may be lucky, really lucky, so
that someone wanders along in a location where few people ever hike, and
thereby one is saved. This last is what occurred as Amy Racina lay dying.

Racina is a very strong person physically and mentally. She had spent
a great deal of time in the wilderness, as a child with her family, and
then later, alone. She reveled in long, solo hikes and was able to cope
with discomforts and problems, such as drenching rain, that dismay less-
audacious urbanites. For her big Kings Canyon adventure, she had done
a 120-mile warm-up hike. It should be made clear that her solo walks in
the wilderness were very different from a stroll in Iowa. She wandered at
altitude and constantly climbed and descended thousands of feet. This
adventure was to cover some 160 miles in seventeen days.

She almost made it.

On August 4, her twelfth day out, she was moving along well, continuing her descent into the Tehipite, a valley she had long dreamed of
visiting. (She later discovered that her grandparents had also visited this
distant valley back in 1924.) She had carefully placed her foot, held on to
a rock and a tree, and had stepped, but her holds gave way and she plummeted 60 feet, crashing onto rock and abrading and harming her body
fearfully. She also had a destroyed knee and two broken legs, which made
it impossible to walk; even crawling was beyond her. She was amazed to

be alive, but realized that she was in real trouble. She had chosen this secluded area because she wanted to be alone—something that would now work against her. Few if any people wandered here; she was slightly off the trail, 25 miles from a trailhead; and she was not expected back for almost another week. She remarked that her "chances of survival are grim." But she has a will of steel, and reminds one of Aron Ralston (see below), who also fought back rather than capitulate to the inevitable.

Despite her horrific injuries and the pain that movement caused, she set about protecting herself and then planning for escape. A number of very positive things were in evidence: She was next to a source of water; her backpack, with its lifesaving content, was within reach (without it, she would have soon succumbed to hypothermia); and her determination to survive was undiminished. She happened to be obsessive concerning her gear and carried only lightweight items and precisely what she required:[1] "I have what I need to give me a chance at survival." She protected herself from the cold night, ate, and then, despite the pain, amazingly, slept. She managed to scrupulously assess her situation and considered threats such as bodily toxins, flooding, falling rock, hypothermia, starvation, loss of blood (which did occur), infection, and animal attacks. But she went forward—like a Beckettian antihero, but with a better chance of success. Now and again, she also had complex metaphysical and theological discussions with herself.

She awoke early on the first full day of her ordeal, went through some maneuvers, and figured out that she was about 1,000 vertical feet and a mile or so above the valley floor. She knew that another trail ran along the valley, and thought that this was a good goal. She knew it would be a horrific task, but worth the effort: If she were to die, not suffering "additional pain and injury will be unimportant." She was able to push herself forward down the slope using her hands, and further facilitated this by getting into the stream where the flowing water helped. She propelled herself along, pulling her pack behind her. It took her one hour to travel 10 yards. This process produced extreme pain, in her damaged hip, for example, but she continued. Astonishingly, she observed that the pain from her many horrible injuries was never as bad as a toothache she had

had some years before. By the end of the day she had traveled a total of 30 yards. She slept.

The second day of torment arrived very early, and while awaiting daylight she read by flashlight! She was aware that she only had a limited amount of warming sunlight so she must move downward quickly. The third day was similar, but a small ledge stymied her progress. She spent her time conversing with herself and God. She had a vision, and she read some more! Every once in a while, she called for help, although it was extremely improbable that anyone would pass nearby or hear her cries: "Heeeeeelp me!" Suddenly she caught two faint whistle toots. She called again, heard the toots again, and then screamed hysterically, and banged on a pot. For a short time there was silence, but then a noise was followed by the arrival of human angels. Three hikers had stumbled upon her and thereby saved her life. Racina does not believe in coincidence; this was a miracle. These people had been sent to rescue her, and they did, by tending to her and running 9 uphill miles to get help, which arrived the next day in the form of EMTs and some helicopters. Jake, the man who stayed with her, told her that had she not "crawled" down to her current location, he would not have heard her cries. He also insisted that the topography would have halted her further progress. She was taken to the Fresno hospital, where she suffered painfully for many weeks.

In most traumatic accounts, the tale concludes quite abruptly after the initial tragedy or rescue. *Angels in the Wilderness* is different. Almost half of the book is given over to Racina's astounding if hard-won recovery, and the latter descriptions are as emotionally powerful and moving as her accident and rescue. Her injuries were much more extensive and horrific than she had imagined, and they required a three-week hospital stay, many (repeated) surgeries, months of hard and painful physical therapy, and a great deal of mental agitation and conjuring to effect a potent recovery. She was assisted in all of this by a large group of exceptionally kind and helpful friends who raised money, collected things she needed, worked with her on her business matters, and cared for her when at first she was a complete invalid. She was very lucky, especially since her $300,000 hospital bill was basically expunged.

Racina often escaped from an ugly and chaotic world, which felt "like shrapnel in [her] soul," by surviving, recovering, thriving, and returning to her beloved wild areas alone for days at a time, which is the second miracle, since no one even knew if she would be able to walk again. This magnificent tale and its miraculous denouement are an inspiration to those who find themselves in exigent situations. Her story made *The Montel Williams Show* and *National Geographic Adventure* magazine.

NOTES

1 She listed every item and offered a combined weight of 33 pounds; this is certainly more reasonable than the enormous 40-, 50-, or 60-pound packs that mountaineers and national-trail through-hikers often haul along, but some of her necessities are questionable. Did she really need a heavy bear canister? (Maybe.) Various bottles and water carriers? (Perhaps.) A notepad? A swimsuit? (Probably not.)

SOURCES

Racina, Amy. *Angels in the Wilderness: The True Story of One Woman's Survival Against All Odds*. Santa Rosa, CA: Elite Books, 2005.

Blue John Canyon, 2003:
Aron Ralston

ARON RALSTON'S PROBLEM WOULD UNDOUBTEDLY HAVE BEEN SOLVED IN
a more-palatable fashion had he informed someone that he was planning
to go to a very specific location, or had he invited someone to accompany
him, or had he altered his plans and accompanied the two women he
had met along the way. Climbing or (in this case) canyoneering alone is,
simply put, stupid.[1]

On April 26, 2003, Ralston decided to visit Blue John Canyon. On
the way in, he met two young women who invited him to try something else, but he declined. He did indicate that they would meet up
later, which is important, because they were the only people who had an
inkling of his location, and might have been worried when he did not
show up. In the end, however, this didn't do him any good. He dropped
down, rappelled, stemmed, passed chockstones, and contorted himself
as he moved through narrow passageways, continuing until he reached
a large wedged stone that had to be circumvented in order for him to
further descend.

He stemmed to the stone and placed his weight on it. It moved, but
held. He crawled to the edge and attempted to hang down and thus lower
himself to the next level. He dangled. He then released, but not soon
enough, for the stone (which he thought weighed about 200 pounds, but
actually weighed much more) tipped and followed him down. He managed to get his head out of the stone's path; the boulder smashed his left
hand and then crushed his right hand and ensnared it. He could not
retract it and despite his pumping adrenaline and the searing pain, he
could not move the rock enough to pull his hand out, no matter how hard

he pushed upward. He was very thirsty, so he drank a lot of water, after which he realized that he had just gobbled up a third of his supply.

Ralston forced himself to calm down and think. He discovered that the boulder sat on three points, with his hand acting as a fourth. He could touch various parts of his unfeeling right hand with his left, but this did nothing for him. He could not move very far and realized that no one knew precisely where he was, so that when he was missed, no one could come searching for him. He surveyed his belongings (food, camera, tool, headlamp, and rope, among many other items) and considered his options, slowly eliminating various rescue possibilities (someone will stumble by, he will be missed by various people at different times). He knew that his water supply was extremely limited, so he only had a few days to live; thus, he realized that rescue was unlikely, "about as probable as winning the lottery."

He tried to chip away at the sandstone block with his multi-tool, which appeared to be a sensible way to escape, but it was as hard and impenetrable as rock, because it was. He continued to hack away at the stone. He told himself (out loud) that he would have to amputate his arm; he then retorted that he did not want to! He was in dire straits with a trapped right hand, but he also had another issue: Although badly swollen and disfigured, there was no pain (not necessarily a good sign). In addition, his thigh was "bruised and abraded in a dozen places," and was painful. He had had the bad luck to drop his keys into a fissure and they were beyond his grasp, but he struggled with different implements and was elated to retrieve them. He continued to chip at the rock and progressed slightly.

Ralston's narrative is extremely detailed, so the reader is able to precisely accompany him as he continued to act and suffer. During the next four days, he did many things. He was able to accomplish these for two reasons. First, he had had many experiences in harsh circumstances. For example, he had set for himself the very difficult goal of climbing all of the Colorado 14,000-foot mountains—in winter, and alone. He also did rescue work. Naturally, he had had many close calls: He had managed to avoid being crushed by a thundering boulder; he had almost drowned; he had ministered to his bad frostbite on his own; and he had convinced two friends to ski a dangerous slope, where they all barely avoided dying in a bad avalanche (they never talked to him again). He seemed to enjoy these potentially fatal situations.

Second, he was a mechanical engineer with five years of work experience at Intel. Since he was unable to sit down, he created, MacGyver-like, an anchor by repeatedly tossing a weighted rope into a crack until it lodged; he then attached the rope to his harness and thereby was able to take weight off his legs for short periods. He then set a second anchor and rigged a pulley system with a 3:1 mechanical advantage (though friction reduced this). He emplaced foot loops at the bottom so that he could use his entire body weight to lift the rock. Sadly, he failed to budge it. As time went by, he heard voices, which turned out to be an animal's scuttling, and then began to seriously contemplate the means of amputating his arm, which distressed and depressed him. He recovered and decided to videotape himself.

The second day of his ordeal passed, and he prepared for the colder night by tying various objects around his bare arms and coiling his climbing rope around his legs. He spent time thinking, praying, philosophizing, and fantasizing, but he remained trapped. The next morning (the third day), he reworked the lifting system, but the dynamic (stretchable) rope he was using, plus the complexity of the system (with carabiners substituted for pulleys), dissipated its lifting power. It did not work. He again contemplated amputation, fashioned an excellent tourniquet, and tried to cut into his skin, but failed.

The fourth day arrived and Ralston was cold, hungry, and thirsty. Although he still had a few ounces of water left, he decided to drink a tiny amount of his urine, which was not as repulsive as he feared it might be. As he dehydrated, his heartbeat weakened but speeded up to 120 beats per minute. He was in bad shape, but nothing was as horrible as his thirst. When he somehow managed to spill a few drops of his precious but dwindling supply, he became even more sad and depressed. His ruminations concerning a rescue concluded in its improbability. Amazingly, though, he was still psychologically capable of videotaping himself, and he spent some time talking to his parents and praising his sister, and later he thanked his friends for the wonderful trips they had taken together.

Next, he reset his hauling system and approached the new attempt very positively. Ralston is an excellent narrator and evoked the situation perfectly: *Okay, now move the boulder, Aron. Do it. Bounce. Harder. Pull on the rope—yank on it. Bounce and yank.* And so on. Lamentably, the chockstone did not move. He then immediately set up his tourniquet and viciously jabbed himself in the arm with his small knife blade. He was amazed. He stopped, drank the last drops of his water, and bound up the wound. The day ended in "Confusion, delirium, and ruthless cold," and he spent much time in a hallucinatory trance-like state. When he did not show up for work earlier in the day, people became concerned, and reported him missing. Naturally, it took time for a serious search to begin.

On the fifth day, hungry, thirsty, dehydrated, and beaten down both physically and psychologically, he nevertheless pressed on, videotaping, considering rescue attempts and how they would play out, dreaming about water, and smashing at the chockstone with a small hard rock, a procedure that was effective but too painful on his left hand to continue. It was at this time, as cold night (and hypothermia) came on, that he realized he was about to die. He then had a waking dream about a little boy (his unborn son) and changed his mind: He would survive! As he continued to suffer, his friends and employer back in Aspen began to take action. They contacted his parents and the police, and attempted to discover where he had gone; since he had told no one and left few hints, this was a seemingly fruitless task. But everyone persevered. Eventually authorities in different Utah park areas went out to trailheads looking for his truck.

It was the sixth and last day, Thursday, May 1, and Ralston could not believe he was still alive, sleepless for 120 hours and thirsty beyond human endurance. He tried to smash the rock again, but it was too painful. He stopped and cleaned the grit up with his knife, accidentally cutting his thumb, which allowed him to discover that the flesh was decomposing much more quickly than he had thought. He thus concluded that the putrefaction was poisoning him, moving up his arm and into his body. This upset him and he angrily lashed out, pulling at his hand roughly, and screaming hysterically. Suddenly he realized that if he twisted his arm enough it would break, which resolved the impossibility of cutting though the bone with his tiny knife. He applied pressure first downward and then upward. He succeeded in breaking his arm. He was so excited that he skipped the emplacement of the tourniquet he had previously designed and proceeded to cut through the soft tissue, tendons, ligaments, and nerves, hoping to cut the arteries last. He then put on the tourniquet, and completed the job at 11:32 a.m. He had freed himself, and lapsed into a state of extreme euphoria.

As he struggled, the search for him continued. And just a short time before he completed the amputation, his truck was discovered, which set in motion a full-fledged rescue by officials from many agencies, including horses and two helicopters.

Astonishingly, he was steady on his feet and levelheaded. He packed up his stuff and left; he felt lightheaded, not because of what he had done, but rather because he was rushing after days of immobility and little sustenance. He stumbled his way through the intricacies of the slot canyon and finally broke out on a wall 65 feet above the ground. Somehow he organized his 170 feet of badly tangled rope, almost lost it over the edge but caught the slithering rope in time, and set up his rappel. He was ready to go when he noticed that he had failed to double his harness belt back through the buckle. But he was anxious to get down: "If I had two hands and weren't in the process of bleeding to death, I would double back the belt, but right now, with water waiting below, it's a risk I'm willing to take."

He very carefully negotiated a lip and then slid down to the ground, and the water he had been dreaming about for days. He immediately swallowed three liters of (dirty) water (which is advised against in such situations, and this did upset his stomach). Now he had to hike 8 miles, so he moved out. It was hard going in the heat, and after a mile, he managed to consume a third of his additional three-liter water supply. He tried a trick: He held some water in his mouth rather than swallowing it. This helped to humidify the air he was inhaling. After 6 miles he met three hikers, two of whom ran back to get help, and soon thereafter, a helicopter picked him up and delivered him to a hospital. Immediately, some personnel returned to the canyon to retrieve the hand for possible reattachment. What they discovered was that the boulder did not weigh 200 pounds, but more like 1,000. They did not have adequate equipment to raise it.

He was well taken care of in the hospital, had three surgeries, and eventually returned home. He became a world sensation and inspired people to press on in the face of adversity. After two weeks, doctors discovered a bad infection in his arm. (He had cut it with a dirty knife.) He had two more operations, and although he returned home, he spent many weeks on intravenous infusions. The lengthy, physically and psychologically painful convalescence was very difficult for him, but eventually he returned to a normal life, devoid of hundreds of journalists, photographers, and well-wishers.

Six months after the accident, he went back to the canyon with four friends and a *Dateline* crew. Ralston continues to ski, climb, and pursue adventure.

These harrowing and amazing events and deadly physical pain, as well as mental anguish, are clearly manifested in *127 Hours*, the Danny Boyle film (starring James Franco) that brings this horrifying experience all too vividly to life. It complements Ralston's account, and inspires one to do his or her very best in the face of overwhelming odds. Along with Joe Simpson's and Doug Scott's escapes, Ralston's triumph must stand as one of the most extraordinary feats in the history of climbing.

Notes

1 JA has done as many as four hundred unaccompanied climbs (e.g., in the Green Mountains, the Blue Ridge, the Rockies, the Alps). Lamentably, often no one knows where he goes, what route he follows, or when he plans to return.

Sources

We based this account on Ralston's extremely fascinating and appositely entitled autobiography. Of its 353 pages, only a handful are allocated to the infamous amputation. The rest of the book deals with his exciting life and what he did during his five-day ordeal, all of which holds the reader in thrall.

127 Hours. Danny Boyle, Dir. Fox Searchlight, etc. 2011.
Ralston, Aron. *Between a Rock and a Hard Place*. New York: Atria Books, 2004.

Everest, 2006:
The Sad and Unnecessary Death
of David Sharp

*They [today's climbers] don't give a damn for anybody else who may
be in distress and it doesn't impress me at all that they leave someone
lying under a rock to die.*
          —SIR EDMUND HILLARY

*When Chaya reached his tent at Camp Four, he collapsed inside it and
cried for two hours [because he was unable to help Sharp].*
            —NICK HEIL

THERE EXISTS AN UNWRITTEN CODE OF CONDUCT, A MOUNTAINEERING
ethic, which attempts to ensure that the brotherhood of the rope remains
intact. There is nothing special about this esoteric-sounding commitment;
it is merely an extension of normal ethical adjurations, which mandate
that, generally, people help their fellow human beings, especially when
no harm accrues to the benefactor, but at times even when the person
must make a sacrifice, risk his or her life in order to save another—a
drowning child, an elderly woman in a burning nursing home, a diseased
person in a contaminated hospital ward, a fellow soldier under attack.
In the past, those who helped may have done harm and subsequently
been sued or prosecuted, and that is why many legislative bodies have
passed Good Samaritan laws to protect those who only had beneficent
intentions. With few exceptions, including Objectivists who denigrate
altruism and are selfishly committed primarily to themselves, most decent

humans (and some domesticated and even wild animals) will offer assistance when necessary.

Most cultures teach their offspring that honesty and caring are virtues, and dissimulation, destruction, theft, and murder are unacceptable and usually punished. Kindness and consideration are human ideals; even when modified by necessity or rapacity, perpetrators know that what they are doing is wrong, a breach of an explicit or unstated ethical commitment. Ethical mandates that obtain in life are not abrogated when a person is removed to the wild; indeed, they are magnified, and in most situations a ranger or hiker, a guide[1] or skier will come to the aid of an injured or sick person trapped alone on a trail, in the desert or mountains, on the ocean, indeed, anywhere such an encounter occurs.

The approximately forty mountaineers who passed by as David Sharp lay dying would never act that way were they not on their lifelong quests to reach Everest's summit. They allowed an expensive and hard-earned personal goal to obviate their good sense, their ethical commitment, their humanness. Had one of them been lying along the trail, it is fairly certain that he or she would have hoped that someone would attempt a rescue, which is usually what does occur. If just one of those many people had really tried to help, Sharp might be alive today. Sadly, this is not an unusual occurrence; see, for example, the situation of the three hanging Koreans described in chapter 6. Nevertheless, the general public was shocked; Sir Edmund Hillary offered harsh criticism (of a fellow Kiwi).

This business is extremely controversial because, concomitantly, it is very easy to criticize and judge from afar, especially when one's $60,000 is still in the bank, when one has not spent years training, and months carrying heavy loads through really dangerous icefalls, acclimatizing, suffering from alien food, intestinal parasites, cold (and heat), frostbite, and risking potential harm or death. It is possible that we might have reacted with nonchalance and summit-fever, if we knew that we could never return, that this was our only chance to achieve what to a general mountaineer is the apex of his or her sport. Sharp's mother is astonishingly open-minded and does not blame those who passed by ("David Sharp [mountaineer]"). Others obviously do.

David Sharp, a lone, unsupported, unguided climber, who carried less oxygen than required, and no radio or telephone, found himself in a horrible predicament on May 15, 2006, as he moved downward; he was incapacitated and needed help. Some forty ascending and descending mountaineers on the north side of Everest passed him, but most failed to render assistance. When Sharp was discovered in Green Boots Cave, he was unable to move, very badly frostbitten, and near death; it was the middle of the night, and by morning, when a rescue might have been attempted, he was in even worse shape. Many people believe that it would have been impossible to successfully bring him down from the death zone. Nevertheless, some climbers did carry him out into the sun, but he remained immobile (Burke). And a Sherpa gave him oxygen and tried to get him to stand and go down, but failed ("David Sharp [mountaineer]").

A different perspective is offered by some of the climbers who passed Sharp, first ascending and then on their way down: They claimed that he was not near death, but rather lucid, and spoke to them, identifying himself and his trekking company ("Everest 2006"). Dr. Jose Ramon Morandeira, an expert in mountain medicine, is unequivocal: "David would have had many possibilities of being saved if someone had cared for him on the spot, and then helped him down. I've seen people in the mountains in a much worse state—and they made it." He insists that in the past most climbers would have helped ("Dr. Morandeira"). Morandeira, however, was not on-site at the time.

But Bill Burke claims that much of the criticism was "harsh and unjustified," especially remarks aimed at Mark Inglis, a double amputee, who had to be carried down because of frostbite, and who was therefore in no position to offer help. Sharp's company, Asian Trekking, also appears to be blameless. Their agreement was for Sharp to climb alone, and the company's representatives did not know what had occurred until it was too late (Burke). As it happens, though, three additional people using this company died shortly thereafter ("David Sharp [mountaineer]").

Nick Heil offers a very broad perspective; he is able to do this because he has written *Dark Summit*, a detailed monograph on the devastating 2006 Everest season (when at least eleven people died). His account puts special emphasis on Russell Brice's Himalayan Experience (HIMEX) group, and especially (but not exclusively) on the fate of Sharp, along with Lincoln Hall and Thomas Weber. Heil indicates that Sharp—who at thirty-four had already tried Everest twice (Heil, 105)—wanted to summit very badly, and was willing to sacrifice appendages to achieve this dubious goal (Heil, 136–37). In 2006, as he operated entirely alone, ferrying loads to his high camps (Heil, 112), an Indian climber was rendered unconscious by cerebral edema high on the mountain. Ironically, many people including a doctor worked feverishly to save his life. He was lowered off the col and a Sherpa carried him to base camp, 14 miles away (Heil, 115, 117). Additionally, Lincoln Hall died, reawakened (à la Beck Weathers), and was rescued. The enormous difference was that Hall was mobile (Heil, 216 ff, 240).

For some reason, Sharp did not elicit enough of this kind of sympathetic help. He was observed on May 11, heading up (Heil, 122). Sometime thereafter, guide Bill Crouse left for his summit attempt just after midnight on May 14, on a very cold night; the temperature was about 40 below zero (Heil, 125, 126). As he proceeded, he and another climber passed an individual "slumped" off the route; it was presumably Sharp, apparently not "using oxygen"; something seemed to be wrong (Heil, 126–27). After summiting, Crouse headed down, and had to pass an unresponsive person moving upward. Later, Crouse looked up and noticed that the person was moving very slowly. Later still, late in the day, he saw him once again: He had managed a mere 100 yards during a two-hour period (Heil, 132, 133). No one knows whether Sharp summited, but eventually, he descended.

Sometime after midnight on May 15, a group of climbers reached Green Boots Cave and were stunned to find an additional person there, still attached to the fixed line. They yelled at him but he failed to respond in any way; he appeared to be unconscious. The men continued up, believing that he could not be helped. Another group followed and reached the same conclusion, although two members indicated that Sharp had replied to them (Heil, 141–43). On May 15, at 9:30 a.m., two descending men found Sharp disconnected from the line and shivering. Their leader below advised them to get him on oxygen, but then to leave. A Sherpa named Dorje gave him some of his own; his client, Max Chaya, was emotionally incapable of helping but simultaneously unwilling to leave. Eventually he did, and when he arrived at camp, he broke down and cried (Heil, 152–54).

Next came two Turkish climbers and two Sherpas who tried to get Sharp up, but failed. They did hook him to one of their cylinders. They too were tired and forced to continue down. Some others then pulled him out into the sun. His limbs were frozen in place, but he did mumble something (Heil, 154–57). What all of this makes clear is that these many men, extremely tired on the way up, now exhausted and in sometimes extreme pain on the way down, could not do much for Sharp, since they were struggling to save themselves. As Inglis notes, "[A]t 8,500 meters it's extremely difficult to keep yourself alive, let alone keeping anyone else alive [and recall that his leader radioed up that Sharp was basically dead and they could not effectively help]" (Heil, 183).

The excellent and moving cinematic overview offered in *The David Sharp Controversy Documentary* presents much slow physical movement, which shows how extremely difficult the climb was, especially on this particularly frigid night. The conditions appear to obviate the possibility of a rescue of a semicomatose person, despite what some armchair critics think. Additionally, there is a great deal of discussion offered by the people involved. Both those (perhaps unfairly) accused of malfeasance and others were deeply affected by what occurred, and at times could barely talk about it. Still, death in the mountains is hardly an infrequent guest. More than two hundred bodies are scattered across Everest's flanks. That Sharp was ill-equipped, started up alone and very late in the day, and therefore may have reached the summit much later than he should have, all played seminal roles here. Some critics indicate that his fate was in his own hands. Nevertheless, mountaineering has changed not least because so many more people now climb. Desensitization and a blasé attitude toward ethical commitment are real problems (*David Sharp Controversy*).

For some, a disagreement concerning calls to an expedition leader far below is a crucial point: Climbers say they called; he says that they did not (*David Sharp Controversy*). For an objective outsider, someone who knows something about mountaineering, the conditions that obtain, and the risks, the calls are of no real consequence. That these autocratic leaders, who stay below, attempt to control their charges, strikes us as unnecessary and at times dangerous. That in this case, he could either give or withhold permission to attempt to save someone's life is egregiously bizarre. A selfish or incapacitated person would ignore him; a small group of dedicated people would have tried (and perhaps failed) to effect a rescue (which sometimes takes days, and the help of as many as fifteen people).

The bottom line is that it is impossible to know how each individual reacted at the moment; some of the participants thought Sharp was dead, or claim to be unsure about matters because of hypoxia and other probable determinants. David Sharp's suffering and death were a direct result of his own attitudes and actions, and some of his peers and even his own mother indicate that he took full responsibility. Still, it is disconcerting and sad that few climbers tried to fully help, that he died, and to think that the same fate can befall anyone who ventures into the wild. Everest does not hold a monopoly on disaster, although many people died there during the 2006 season. Let Mogens Jensen, who was there, have the last word: "I never understood the controversy about David Sharp. . . . There is no controversy [because it is almost impossible to get a comatose person or body down from that altitude]" (Heil, 169).

Notes

1 The famous Chamonix guides are ethically obligated to stop their guiding, even though their clients have paid them, and go to the aid of an injured or exhausted stranger, which is precisely what occurred to the senior author of this book as he and his brother climbed Mont Blanc. They waited patiently while the rescue took place. (This, by the way, was the only time that either of the authors ever used a guide during more than half a century in some thousand climbs in various parts of the world.)

Sources

Multiple sources were consulted for this narrative; they are identified (parenthetically) in the text.

Burke, Bill. "The Tragic Death of David Sharp." *Eight Summits.* 2013. eightsummits
    .com/bills-articles/the-tragic-death-of-david-sharp/.
The David Sharp Controversy Documentary. Dir., Richard Dennison. 2014.
"David Sharp (mountaineer)," Wikipedia. en.wikipedia.org/wiki/
    David_Sharp_(mountaineer).

"Dr. Morandeira: Could David Sharp have been saved? Definitely." ExplorersWeb. www.explorersweb.com/everest_k2/news.php?id=10081.

"Everest 2006: 'My Name is David Sharp and I am with Asian Trekking.'" EverestNews .com.

Heil, Nick. *Dark Summit: The True Story of Everest's Most Controversial Season*. New York: Henry Holt, 2009.

K2, 2010:

Little Lies, Damning Lies: Christian Stangl's Ascent Hoax, and Kanchenjunga, 2009: Oh Eun-Sun's False Claim

IN SOME INSTANCES, CONTROVERSIAL, FRAUDULENT, OR TRAGIC CONSE-quences intersect with each other. In Christian Stangl's case, this does not occur; here we have a straightforward hoax, a blatant lie, one that covers a lot of ground because Stangl was still 3,000 feet from the summit he claimed to have reached. Despite diverse precedent, it strikes us as very peculiar—indeed, incomprehensible—that a competent and respected person would attempt to deceive. First, he must realize that there is a good chance he will be discovered, and then he will have to continue to assert his claim to a skeptical world, which can be embarrassing, or admit culpability; and second, he is acting unethically, dishonestly, dishonorably, and it is honor and its many tangible concomitants that he seeks. Very few people break the world record for global circumnavigation or discovery of America or arrival at the North Pole or any other great deed and keep it to themselves. They are proud of their hard-won accomplishments and wish to be honored (with a big grant from Queen Isabella, or a New York ticker-tape parade).

But since even respected scientists sometimes dissimulate (in many ways), despite their goal of discovering truth (and the fact that replication will eventually prove they are wrong),[1] it is obvious that adventurers may delude themselves into hoping they can get away with murder—so to speak. Mark Horrell comes up with eight reasons to claim a summit even though it eluded the climber. In addition to fame and remuneration, one may wish to impress sponsors or clients, or get a bonus, or simply be mistaken (Horrell).

Stewart Green tells us that on August 12, 2010, Christian Stangl summited K2 alone after a seventy-hour marathon. He shot some photographs, descended, rested along the way, and eventually returned to base camp. Some people were skeptical, since he only had a single (faked) image (in reality, shot 3,000 feet under the summit) to prove that he had reached the top; no one had seen him high on the mountain (and there were no signs that he had passed various points); he did not have any data from GPS readings; and his axes and other equipment were found at Camp Three. At first, he vehemently defended his accomplishment. Later, at a press conference shortly after he returned, he admitted that he had not reached the K2 summit, but he bizarrely claimed that he did not mean to dissimulate: "[H]ypoxia-induced hallucinations" caused him to make his claim, something that might seem credible to people who were not on the mountain at the time, because Stangl has a stunning résumé. His fear of failing on this, his seventh K2 attempt, allowed him to twist the truth. The result is that a great mountaineer's integrity has been called into question, and Mammut, his sponsor, was very disenchanted with him (Green).

Vinicio Stefanello points out that although at first Stangl insisted that he had made the top, he then capitulated and admitted that he had lied. That he fully confessed, and on a live television broadcast, is apparently a unique development, which took a great deal of courage. Stefanello, generalizing from this experience, takes mountaineering to task: It is in crisis, caught up in summit fever, and should return to its roots: climbing for its own sake, not for sponsorships or rewards (Stefanello). Lamentably, he is correct: Far too many people now climb for the wrong reasons, sometimes compulsively, which results in unnecessary risk and, upon failure, dissimulation. We can no longer trust solo climbers who make claims without adducing solid evidence.

In a powerful coda to this grotesque affair, Stangl's sponsor, Mammut, announced that on July 31, 2012, Stangl finally reached the summit of K2. He provided precise evidence of his achievement through ongoing coordinate readings and a summit video. His goal, all along, has been the triple Seven Summits, that is, the three highest peaks on each of the seven continents ("Christian"), a feat he achieved shortly thereafter.

Coincidentally, there took place in 2009 another deception perpetrated by another extraordinary mountaineer. At that time, three climbers were vying for the extreme honor of being the first female to reach the summits of all fourteen 8,000-meter peaks. They were under great pressure—from themselves and probably from their countries and sponsors. It was a close race among Gerlinde Kaltenbrunner (an Austrian), Edurne Pasaban (a Spaniard), and Oh Eun-Sun (a Korean). Oh won; even Kaltenbrunner admitted this, when Oh claimed Kanchenjunga's summit. As it happens, Mark Horrell was on Gasherbrum I, a year before, and was unable to continue, whereas Oh reached the summit. Horrell was skeptical but allowed it to pass. Kanchenjunga, however, was another story (Horrell).

Korean culture is extremely demanding: Shame is worse than death; parents push their children so hard that they commit suicide; and mountaineers have the reputation of being unrealistically desirous, ambitious, and aggressive in their goals. They wish to reach the summit regardless of cost, and will push on when others turn back. Their motto might be the "summit or die" catchphrase a Korean climber uttered when he tried to make clear how he and his countrymen felt about their objective. Oh, inured to these general and specific cultural demands, lost sight of essential guiding principles such as truth and integrity, and substituted (faked) success in the eyes of the world. She was not allowed to fail, she could not fail, and so, as Angela Benavides pointed out, she claimed the summit of Kanchenjunga, her last fourteen thousander, when in reality she had probably failed. Both the Korean Climbing Federation as well as Elizabeth Hawley, the Kathmandu-based historian of Himalayan climbing, rejected her claim.

Oh is infamous for failing to provide proof for her previous summits. Benavides noted many concerns related to Kanchenjunga: Oh went up in very bad weather, moving slowly below and then speeding up high on the mountain, which is most unusual and unrealistic; a summit photo did not appear for many weeks, and when it did, it showed rubble whereas the summit is snow-covered; she did not see the oxygen cylinders on the summit; her banner was found below the top; no confirming evidence was ever presented; finally, one of her Sherpas told Pasaban that they had failed, but he refused to speak up because he did not want to lose his livelihood, though for a payment he indicated that he would provide proof (Benavides, part 1). Sometime after continuing to insist that she had summited, Oh admitted, in an interview with *Der Spiegel*, that she had never reached the top of Kanchenjunga: "The weather was very bad, so we did not go to the actual summit. But where I stand, it is the summit for me" (Benavides, part 2).

This personal truth, which dissimulators like to cite, is the bane of historians and those who care about what really occurred, not what happened in a climber's heart and soul; this is analogous to the lies both scientists and the downtrodden perpetrate in order to achieve a "higher purpose." But it must be clear to readers that there is an enormous difference between these minor deceptions followed by confessions (not to mitigate ethical responsibility) and the ongoing series of lies that Cook perpetrated, and which are still being defended more than one hundred years later. (See above.)

Notes

1 Recent severe instances of scientific misconduct (which comprises fabrication, falsification, and plagiarism) are far too numerous to enumerate, but include the *Cell*/Baltimore, Jan Hendrik Schön, and Marc Hauser cases. See William Broad and Nicholas Wade's *Betrayers of the Truth* and Marcel C. LaFollette's *Stealing into Print*, among many other monographic treatments. More successful and (profitable) dissimulation exists in the art world, where forgers create (older) masterpieces and sell them for enormous sums of money, often eluding detection for decades or longer. See, for example, the forgeries of Han van Meegeren, Elmyr de Hory, and John Myatt. (And finally, consider the witticism that states the great Corot painted three thousand paintings, five thousand of which are in America.)

Sources

Christian Stangl
"Christian Stangl Overjoyed to Reach the Summit of K2—Mammut." August 13, 2012. www.mammut.ch/basecamp/en/entries/basecamp-news/christian_stangl_successful_ascent_on_k2?iframe=1.

Green, Stewart. "Austrian Climber Christian Stangl Tells Big Fat Lie about Ascent," About Sports. 2010. climbing.about.com/b/2010/09/10/austrian-climber-christian -stangl-tells-big-fat-lie-about-k2-ascent.htm.

Horrell, Mark. "8 reasons why false summit claims are made." *Footsteps on the Mountain.* December 10, 2010. www.markhorrell.com/blog/2010/false-summit-claims/.

Stefanello, Vinicio. "Christian Stangl Confesses: His K2 Summit Fruit of the Imagination." PlanetMountain.com. September 8, 2010. www.planetmountain.com/en/ news/alpinism/christian-stangl-confesses-his-k2-summit-fruit-of-the-imagination .html.

Oh Eun-Sun

Benavides, Angela. "ExWeb Special Report, Part 1: Oh Eun-Sun Loses Summit Status at AdventureStats." ExplorersWeb. December 9, 2010. www.explorersweb.com/ everest_k2/news.php?id=19768.

Benavides, Angela. "ExWeb Oh Eun Sun Special Report, Part 2: The Scoop." Explorers Web. December 10, 2010. www.explorersweb.com/everest_k2/news.php?id=19770.

Horrell, Mark. "8 Reasons Why False Summit Claims Are Made." *Footsteps on the Mountain.* December 10, 2010. www.markhorrell.com/blog/2010/ false-summit-claims/.

Tunnel Creek, 2012:
Avalanche

On February 19, 2012, sixteen skiers and snowboarders took a lift and then walked across to the out-of-bounds area called Tunnel Creek in Washington's Cascade range in order to ski or board (usually, ride) back down. Their impact on the snow caused a devastating avalanche and three exceptional people died. This tragedy so impressed the editors of the *New York Times* that they did something that is probably unprecedented: They created a special fourteen-page, magnificently and colorfully illustrated, advertisement-free section (written by John Branch) that was devoted entirely to this single occurrence. Ironically, although the tragedy took place out of bounds, it was just off Stevens Pass ski resort rather than deep in a helicopter-accessed backcountry location.

Avalanches are extraordinarily destructive. Every year, individuals, groups, and villages, in Switzerland, for example, are overcome by vast quantities of flowing snow pouring down at as much as 300 miles an hour. In 1618, a single avalanche in Pleurs, France, killed some 2,430 people; at least 35 Americans were killed by avalanches in 2001–2002 (Hartemann, 21–22). The yearly, worldwide toll is around 200 people. The authors, naturally, have encountered distant harmless avalanches, in Utah, for example, but have also climbed in the Rockies many months after an avalanche had occurred. It is impossible to adequately describe the extensive devastation: Tens of thousands of trees lay twisted and broken along a wide swath of formerly forested land.

The skiers and boarders at Tunnel Creek were all professional experts, and many had skied these meadows and gullies before. They were not foolhardy adventurers hoping for an extreme run on an 80- or 90-degree cliff, one in which a single slip or error can prove fatal. Instead, they were just out for a pleasant afternoon in new deep powder, but happened to find themselves in the wrong place at the wrong time. Some had read the avalanche reports but had not paid strict attention to the avalanche forecast (considerable to high), nor scrupulously analyzed the snowpack (with its 32 inches of fresh snow).

But the ski patrol had: They began very early to set off charges along the ski area slopes in order to release some of the new powder. Tunnel Creek, however, is out of bounds. Despite this, these people were well prepared: Wenzel Peikert brought his beacon, probe, and shovel along, as did all but one of the others. The beacon or transceiver emits a signal that allows searchers to easily locate a victim; a probe is a long staff that one uses to search for a buried person; the shovel increases digging speed. Professional skier Elyse Saugstad even wore avalanche wings, air bags that inflate through the release of compressed gas from a canister; they help to keep one near the surface. They all apparently had helmets. Some of the information gathered later was available because two persons wore helmet cameras.

As the individuals in the large group walked along the trail to the Tunnel Creek side, they passed a beacon check station, which emitted a series of beeps indicating that the hikers' beacons were all operative. Some of the more cautious skiers and boarders felt uncomfortable because the group was so large, and it is people who often cause avalanches. Nevertheless, they all grabbed partners and set off. Just as one is supposed to have a swim buddy in the ocean, when skiing out of bounds in a potentially dangerous (avalanche-prone) situation, one should have a ski/board partner nearby. The same is true for mountaineers, although many people do solo climbs of smaller (and even larger) peaks.[1]

They began by skiing and boarding through a forested area, around trees and then into the comparative open. Three went left, which they considered the safer route; twelve went straight down; and Erin Dessert, the only person without a beacon, felt uncomfortable so she went off to the right. After the snow released and poured down the steep slopes and narrow ravines, its power was exacerbated in the narrow funnel-like defiles. Had this been a completely wide-open slope, things might have gone differently, but because the area was so delimiting, the snow and its speed and pressure were increased. It was like water cascading through a narrow arroyo in a flash flood.

Saugstad was caught, and as she tumbled down she released her air bags and tried to keep her hands in front of her face to maintain a breathing space when she finally stopped, at which time she, naturally, became entombed in the rock-hard snow. This is a situation that does not allow for any movement but in which, when buried, one may continue to breathe for thirty minutes or more. Saugstad still had one ski attached to a boot, was fully encased, and could not move. But she was extremely fortunate, for although the avalanched snow was 20 feet deep in some places, Saugstad, impossibly, could see the sky through a thin layer of fluffy flakes, and her hands were above the surface! Wenzel Peikert skied down, tripped his beacon, discovered her, and dug her out. (The online version of Branch's article contains a short video clip of Saugstad describing what it felt like to be hurled along; it was frightening, and she was afraid that she might die.)

Rob Castillo was caught as he stood above some very large trees; he stuck his head between two and held on as the snow pummeled him. Many of the trees around him were snapped in half, but his protectors held. After the avalanche passed by, he was left uncovered by the snow, but when he looked for the three people who had been above him, all he saw was emptiness. He was soon joined by two other survivors and they immediately began to monitor their beacons in order to locate buried people. Castillo also called 911. The ski area mustered rescue teams, although they did not arrive immediately. A short way down, Castillo found one of his partner's skis in a tree. Tim Carlson and Ron Pankey continued to the bottom of Tunnel Creek, where they discovered a debris mound. Their beacons began to beep wildly. They homed in on the precise spot, dug, and immediately found Jim Jack; his body was badly contorted and he was not breathing. They tried to revive him but failed. They then located Johnny Brennan, but he too was already gone. A third victim, Chris Rudolph, was also laboriously dug out, but CPR failed to revive him. (An eleven-minute YouTube video presents the disaster, contains original footage derived from the cameras worn by two people, and offers sad remarks from the survivors as well as relatives of the victims.)

Three of the original sixteen-member party perished in the avalanche. It is crucial to keep in mind that these were all professional skiers, boarders, and industry personnel. They all knew what they were doing, and all but one were equipped with protective avalanche equipment. The lesson to be garnered here is that the mountains are always potentially dangerous places, especially in avalanche or lightning country. This calamity had a potent effect on many concerned people, but especially on the victims' loved ones.

One might like to say that we can learn from our mistakes, but when dealing with unpredictable events, there is little one can do short of staying off the mountain. One sadly recalls that more than one hundred years ago, an avalanche in the vicinity of Tunnel Creek killed ninety-six people.

Notes

1 As mentioned above, JA has done perhaps fifty winter, and naturally, also many hundreds of summer climbs, alone, in Colorado, Vermont, and Maine, for example, on mountains—Bierstadt, Mansfield, Katahdin—where the weather was sometimes horrendous, and he was often the only person climbing. This can be very dangerous, and even life-threatening. As for helmets, JA spent 1954–1965 avidly skiing in New England, especially Vermont, and in Austria, and never encountered anyone wearing a helmet, but the shift to out-of-bounds and extreme skiing and boarding demands head protection, so the current helmet trend is an excellent development. Nevertheless, helmets do not eliminate concussions and brain damage, as can be seen in the distressing out-of-bounds skiing accident that Michael Schumacher, widely regarded as one of the greatest Formula One racers of all time, had in France: His helmeted head hit a rock, resulting in a critical condition (Nadeau). Six months later, he left the hospital conscious but barely functioning.

Sources

Branch, John. "Avalanche," *New York Times*. December 23, 2012: 1–14 NY.

Branch, John. "Snow Fall: The Avalanche at Tunnel Creek." nytimes.com/snow-fall. Accessed January 3, 2014.

Hartemann, Frederic V., and Robert Hauptman. *The Mountain Encyclopedia*. Lanham, MD: Taylor Trade, 2005.

Nadeau, Barbie L. "Formula One Champion Michael Schumacher in Coma After Ski Accident." *The Daily Beast*. December 30, 2013. www.thedailybeast.com/articles/2013/12/30/formula-1-champion-michael-schumacher-in-coma-after-ski-accident.html.

"The Avalanche at Tunnel Creek: Disaster on the Mountain (*New York Times*)." YouTube. December 21, 2012. www.youtube.com/watch?v=cjzT15-oQq0.

Everest, 2014:
A Sherpa Tragedy

THE SHERPA PEOPLE WERE PROBABLY A FAMILIAL, KINSHIP GROUP, CLAN, or tribe that emigrated across a high pass from Tibet into Nepal and eventually India and other nearby lands about five hundred years ago. As the Sherpa communities grew, their numbers increased to 20,000; today, a figure as high as 150,000 is sometimes cited. They are considered an ethnic group, similar in essence to, though certainly distinct from, for example, the Pakistani Balti or the Chinese Han. The Sherpa inhabit high-altitude villages in rural areas of Nepal, one of the world's poorest countries. Recently, some of them have migrated to urban centers such as Kathmandu, where most of the inhabitants are poor, but here there also exist middle and aristocratic classes. The urban Nepali are Hindus; the Sherpa are Buddhists. Because they have lived at altitude for many thousands of years (in Tibet and Nepal), they are born with a high degree of acclimatization, unlike those whose ancestral roots have been at sea level for millennia. Thus, they are already acclimated, so that Everest base camp, at about 18,000 feet, presents few problems for them. They are at ease as they ascend, and can often flourish even in the death zone (above 8,000 meters, or 26,000 feet).

In the distant past, Sherpas, primarily in the Himalaya, as well as other ethnic groups, primarily in the Karakoram, have worked as porters, high-altitude porters (HAPs), guides, mountaineers, and recently even as real colleagues, climbing alongside foreigners—that is, Westerners and Asians, who come to these ranges to attempt to reach summits. Since the per capita income in Nepal is something like $750 per year, the opportunity to earn many thousands of dollars, plus bonuses, for a few months of (potentially deadly) work is very difficult to resist. Sherpas climb. They also die. (Sherpas perish primarily in avalanches, and of the 264 climbers who have lost their lives on Everest, one-third have been Sherpas [*Everest*].) So, just as their foreign guests have been hurt and killed in the Himalaya, so have the Sherpa, but the 2014 tragedy on Everest is in many ways unprecedented. It has been called the worst accident in mountaineering history, and when one considers that thirteen human beings lost their lives (and three are still missing) in a single stroke—of a falling serac and avalanche—it is. The consequences of this horror were also most astounding.

From the earliest period of Alpine mountaineering, amateurs and even professionals were accompanied by guides and/or porters. Expeditionary siege tactics reached their apex in the early twentieth century when the Duke of the Abruzzi was accompanied by nine hundred porters carrying, among other items, alcohol and a brass bed. But things have changed, and now Alpine ascents are favored. One might presume that only a handful of people are interested in risking their lives in order to reach the summits of the world's higher mountains, including Denali, Aconcagua, Kilimanjaro, K2, Everest, and other 8,000-meter peaks. But this is incorrect. Apparently almost everyone wants to reach a summit. And so base camps are filled with many expeditions, each of which has multiple members. Nevertheless, those enormous porter lists have concomitantly diminished.

Thus, it comes as a real shock to discover that in April 2014, there were 600 Sherpas (assisting 39 expeditions with about 400 members) at Everest base camp. After the avalanche in the Khumbu Icefall killed 13 of them, 500 decided to leave, even before the real climbing season began. They felt that they had been mistreated, that climbers had taken advantage of them, and so they refused to carry on. Freddie Wilkinson (seconding Ed Viesturs) points out that because Sherpas pass through the dangerous Khumbu Icefall so many times (while expedition clients are off acclimatizing on nearby peaks, so as to avoid the danger), they bear the brunt of the Icefall's wrath disproportionately. They should organize and receive better treatment and additional remuneration (Wilkinson). And they are doing so: The Sherpas' action, like their unified demands presented to the Nepalese government, were unprecedented.

Early in the morning of April 18, 2014, about thirty Sherpas went up through the dangerous Icefall: Their work includes emplacing ladders across crevasses, and setting fixed lines higher up on the mountain. This day they were ferrying equipment to higher camps (Barry, A8). Suddenly, a large serac broke off and caused an avalanche that overwhelmed them; thirteen were buried and lost their lives; three were missing. Although accidents and death are fairly common in the high mountains, this horrific tragedy immediately changed things for everyone concerned. Both the Sherpas and the Westerners were upset, saddened, and angry. Seven men were rescued (Pokharel) and hospitalized; the dead were brought off the mountain. The climbing season sputtered to a halt before it truly began. Expeditions were canceled and many, though not all, of the disappointed clients decided to go home despite their investment of time, training, and an enormous amount of money (tens of thousands of dollars). The Icefall was very dangerous; additionally, to those who truly care, it seemed the right (ethical) thing to do.

On May 4, little more than two weeks after the debacle, the Discovery Channel aired *Everest Avalanche Tragedy*, a ninety-minute documentary, followed by a second ancillary program, on the preparations for the 2014 climbing season on Everest. It covered the march in to base camp, interviews with and comments of various Western climbers, discussions by surviving Sherpas, and vivid and powerful cinematic coverage of the tragedy, rescue attempts, and discovery and helicopter retrieval of the bodies. (The latter is extremely important for Sherpa families, because Buddhism requires a final ceremony and cremation that seems to be even more critical than the last rites demanded by some other religions and cultures.)

The reason that Discovery and NBC were at base camp in such large numbers and with such an abundance of generators, cameras, transmitters, producers, crews, and high-altitude cameramen (and were thus able to create so much superb original footage) is that they were planning to broadcast live and film Joby Ogwyn as he flew off the summit of Everest in a wingsuit, eventually landing in base camp, something that has never been done before. Because of the Sherpa deaths, the jump and filming were canceled, but all of the film shot earlier, plus the cinematic work done as the rescue unfolded, allowed the producers to quickly put together *Everest Avalanche Tragedy*.

This film shows how many Western climbers immediately rallied, prepared, and quickly made the two-hour ascent to the site to try to rescue the buried men. Others set up radio links and acted as communication officers. The brief remarks many of these men, such as Todd Burleson, offered were accompanied by extremely emotional responses, sadness, and tears for the cook, porters, and guides who had become their friends. The few who were hurt but survived were led down. It is not impossible that if some or all of the buried and missing had been wearing transceivers, more would have survived. Tragically, not a single one of the sixteen Sherpas was so equipped. Nevertheless, some, like Janbu Sherpa, saw the ice coming and managed to survive because it cascaded rather than burying. *Everest Avalanche Tragedy* is dedicated to the memory of each of the named victims.

This has been called "The darkest day Mount Everest has ever known." See EverestAvalancheTragedy.com for details, a truly amazing three-dimensional video of the route, and an opportunity to aid the Sherpa victims' families. The *Wall Street Journal* produced a website that presents an extended overview of the tragedy, including personal remarks on those involved, and extraordinary video intercalated directly within the text. See Gordon Fairclough, Raymond Zhong, and Krishna Pokharel's "Death at 19,000 Feet: Sherpas, Fate and the Dangerous Business of Everest," *Wall Street Journal* (updated May 22, 2014, WSJ.com/Everest).

Sources

The historical material on the Sherpa communities presented here derives from the authors' personal knowledge. Readers interested in additional information can look at Sherry Ortner's sociological studies, especially her Life and Death on Mount Everest: Sherpas and Himalayan Mountaineering *(Princeton: Princeton University Press, 1999), the many journal and magazine articles that exist, as well as apposite websites. The tragic events recounted are documented in the usual way within the text.*

Barry, Ellen, and Graham Bowley. "Deadliest Day: Sherpas Bear Everest's Risks," *New York Times*. April 19, 2014: A1, A8.

Everest Avalanche Tragedy. Liz Fischer and Betsy Wagner, Exec. Producers.
NBC News Peacock Productions, 2014. Aired on the Discovery Channel,
May 4, 2014. (Simulcast in 224 countries.)

Pokharel, Krishna. "Avalanche on Everest Kills 15 Guides," *Wall Street Journal.* April
19–20, 2014: A7.

Wilkinson, Freddie. "The Risks of Everest Are Deadlier for Some," *New York Times.*
April 20, 2014: sr 5.

CONCLUSION

THE FORGOING COLLECTION OF ACCOUNTS PROVIDES OVERVIEWS OF adventurers who have created controversial situations, fabricated reality, and either acted in such a way or been caught in a situation that resulted in real tragedy. Sometimes people are directly responsible for the very bad choices they have made, but often fate provides an unexpected natural occurrence, such as a major prolonged storm or an avalanche or an earthquake, and there is little that mere humans can do to counter these things. It also occurs that a real triumph emerges from a potential disaster, but not always, as the graves in the sky attest. High on Everest's South and Northeast Ridges, well into the lethal zone, Sagarmatha watches silently over two hundred cadavers, perfectly preserved by the dry, glacial air above 28,000 feet. Tossed and scattered like dolls by an angry child, they are the grisly reminders of the exacting price of a walk into the death zone, for fame, fortune, or human folly.

Those who pass them, famous or forgotten corpses, are close to the doors of death themselves: parched, dehydrated, faint, and thirsty for oxygen, they walk slowly, laboriously, humming throbbing mantras in their clouded minds, bodies eating their own muscles in the preternatural, ultraviolet sky. They woke early in the mineral night, giddy with apprehension, nauseated with thirst, in the vast garbage dump of the South Col; Lhotse to the South, Chomolungma under vacillating Polaris in the stratospheric predawn. Lurking in the skyward abyss, the great winds dance on icy ridges, under the watchful gaze of their father, the jet stream. Bitter cold, fallow light, and the rancid smell of tea surround the living, while the dead smile in vain, embalmed in their marmoreal tombs. The frightful clatter of metallic tools echoes into the night: crampons, ice axes, oxygen tanks. The tedium of strapping, latching, buckling, and readjusting, slowly fades into sweet nothingness: ready or not, it is time to go; to say goodbye to the lifeline of the camp, for a last push into the ether, where the dead forever stand guard at the Hillary Step. Will we even remember climbing the ridge? The small things: ice crystals, sweat, quartz, a tiny fly in the snow, the feeble drum of our heart? The big things: the curving skies, hallowed glaciers, jagged towers, and the impossible geometry of the highest peaks? The distant world, poignantly green on the horizon? Will we even know that we died in the sorrowful skies?

SOURCES

For those readers who are fascinated by disaster, an excellent website, "Ten Tragic Mountaineering Accidents" (listverse.com/2011/07/28/10-tragic-mountaineering-accidents/), leads to additional material.

GLOSSARY

This is not meant to be a comprehensive glossary; it includes many of the unfamiliar terms that turn up in this book.

5.15: The highest designation in the Yosemite Decimal Classification, a system used to indicate difficulty in rock climbing. The numbers 1 through 5 relate to movement prior to climbing; 5.1 through 5.10 become progressively more difficult; above 5.10, only extremely competent climbers can reach the top. Only a handful of people can succeed on a 5.15 route. (JA recently heard of a 5.16!)

8,000-meter peaks: The fourteen highest mountains on Earth. Ambitious climbers set a goal for themselves: to climb all fourteen, and without supplementary oxygen if possible.

ABC: See *base camp.*

Abseil: See *rappel.*

Acclimate (acclimatize): The ability of the body to adjust to higher altitudes. This is accomplished by ascending slowly for short distances (1,000 vertical feet per day is ideal, though extremely impractical), then descending, sleeping, and repeating the process. All of this is usually unnecessary until one reaches about 15,000 feet; nevertheless, some people have serious trouble as low as 8,000 feet above sea level. There does not seem to be any specific characteristics that control this ability, although infants and very young children are more susceptible to acute mountain sickness than adults.

Acute mountain sickness (AMS): An ailment that strikes some climbers, especially if they ascend too quickly. Symptoms include coughing, nausea, headache, and a sickly feeling. Much worse, and potentially fatal, are pulmonary and cerebral edema (in which water accumulates in the lungs and brain).

Aid: Devices such as pitons or ascenders used to help a rock climber move up a face.

Alpine style: A type of mountaineering that features light packs, speed, and few ancillary materials or people. Its antithesis, now frowned upon, were enormous expeditions with as many as nine hundred porters. Today, commercial expeditionary climbing still exists, but on a smaller scale.

Amputation: Severe frostbite and subsequent gangrene may result in the necessity to amputate fingers and more frequently toes. It is difficult to climb rock at a high level without toes, but mountaineers learn to walk again and can continue to ascend even the higher peaks. Maurice Herzog lost his fingers but went on to a storied career as mayor of Chamonix and author of *Annapurna*. Not long after Aron Ralston amputated his own forearm, he was back climbing. And Beck Weathers underwent very severe losses but somehow returned to his work as a pathologist, at least for a time.

AMS: See *acute mountain sickness*.

Arête: A narrow ridge of rock.

Ascender: A mechanical device that allows one to attach to a fixed line and move up safely. When weight is placed upon it, a cam locks and the climber is held in place.

Avalanche: The release of anything (mud, rock, rubble, but here, snow and ice) that cascades downward, sometimes with extreme force and at very high speed. Anyone caught in its path may be swept away and then buried. Unaided escape after burial is very difficult. Various methods, devices, and trained animals all help to rescue victims.

Base camp: The first camp on an expeditionary climb. It is located at the base of the mountain and serves as headquarters for supplies, the base camp manager, medical personnel, communications, and so forth. Usually, but not always, the next highest location is Advance Base Camp (ABC).

Belay: (v and n) To protect by attaching a rope to another person and/or some solid object. In a moving belay, two or more mountaineers climb simultaneously.

Belay plate: A device, similar to a figure eight, that allows the belayer to control the speed of the down-flowing rope.

Bergschrund: A gaping crevasse that forms at the top of a glacier where it meets the rocky aspect of the mountain.

Bivouac: (v and n) To spend a night on the mountain without a tent or sleeping bag; some climbers carry bivvy sacks, which offer minimal additional protection. At high altitude and in frigid conditions, it is a very dangerous practice.

Board: (n and v) A snowboard, and to ride one. Normally, the verb *ride* is used, but we use *board* to eliminate confusion.

Brotherhood of the Rope: A metaphoric phrase that describes a commitment on the part of roped climbing partners, especially mountaineers. It implies that the men and (and women) respect, care for, and protect each other.

Chimney: (n and v) A narrow, vertical, two- or three-sided rock cleft, large enough for a person to enter, to climb such a configuration by pressing the body against the walls. If it widens too much, one must stem.

Chockstone: A substantial block of stone that is wedged (balanced) between the sides of a narrow canyon. Because it is larger than the opening, it cannot fall directly downward, but it can release under the right conditions: external (lateral) pressure, falling rock, flooding, earthquake. Caution is advised when crossing beneath chockstones.

Cirque: A steep, bowl-shaped valley formed by a glacier. It sometimes contains water.

Col: A declivity on a ridge; a pass.

Cornice: Solidified snow or ice that overhangs a ridge or summit. Some cornices extend out quite far and will break off under pressure. The great climber Hermann Buhl fell to his death from a collapsing cornice.

Couloir: Gully, often steep and covered with snow, ice, or loose rock.

Crampons: Adjustable metal frames, each of which contains twelve sharp points; they are attached to boots in order to allow one to grip hard ice. In combination with two small axes, they are also used to climb vertical ice.

Crevasse: A split in a glacier or deep snowfield. Some are barely noticeable on the surface; others are wide and very deep. Snow bridges may fool climbers; when they place weight on them, they can collapse, causing the people to fall in. Unbelayed, they may be hurt or killed.

Cwm: (pronounced koom) A valley or cirque.

Death zone: The altitude above about 26,000 feet. The body begins to degenerate, and if a person spends too much time here, he or she can die.

Dihedral: A point where two rock walls come together at an acute angle, up to approximately 90 degrees.

Étrier: A short ladder-like device that can be attached to rock to aid in climbing.

Expeditionary style: (Also called siege tactics.) A method of getting up big (Himalayan) mountains by employing many climbers and porters, setting up camps, and supplying them with material and food. All of this takes a great deal of time. Its antithesis is Alpine style, which is favored today, sometimes even on big, lengthy climbs. Here a few people carry most of what they need, abjure camps, and head up as quickly as they can. Naturally, prior acclimatization and good weather play a very important role here.

Exposure: The abyss that looms below a climber. Exposure psychologically exacerbates steepness or difficulty to the point where something easy may become impossible due to fear or physical debility (such as *sewing machine leg*; see below).

Fall line: The line down a slope along which gravity would carry a falling object.

Firn: Old snow turning to ice.

Fixed line: A rope or series of ropes set in place on especially steep or icy slopes. They are anchored at top and bottom by ice screws or snow pickets. When conditions change or too much weight is placed on the anchors, they may pull out. This can result in harm or death to those attached to the line by ascenders.

Free: *Climbing free* means going up without the help of anything other than the rock face and one's body (fingers, feet, legs).

Glissade: To purposely slide on fairly steep ice or snow on the soles of the feet or in a sitting position. It is necessary to have an ice ax in hand to help control one's speed.

HACE: See *High-Altitude Cerebral Edema*.

HAP: High-altitude porter, especially in Pakistan. These men climb above base camp.

HAPE: See *High-Altitude Pulmonary Edema*.

Heli-skiing: Skiers and snowboarders are transported by helicopter high into out-of-bounds areas, in Alaska, for example. They then ski and board back down in deep powder, often on very steep terrain. It can be quite dangerous, but the participants think it is worth the risk.

High-Altitude Cerebral Edema (HACE): A condition in which water accumulates in the brain; unless one descends, it is likely to prove fatal. It is even more dangerous than HAPE.

High-Altitude Pulmonary Edema (HAPE): A condition in which water accumulates in the lungs; unless one descends, it is likely to prove fatal.

Hypothermia: Loss of body heat. Just a few degrees make a big difference, and 10 degrees, from 98.6 to 88.6, is probably fatal.

Hypoxia: Depletion of adequate oxygen to maintain life in a normal way. As oxygen intake is reduced, the physical body and mental activity are concomitantly harmed.

Ice screw: A tubular screw surmounted by a ring to which a carabiner can be attached. It is screwed into ice to offer an anchor point for a belay.

Marteau-piolet technique: One climbs very steep ice with two short axes, synchronizing hand and foot movement, so that three anchor points are present at all times. It is best understood by contrasting it with ascending less steep ice or snow, where the crampons and the longer ice-ax, which must always be positioned on the upslope, provide two fixed anchors. In the marteau-piolet technique, one can climb in a rope with protection; solo with protection; two climbers simultaneously without protection; and solo without protection; the latter being the fastest, most dangerous approach.

Pendulum: To swing back and forth on a hanging rope. This is a useful climbing maneuver, but when it occurs inadvertently, it can be harmful, or fatal.

Picket: An approximately 2-foot, aluminum I-beam containing a hole through which a carabiner can be threaded; it is pounded into the snow in order to act as an anchor for a belay.

Protection: The devices that one places in rock crevices, ice, or snow in order to provide an anchor for a belay.

Prusik: An extremely useful knot, widely used before ascenders were invented. A thinner but strong string is wound three times around the hanging rope and tied off in a loop. Two of these will alternately hold the body weight without slipping, but when unweighted, will easily slide upward, thereby allowing the climber to move slowly up the rope.

Randkluft: A gap between glacial ice and rock. (See also *bergschrund*.)

Rappel: (v and n) To use a rope to lower oneself quickly down a sheer cliff. There exist various methods and devices that help in this endeavor. (Also, *abseil*.)

Rimaye: A crevasse high on the glacier.

Rope: Used primarily for protection in belays. The static variety does not stretch and is not used for serious belaying, since the shock on a climber would be severe. Instead, dynamic rope is employed. When it is weighted, it stretches a bit, which protects against shock to the body.

Self-arrest: When a mountaineer slips and falls on a steep slope and begins an uncontrollable downward slide, she must flip onto her stomach with her head upward and begin to drag an ax along the ice or jam it into the snow, if possible. This will slow one down and eventually halt the slide. This maneuver may be impossible to perform if the ice is too hard, the slope too steep, or the person incapacitated.

Serac: An enormous block of ice that hangs above a glacier. It moans and crackles, and sometimes very large chunks, the size of a house, break off and cascade downward.

Seven Summits: The highest point on each of the seven continents. Even today, only a few people, comparatively speaking, have managed to climb all seven. Even fewer have done so without using bottled oxygen.

Sewing machine leg: A condition, usually caused by fear (sometimes it occurs because of physiological strain), in which the leg trembles or vibrates. It is most common when one is climbing vertical rock. Pushing the heel down may help to alleviate it.

Sherpa: Originally a family or clan, now an ethnic group of people who live primarily in rural Nepal. They arrived about five hundred years ago, after leaving Tibet. They are Buddhists and excellent climbers, acclimate well to high altitudes, and act as guides for Western climbers.

Short-rope: (v) To pull or hold back another climber through a 3-foot length of rope attached to their harnesses. It can help a weaker person climb or descend safely.

Snow blindness: Because sunlight reflects brilliantly off unrelieved snow and ice, and because the atmosphere is thinner at altitude, radiation increases. Therefore, the eyes require the protection of very dark glacier glasses. Without them, a painful condition called snow blindness occurs, which obviously makes climbing difficult, or impossible.

Stem: To spread the arms and legs widely so that they press upon the walls of a narrow enclosure (such as a rock chimney). The pressure keeps a climber from falling as he or she moves up or down.

Storm: Heavy rain and especially snow often accompanied by wind; not as bad as a blizzard, but bad enough. The authors once found themselves near the summit of Idaho's Borah Peak. Suddenly, a comparatively mild storm rolled in, created whiteout conditions, and covered the formerly barren ground with a white covering—all in less than five minutes. Here, *storm* and *blizzard* are used interchangeably.

Tie in: To attach a rope to one's body, formerly, by looping it around the waist, now, by tying it to a harness. The rope extends to another climber who has also tied in.

Transceiver (or beacon): A device that one can carry when in avalanche country. It emits a signal that allows searchers to quickly locate a buried victim. They are slowly becoming more common, although many climbers do not carry them unless impelled to by ski areas or peers.

Traverse: (v and n) To move horizontally (approximately perpendicular to the fall line) across a slope. The steeper the incline, the more dangerous the movement.

Wand: Bamboo (or thin metal) shaft (2 to 4 feet long) topped with a small, colorful (plastic) flag. They are placed every 100 to 200 feet in snow or ice to mark the way so that climbers can return in relative security. They are especially useful in whiteout or stormy conditions, when even a deep trail can be obliterated in a few minutes.

Whiteout: A condition that derives from blowing snow or low-lying clouds and, like pea-soup fog, makes it difficult or impossible to see.

ABOUT THE AUTHORS

Frederic V. Hartemann (PhD) is a physicist at Lawrence Livermore National Laboratory. His professional work appears in the premier physics journals. Fred is an avid mountaineer and has been active for thirty-five years. He has climbed in many European and all North American countries. He is the coauthor of *The Mountain Encyclopedia*, among other works.

Robert Hauptman (PhD) is a retired university professor and the editor of the *Journal of Information Ethics*. He too climbs regularly and in many different lands. He has managed to stand on the highpoint in forty-five states. He is the coauthor of *The Mountain Encyclopedia*, one of his approximately seven hundred publications.